"She's done it again! Diana Butler Bass has this unique ability to articulate clearly and compellingly what you've previously experienced as an intuition, a sense, a nudge. Many of us are aware of the massive shifts going on all around us, and here Diana gives us the gift of naming it, explaining it, and presenting the evidence. She's spot-on prophetic, compelling, and most important, hopeful."

—Rob Bell, author of *Love Wins*

"In this readable and engaging exploration of our present puzzling spiritual situation, Diana Bass takes a welcome stride beyond the already tired discussion of what so many people mean when they say they are 'spiritual but not religious.' She points the way beyond either clinging to or rejecting creeds and institution-bound religion to a faith centered not on 'what' we believe (or do not believe) but on what she calls the 'how' question, the search for what is 'actionable.' The book is refreshing, evocative, well informed, and original. It will appeal to both professional and laypeople."

—Harvey Cox, author of *The Future of Faith*

"American religious life is clearly changing, and fast. Diana Butler Bass explains how experience, connection, and service are replacing theology as keys to the next Great Awakening. It's a fascinating story."

—Bill McKibben, author of *Eaarth* and founder of 360.org

"Some people speak well, some people say what must be said, but fewer have both the experience and competence to speak so all can understand and even agree. Diana Butler Bass does all of the above—and even better, she does it with faith and love. Join her in rebuilding religion from the bottom up!"

—Richard Rohr, O.F.M., Center for Action and
Contemplation and author of *Falling Upward*

"Butler Bass has always had something significant to say in each of her books, but here she outdoes even her own winning record. Rich with tempered but optimistic insights and blessed with up-to-date statistics and the scholarship to support them, *Christianity After Religion* should be required reading for every thinking Christian. It is one blockbuster of an analysis that is also a delight to read."

—Phyllis Tickle, author of *The Great Emergence*

"Diana Butler Bass is traditional without being a traditionalist. She's smart but not a stuffy academic. She's a mystic but still down to earth. She has a good nose to sniff out crappy religion, but she also has the eyes to see new life budding from the compost of Christendom. Diana reminds us here that, before every great awakening, folks say it is impossible . . . and after every great awakening, folks say it was inevitable."

—Shane Claiborne, author and activist

"*Christianity After Religion* is an important and life-giving book, written by an engaged Christian who is already well-established as one of our finest religious writers. Diana Butler Bass has a keen eye for what is happening in the Christian world these days—so keen, she is able to see through the bad news for the good news that is emerging. With her historical scholarship, her hopeful eye to the future, her on-the-ground experience with the church, and her gift for lovely, lucid prose, the author has given us a book that can help us reclaim the best of our faith tradition."

—Parker J. Palmer, author of *Healing the Heart of Democracy* and *Let Your Life Speak*

"Interesting, insightful, impressive, and important, this gracefully written book establishes Bass as one of our foremost commentators on twenty-first century Christianity."

—Marcus Borg, author of *Speaking Christian*

"Of Diana Butler Bass's many excellent books, this is the most substantive, provocative, and inspiring yet. Building on substantial historical and sociological analyses of past and present, it leads to a powerful finale of sage guidance for the future. Along the way, the book overflows with generous insights—about scripture, about movements and institutions, about the point of religion and spirituality, about Christian identity, and about how endings and beginnings can be contained in the singular seed of the present moment. I expect (and hope) that this will be the must-read 'church book' for every Christian leader—clergy and lay—for years to come."

—Brian D. McLaren, author of *A New Kind of Christianity* and *Naked Spirituality*

# CHRISTIANITY
# AFTER
# RELIGION

# CHRISTIANITY AFTER RELIGION

## THE END OF CHURCH AND THE BIRTH OF A NEW SPIRITUAL AWAKENING

## DIANA BUTLER BASS

HarperOne
*An Imprint of HarperCollinsPublishers*

FIRST HARPERCOLLINS PAPERBACK EDITION PUBLISHED IN 2013

Library of Congress Cataloging-in-Publication Data
Bass, Diana Butler.
    Christianity after religion : the end of church and the birth of a new spiritual awakening / Diana Butler Bass. — 1st ed.
        p. cm.
    Includes index.
    ISBN 978-0-06-200374-4
1. Christianity—21st century. I. Title.
BR121.3.B37    2012
277.3'083—dc23                                        2011032681

13  14  15  16  17  RRD(H)  10  9  8  7  6  5  4  3  2  1

*To Marcus, Marianne, Henry, and Abbey.*
*You have gladdened my heart along the way.*

# Contents

# PART III
## *Awakening*

# The Beginning

I OPENED MY LOCKER—IT WAS as overstuffed and unorganized as usual—and out fell a copy of the New American Standard Version of the Bible. The Word of God hit the sandaled feet of a girl with a locker near mine.

"You're so religious," my high-school companion growled. "A Bible at school? Are you becoming a Mormon or something?"

"No," I replied. "I'm not a Mormon." I had recently joined a nondenominational church, however, a church that took the Bible both seriously and literally. I was only vaguely acquainted with scripture through childhood Sunday school. But my new church friends knew the Bible practically by heart. I was trying to make up for lost time by reading it at lunch.

"What sort of religion makes you bring a Bible to school? Are you a religious fanatic?"

"I'm not religious," I responded. "I've got a relationship with

God. I don't really like religion. Religion keeps us away from Jesus. It is more a . . ." I wasn't sure how to put it. "It's a spiritual thing."

My answer did not register. She turned away, flipping her long Marcia Brady–like hair impertinently in my face, and walked off.

It would be at least another decade before I would hear someone confess to being "spiritual but not religious." I was only trying to describe something that had happened to me, an experience I had with God. A few months earlier, I had started attending a new church, one where the pastor urged members to get born again. I wasn't entirely sure what that meant. But I listened to friends testify to God's presence in their lives; they said Jesus was their friend and that they felt the Holy Spirit in their hearts. Although I had grown up in a Methodist church, I had never heard anyone talk about God with such warmth or intimacy. So, one Sunday during communion, as I ate Saltine crackers followed by Welch's grape juice, I actually felt Jesus. He was there. He showed up again a few days later at youth group at a backyard pool party as we all sang, "I Wish We'd All Been Ready," a popular song about the Rapture and the end times. I didn't know how to explain it, but God had touched my heart, and I felt fresh and new, relieved that God was there. I figured this was what the pastor meant by getting "born again."

I told a friend and asked him, "What's this religion called?"

He laughed, saying, "It isn't a religion; it's a relationship."

At the time, I felt pretty special, that God had chosen me, or the small group of "us," for this experience. What I didn't know was that millions and millions of other people shared our story—of growing up in a formal religion, finding that somehow chilly or distant, and rediscovering God through a mystical experience. Many of those people would call it being "born again," but others would speak of being "filled with the Holy Spirit" or being "renewed" by God. They left traditional religion in search of new communities; they tried to reform their old churches by praying for the Spirit. They embraced all sorts of theologies, from fundamentalism to medieval Catholic mysticism, from Pentecostalism to doctrines of their own design. They got baptized (or rebaptized), formed alternative communities, wrote praise songs, and raised their arms in ecstatic prayer.

And it was not only Christians. Many of my Jewish friends recount similar experiences of finding God anew in those days, as do those who grew up in agnostic or secular families. Millions reconnected with their Higher Power in recovery groups. Religion morphed from an external set of rules into a vibrant spiritual experience of God. Somehow, the word "religion" did not seem quite adequate to explain what had happened. For those of us who followed Jesus, we had stumbled into a world of Christianity after religion, a spiritual space beyond institutions, buildings, and organizations, a different sort of faith.

With hindsight, it is a little easier to understand. The 1970s were a time of profound change, a rearrangement of social relationships, a time of cultural upheaval and transformation. There were spiritual aspects to that change as well as political and social ones. Institutions and practices that once composed what was "normal" in American life began a prolonged period of decline, a failure that happened in fits and starts and that continues even today. As the old ended, Americans began an extended experiment in reordering faith, family, community, and nation.

In 1962, only a couple of years after I was born, pollsters found that 22 percent of Americans claimed to have had a "mystical experience" of God. In 1976, the year my Bible nearly broke my classmate's toe, that number had risen to 31 percent of the population. Back in those days, we thought we were in the middle of a revival. Apparently, however, it did not end. By 2009, 48 percent of Americans confessed that they had had a mystical encounter with the divine. This was not merely some sort of short-lived emotional outburst of renewed faith. Instead, the numbers indicate that, during the past thirty years, American faith has undergone a profound and extensive reorientation away from externalized religion toward internalized spiritual experience.

For much of this time, most journalists, historians, and theologians equated this change with a resurgence of conservative Christianity, believing that America had just experienced a massive evangelical awakening akin to the First Great Awakening in the 1740s or the Second Great Awakening in the early 1800s. In more recent years, however, something else has become clear. Not everyone who has experienced God afresh is an evangelical, fundamentalist, or Pentecostal. Indeed, they hail from many sorts of faiths, and many are not Christians.

And what is equally true, not all of those who first understood their experience of God in the context of evangelicalism stayed evangelical. Of friends from my high-school youth group, only a very few remained on the evangelical path. Others—including myself—migrated back to the old churches we once deserted; some became Buddhists, Hindus, or Jews; more than a few became inveterate seekers, agnostics, and atheists. One experienced Allah in her prayers; another met God in nature, magic, and ancient Celtic legends. Along the way, we found plenty of other people who had met and experienced God and never called themselves "born again." The 48 percent is, if nothing else, a theological motley crew, diverse and pluralistic in their spirituality, as ineffable as the divine itself. But whatever the differences between these people, it appears that a good many of them are traveling new paths of meaning, exploring new ways to live their lives, experiencing a new sense of authenticity and wonder, and practicing new forms of community that address global concerns of human flourishing.

Fundamentalist preachers look at this situation and shake their heads, warning against the devil appearing as an angel of light, decrying how easy it is to fall into heresy, and how the evil one roams about tempting God's children. To them, the 1970s revival went on the skids—neither their converts' lives nor their attempt to convert culture unfolded as planned. They are busily training new troops to correct the course and return America (and the rest of the Christian world) to old-time religion and God's righteous path. They envision a global sawdust trail to convert the heathen masses and restore biblical inerrancy, family values, social order, clerical authority, theological orthodoxy, sexual purity, free-market capitalism, and Protestant piety.

But there is another way of looking at things. What if the 1970s were not simply an evangelical revival like those of old, but the first stirrings of a new spiritual awakening, a vast interreligious movement toward individual, social, and cultural transformation? Have we lived the majority of our lives in the context of this awakening, struggling toward new understandings of God, how we should act ethically and politically, and who we are deep in our souls? What if the awakening is not exclusively a Christian affair, but rather that a certain form of Christianity is playing a significant role in forming the contours of a new kind of faith beyond conventional religious boundaries? Is America living in the wake of a revival gone awry or a spiritual awakening that is finally taking concrete—albeit unexpected—shape?

Strange as it may seem in this time of cultural anxiety, economic near collapse, terrorist fear, political violence, environmental crisis, and partisan anger, I believe that the United States (and not only the United States) is caught up in the throes of a spiritual awakening, a period of sustained religious and political transformation during which our ways of seeing the world, understanding ourselves, and expressing faith are being, to borrow a phrase, "born again." Indeed, the shifts around religion contribute to the anxiety, even as anxiety gives rise to new sorts of understandings of God and the spiritual life. Fear and confusion signal change. This transformation is what some hope will be a "Great Turning" toward a global community based on shared human connection, dedicated to the care of our planet, committed to justice and equality, that seeks to raise hundreds of millions from poverty, violence, and oppression.

This awakening has been under way for some time now and has reached a crucial stage, as a new "Age of the Spirit" has dawned. Theologian Harvey Cox points out that this turn toward spirituality as the new form of faith started in the previous century. The 1970s were a significant period in a long process of moving away from old-style religion toward new patterns of faith. In the last decade, this shift has accelerated exponentially, sweeping millions more into both discontent and the longing for change.

Exponential change creates exponential fear along with exponential hope. Massive transformation creates the double-edged cultural sword of decline and renewal. Exponential change ends those things that people once assumed and trusted to be true. At the same time, upheaval opens new pathways to the future. Change is about endings and beginnings and the necessary interrelationship between the two.

Most people accept that technology, politics, and social conditions change. But many also think that religion will shield them from the consequences of change in these secular arenas. Others think that a return to the "faith of our fathers" will slow or stop worrisome or unwanted social change. Neither of these perspectives is true. Faith can neither insulate from nor prevent change. Instead, faith is swept up in the waves of global change, as every aspect of human experience is undergoing profound rearrangement. In some arenas of contemporary life, especially in Africa and South America, religion is actually leading other sorts of change. Religion rarely protects people from change. Perhaps a call to return to older forms of faith may delay change—only, however, in the way that Roman persecutions slowed the spread of Christianity or late medieval inquisitions turned back the advance of Protestantism. History teaches that the "faith of our fathers" may have won some battles, but has lost many a war.

Is there a better way to understand change and faith in these days when the ground seems so unsteady beneath us? Religion, faith, spiritual experience, mysticism, church, theology—all these are holy things, profound ways of relating to God. Yet they all exist in the context of the world, equally as dependent on the vicissitudes of human experience as any surety of divine revelation. Religious expression is not immutable; it changes all the time. Faith roils right along with other global pressures. Christianity is no exception to the historical transformation of our times, and to view faith as either irrelevant to or outside of the purview of global cultural change is foolish.

This book is concerned with religion and change—specifically how Christianity, especially Christianity in the United States, is changing and how people are questioning conventional patterns of faith and belief. At the outset, let me be perfectly clear. I do not think it is wise to adapt religions to contemporary tastes willy-nilly. As the gloomy nineteenth-century Anglican dean William Inge once said, "Whoever marries the spirit of this age will find himself a widower in the next." I do, however, think it is exceedingly wise for faithful people to intentionally engage emerging religious questions in order to reform, renew, and reimagine ancient traditions in ways that make sense to contemporary people.

The 1970s were the beginning of the end of older forms of Christianity, and now, decades later, we are witnessing the end of the beginning. What follows is a sustained reflection on how religion has changed in our lifetime—a life lived between the beginning of an end and the end of that beginning—and what that means for Christian faith and practice. Much has changed. Where Christianity is now vital, it is not really seen as a "religion" anymore. It is more of a spiritual thing.

# PART I

## The End of Religion

What is bothering me incessantly is the question what Christianity really is, or indeed who Christ really is, for us today. . . . We are moving toward a completely religionless time; people as they are now simply cannot be religious anymore. Even those who honestly describe themselves as "religious" do not in the least act up to it, and so they presumably mean something quite different by "religious."

What does that mean for "Christianity"? If religion is only a garment of Christianity—and even this garment has looked very different at different times—then what is a religionless Christianity?

DIETRICH BONHOEFFER
*Letters and Papers from Prison*

# CHAPTER ONE

# The End of the Beginning

E VERY SPRING, I LOOK forward to the Easter issue of the national newsmagazines. The cover is usually beautiful, bearing an image of Jesus or other religious art that accompanies a story about faith in America. As with the Christmas issue, the secular magazines offer up a heart-warming religion story as a nod to the season.

When I pulled the April 4, 2009, issue of *Newsweek* from my mailbox, nothing could have surprised me more. The cover was black, emblazoned with a headline in large red type: "The End of Christian America." I flipped open the story, written by *Newsweek* editor Jon Meacham, and read the lead:

> It was a small detail, a point of comparison buried in the fifth paragraph on the 17th page of a 24-page summary of the 2009 American Religious Identification Survey. But as R. Albert Mohler Jr.—president of the Southern Baptist Theological Seminary, one of the largest on earth—read over the document after its release in March, he was struck by a single sentence. For a believer like Mohler—a starched, unflinchingly conservative Christian, steeped in the theology of his particular province of

the faith, devoted to producing ministers who will preach the inerrancy of the Bible and the Gospel of Jesus Christ as the only means to eternal life—the central news of the survey was troubling enough: the number of Americans who claim no religious affiliation has nearly doubled since 1990, rising from 8 to 15 percent. Then came the point he could not get out of his mind: while the unaffiliated have historically been concentrated in the Pacific Northwest, the report said, "this pattern has now changed, and the Northeast emerged in 2008 as the new stronghold of the religiously unidentified." As Mohler saw it, the historic foundation of America's religious culture was cracking.

"Cracking" may seem too negative a term, but the *Newsweek* analysis of the polling data is certainly on target. In the last decade, Christianity in the United States has undergone tectonic shifts that have altered the nation's religious landscape.

For a couple of years prior to the *Newsweek* story, I had been pointing out to denominational executives, seminary presidents, and clergy leaders that the demographics of Christianity as a whole—not just liberal religion or Roman Catholicism or mainline Protestantism—were changing in unprecedented ways and that surveys indicated less religiosity in the United States than was historically the case. People were skeptical, insisting that evangelical, conservative, and megachurch Christianity was still growing. But there it was in black and white (and red) in *Newsweek*. Christianity of all sorts is struggling in America. "This is not to say that the Christian God is dead," Jon Meacham stated, "but that he is less of a force in American politics and culture than at any other time in recent memory. To the surprise of liberals who fear the advent of an evangelical theocracy and to the dismay of religious conservatives who long to see their faith more fully expressed in public life, Christians are now making up a declining percentage of the American population."[1]

For those old enough to remember—or for eager history students—the April 2009 *Newsweek* cover harkened back to another newsmagazine cover. Forty-three years earlier, in April 1966, *Time* had a similarly bleak black-and-red cover story entitled, "Is God Dead?" That story proclaimed a radical new theology, as stated by religion professor Thomas Altizer: "We must recognize that the death of God is a historical event: God has died in our time, in our history, in our existence." Of course, God had not died, and the United States was a decade away from electing Southern Baptist Jimmy Carter as president in the evangelical revival that swept the country in the 1970s. But memory of the cover remained, permanently making readers skeptical of such pronouncements on the part of the mainstream media. Although the old "God is dead" theologians actually made some reasonable and relevant philosophical points, *Time* treated their work as a fad and got the story wrong. As a fad, "God is dead" gave way to Jerry Falwell and Pat Robertson and the religious Right, a reborn born-again revivalism that reshaped twentieth-century faith. The ensuing religious fervor made a laughingstock of the 1966 *Time* cover, and historians of religion ridiculed it in textbooks as an example of how not to analyze religion in America.

Because of the *Time* magazine "God is dead" cover debacle, *Newsweek* readers eyed "The End of Christian America" rather cynically. Yet the *Newsweek* story is not of a few university professors theorizing about secularism or existentialism. *Newsweek* reported on two major polls in American religion, both significant, sophisticated, and scientifically grounded research about grassroots American beliefs. According to *Newsweek,* these polls found that the percentage of self-identified Christians has fallen 10 points since 1990, from 86 to 76 percent, while the percentage of people who claim they are unaffiliated with any particular faith has doubled in recent years, rising to 16 percent. The number of people willing to describe themselves as atheist or agnostic has increased about fourfold from 1990 to 2009, from 1 million to about 3.6 million.[2] In other words, the *Newsweek* story did not report what theologians think about religion; the *Newsweek* story reported what the American people are thinking about religion. This was a very different story.

According to Meacham, the conservative Southern Baptist Al Mohler stated: "A remarkable culture-shift has taken place around us. The most basic contours of American culture have been radically altered. . . . Clearly, there is a new narrative, a post-Christian narrative, that is animating large portions of this society."[3] He got that right.

Despite the good reporting in the *Newsweek* story, the editors may have come a little late to the conversation. For more than two decades, theologians, historians, and social scientists have been noting unanticipated shifts in religious life and discussing "the end of Christendom" and the emergence of "post-Christian" Western culture. Much of their work has focused on Europe and Great Britain, intellectually hedging their bets with vague appeals to American exceptionalism (saying things like, "The United States does not quite fit the religious pattern of other Western nations").

Since the mid-1990s, however, observers of contemporary religion have increasingly argued that Christian belief and practice are eroding even in the United States. Traditional forms of faith are being replaced by a plethora of new spiritual, ethical, and nonreligious choices. If it is not the end of religion, it certainly seems to be the end of what was conventionally understood to be American religion. Put another way, the shift that I experienced in the 1970s may have come to a conclusion. The process of leaving religion, one that started three or four decades ago, seems to have reached a tipping point. We have most likely come to the end of the beginning of a great transformation of faith. What was is no longer. And, as a result, discontent, doubt, disillusionment, and for some, despair, are the themes of the day.

## Rumblings

For the last dozen years, I have been studying what nurtures vital congregations and writing books about good churches. In the process, I have visited hundreds of strong Christian communities, small and large, old and new, modest and wealthy. Most of those congregations are "mainline Protestant" churches, a historic moniker describing denominations whose roots stretch back to the European founding of America. Although these old churches are often ignored or dismissed, I discovered that there exists an unnoticed spiritual vibrancy in some mainline congregations, based around a serious engagement with faith practices such as prayer, hospitality, and enacting justice.

Most of my work explored success stories—churches that are making it despite difficult times for their denominations more generally. However, I began to wonder if I was avoiding a more perplexing question. Despite such examples of vibrant faith, why is Christianity in the United States struggling to maintain its influence, institutions, and numerical strength?

During the same dozen years in which I analyzed successful local religious communities, new surveys and polls pointed to an erosion of organized Christianity in nearly all its forms, with only "nondenominational" churches showing a slight numerical increase. It began to appear that vital churches might well be only islands of success in the rising seas of Western unbelief and the high tides of cultural change are leaving traditional religion adrift. All sorts of people—even mature, faithful Christians—are finding conventional religion increasingly less satisfying, are attending church less regularly, and are longing for new expressions of spiritual community. As I traveled the country sharing my research with pastors, they began to relate on-the-ground stories that echoed the polling data. "People just don't come to church anymore," pastors told me. "It doesn't really matter what we do or how solid our community is. Even those who consider themselves 'good' members only come once a month or so now."

At first, I didn't pay much attention to these complaints. After all, religious leaders always seem overly concerned with attendance numbers, their need to recruit Sunday school teachers and committee members, and how much money is tossed into offering plates. Ever since the Great Awakening in the 1740s, American pastors prove that God is blessing their church, their revival, or their religious tribe by inflating numbers of the faithful, while others try to rouse the spiritually lazy by criticizing their lack of church attendance. American ministers vacillate between bragging about and bemoaning the number of people who attend church, in each case using numbers to underscore some theological point. As a result, most of us who study American religion are often skeptical of pastoral reports of increase and decline.

Whatever the history of ministerial exaggeration, I became convinced that the numbers were not being manipulated this time. The survey data were too consistent and coming from too many different sources for too many years. Academic polls, journalistic ones, denominational surveys, and polls with heavy theological agendas—all indicated that inherited religious identities, like "Protestant," "Catholic," and "Jewish," were in a state of flux in the United States, that actual attendance at weekly religious services is significantly down, that people mix and switch religions more easily than in the past, that traditional religious institutions are in a sustained decline, and that even general belief in God has eroded over the last thirty years.

Many individual congregations may be successful, yes. But the overall picture for religious life in the United States is not terribly encouraging, especially for Christians. Put simply, religious patterns in the United States are beginning to resemble those of other Western industrialized countries and no longer indicated the American sort of spiritual exceptionalism boasted about by previous generations. As sociologist of religion Mark Chaves, from Duke University, says, "The evidence for a decades-long decline in American religiosity is now incontrovertible—like the evidence for global warming, it comes from multiple sources, shows up in several dimensions, and paints a consistent factual picture—the burden of proof has shifted to those who want to claim that American religiosity is not declining."[4]

More anecdotally, perhaps, it has also become clear that more people are angry—or are willing to express their anger—about religion, most especially Christianity, than at any other time in the last century or so. Some comments are predictable ("I've invented my own religion" is a line I have heard far too many times), but others are tragic—including the one I heard from a businessman who had not attended church in more than twenty years, since his infant child had died. "At the funeral," he said shakily, "the pastor said our baby died because we hadn't prayed enough. It was our fault, he said, and that our lack of faith killed our son. Well, I walked out of church that day, and I have never returned."

But anger is not the only emotion people express when talking about religion. Many people are just bored. They are bored with church-as-usual, church-as-club, church-as-entertainment, or church-as-work. Many of my friends, faithful churchgoers for decades, are dropping out because religion is dull, the purview of folks who never want to change or always want to fight about somebody else's sex life; they see the traditional denominations as full of Mrs. Grundy priggishness. On Sundays, other things are more interesting—the *New York Times,* sports, shopping, Facebook, family time, working in the garden, biking, hiking, sipping lattes at the local coffee shop, meeting up at the dog park, getting the kids to the soccer game. Or just working. With tough economic times, lots of people work on Sunday mornings, the traditional time to attend to religious obligations.

In previous generations, scholars referred to eleven o'clock on

Sunday morning as the most segregated hour in America, meaning that white people went to one church, black people to another. Now, the line of segregation is between those who go to church and those who do not. And, judging by the number of cars parked in driveways on Sunday morning in most American cities and suburbs, it is not hard to figure out which group is growing.

## Bear Market: The Great Religious Recession

It may seem overly dramatic to speak of the "end of religion," especially in a country like the United States, which appears (especially to outsiders) to be particularly partial to God. In recent years, however, a number of fine scholars and writers have written about the religious change in which we now find ourselves, from Harvard professor Harvey Cox ruminating on the end of the "Age of Belief" in his book *The Future of Faith,* to journalist Phyllis Tickle writing of the end of Christendom in her *The Great Emergence,* to author Brian McLaren describing a "new kind of Christianity" in a book bearing that title.[5] Certainly change is the cultural moment; transformation is the air we breathe. But an end to, of all things, religion?

Throughout the twentieth century, some insightful Christian thinkers began to wonder if Western Christianity was coming to some sort of end. As early as 1912, Wellesley College professor Vida Scudder opined that "conventional" European Christianity was "passing and will soon be forgotten"; it would be replaced by a new faith of "high adventure."[6] Some thirty-odd years later, German theologian Dietrich Bonhoeffer, writing from a Nazi prison camp, speculated that Christianity might be "over" as a religion, adding that all religion as a "historical and temporary form of human expression" may well be dying. Religion was ebbing away. Pondering this change, he wondered, "What is a religionless Christianity?"[7]

Radical theologians of the 1950s and 1960s took up this line of questioning and extended it to include God, whose death appeared imminent. Indeed, in the middle decades of the twentieth century, religion—and God along with it—looked to be in sad shape. Churches started to empty as those of the postwar generation rejected their parents' conventional faiths and opted to become religious seekers instead. At that time, Harvey Cox wrote of a "secular city," arguing against church-as-institution or traditional denomination in favor of a God who is active in the secular realm. Roman Catholics embarked on a process of modernizing their church in the great council of Vatican II. Indeed, for the intellectuals of the mid-twentieth century, Christianity seemed to be, as Scudder and Bonhoeffer had suggested, in serious trouble, if not dying altogether.

For other people, however, things did not seem as dire, for these same intellectuals paid scant attention to the intrinsic churchgoing habits of heartland America and even less to the energetic springs of a vibrant new evangelical religion. For many American pastors and revivalists in the offices of evangelical ministries and mission agencies and at the prayer meetings of Pentecostals, all the talk of God's death, religionless Christianity, and church decline fell flat. Some forms of religion may be dying, they proclaimed, but not theirs. "We're not a religion anyway," they insisted. "We're about having a relationship with Jesus." Their version of Christianity—the only "true" one from their point of view—remained robust; only liberal, overly intellectualized, apostate religion was dying. Conservative Christianity—real, potent, theologically orthodox, and politically right-wing Jesus religion—was just fine, thank you.

Their assessment seemed true for two or three decades, but it is no longer the case, for in the first decade of the twenty-first century, even the most conservative Christian churches have stopped growing. Membership gains have slowed to a crawl, and in some cases membership is dwindling. Churches in the Southern Baptist Convention, the Missouri Synod Lutheran Church, and the conservative Presbyterian Church in America are reporting losses that resemble declines their mainline counterparts suffered in the 1970s. New megachurches spring up and are successful for a time—until they are forced to close down and sell their buildings. Even the Catholic Church has barely maintained its share of the population, mostly because immigrant Catholics offset the massive loss of U.S.-born members. The old argument that liberal churches are in decline and conservative ones are growing is not true. The denominations that once seemed impervious to decline are beginning to look like most other American religious groups. Everyone is in the same situation: a religious bear market. Indeed, the first decade of the twenty-first century could rightly be called the Great Religious Recession.

## Anne, Ellen, and Sheila

On July 28, 2010, novelist Anne Rice posted her resignation on Facebook: "Today I quit being a Christian. I'm out. I remain committed to Christ as always, but not to being 'Christian' or to being part of Christianity." She further explained:

> I refuse to be anti-feminist. I refuse to be anti-artificial birth control. I refuse to be anti-Democrat. I refuse to be anti-secular humanism. I refuse to be anti-science. I refuse to be anti-life. In the name of Christ, I quit Christianity and being Christian. Amen.

Within twenty-four hours, more than four thousand people gave Rice's Facebook declaration a thumbs-up, and tens of thousands more shared or retweeted it. It seemed particularly strange, because Rice had returned to her childhood Catholicism with some fanfare about a decade earlier. She wrote of her reconversion to religion in her autobiography: "In the moment of surrender, I let go of all the theological or social questions which had kept me from [God] for countless years. I simply let them go. There was the sense, profound and wordless, that if He knew everything I did not have to know everything, and that, in seeking to know everything, I'd been, all of my life, missing the entire point."[8] She rejoined the Catholic Church. When she reembraced the church, Rice's affirmation of faith had been big news. Now, the prodigal daughter was going the other way—walking away from all organized religion as a self-confessed "outsider" critical of the church. Major papers, online news sites, and television stations carried word of her rejection of Christianity. Within days, Rice's anti-profession of faith was all over the Internet, on talk shows, in sermons, on blogs, and the subject of coffee-shop conversations.

Of course, when a noted public figure makes such an announcement, it is big news. But Rice's confession did not go viral simply because she is famous. Rather, popular discontent with Christianity is such that millions of Americans could relate to her words. She struck a cultural chord. She said what others only suspect or feel or secretly think—that there is a profound and painful disconnect between what Christianity (and other religions as well) has become and what we perceive that it should be.

A few weeks before Rice's Facebook testimony, I delivered a keynote address at a conference of mainline Protestant clergy and leaders. Their conference theme was "Who Are You Christians Anyway?" The question is a good one. Although the United States remains the country with the largest number of Christians in the world, even here Christianity is experiencing a decline in demographics. As noted in the *Newsweek* article, the actual percentage of Christians has dropped significantly in recent years. Many people feel increasingly anxious about identifying themselves as Christians. Some obviously reject Christianity in favor of other spiritual alternatives, while others use different terms, such as "Jesus follower," to identify themselves.

I had been writing about this shift in a series of blogs that appeared in the weeks before Anne Rice's announcement. The comments to these posts revealed that many of my readers were honestly and anxiously wrestling with religion. One minister wrote about the "difference between religion and faith," saying that "religion seeks conformity and control—scriptural infallibility and literalism, imposition of beliefs upon others—and cannot abide any other way of encountering God that falls outside of its defined boundaries. Faith seeks freedom and life for all to experience God on their own terms and in their own ways—and then allows for communal experiences and collaboration to build a better world." A self-described forty-something said, "I increasingly find the Catholic church and mainline Protestant churches to be irrelevant. Many churchgoers seem to be content with the status quo and are uncomfortable being challenged, especially on issues of social justice. . . . We are currently experiencing the death throes of a dinosaur." The following sharp assessment came from an Anglican in Sydney, Australia: "I'm continually being disappointed by (bordering on disillusioned by) the institutional church. Institutional self-preservation seems more important than those on the front line who still minister to the physically, emotionally, and spiritually needy. . . . [Church] just doesn't seem relevant to 'modern' lives." And in an equally blunt observation, another noted, "Christianity has become a culture unto itself and has merely skimmed over what Jesus has said and is saying."

Just a few days before Anne Rice proclaimed that she quit and generated a media sensation, a humble testimony appeared in the comment stream. In an entry dated July 25, 2010, a woman identified only as "Ellen" shared her churchgoing experience with the blog community:

> I awoke this Sunday morning grateful that I didn't have to go to church anymore. I still believe in the living God but after years of moving from church to church, I feel that I can wing it for now without risking my immortal soul. I grew up as the minister's child in a white-bread mainline church that was orderly, kind

and very nice. I lived in a constrained, polite fishbowl, which I put behind me as soon as I left for college. . . . As a young mother, I chose the Episcopal church in part for the liturgy, but also as a middle ground between my husband's Roman Catholic upbringing and my Protestant one. I lived in a conservative diocese which fought women's ordination in the ugliest way imaginable, while at the same time seeming to turn its back on the poor and needy. I moved to the Roman Catholic church, which made no pretense about women's rights, but at least has a marvelous tradition in serving the outcasts and those in need. I think my best church years were within that fold. But there was always the nagging question of the Eucharist. How did it become so closed and regulated? Where did the idea of restricted access come from? Eventually I got interested in a non-denominational church, because it seemed to take the faith walk most seriously. . . . The church preached the Bible only, but of course only the parts that pounded the tithing message, the "name it and claim it" message, and endless salvation threats. I left in disgust when disagreeing with the pastor meant you were not being faithful to God. I knew when I left that I wouldn't be going anywhere else for a time. For a while I kept up the discipline of daily Bible reading and prayer, but it wasn't really feeding my soul. It had become another ritual. . . . But I realized my spiritual formation was ongoing and had been a compilation of the many Christian traditions I had been a part of. I had read the Bible cover-to-cover two or three times and had been in many Bible study groups and felt perhaps I had enough of a biblical foundation to safely put the good book aside for the time being. I enjoy reading religious books, blogs and listening to podcasts of sermons, too. But I feel most churches are way too fixed on self-preservation and preaching the gospel rather than living it. So, for now, my offering goes to Doctors Without Borders and other charities. My work is my ministry as I meet the broken-hearted and lost every day. I quietly encourage the faith of the dispirited, pray for others and try to walk humbly with my God.[9]

Ellen had been a mainline Protestant, Anglican, Roman Catholic, and evangelical. Each church had failed to live out the love of God in practical, relevant, inclusive, and healing ways. Each was too interested in its own agenda to be able to make a real difference to Ellen's life and world. Anne Rice is not the only Christ follower discontented with Christianity. Unfamous Ellen is too.

In 1985, sociologist Robert Bellah introduced his readers to Sheila Larson, a nurse whom he interviewed for his book *Habits of the Heart*. Sheila had drifted away from church and named her religion after herself, dubbing her faith "Sheilaism." She said: "I believe in God. I'm not a religious fanatic. I can't remember the last time I went to church. My faith has carried me a long way. It's Sheilaism. Just my own little voice." Sheila became a paradigm for late twentieth-century faith—individualistic, therapeutic, private, and inner-directed. "It's just try to love yourself and be gentle with yourself," Sheila explained. "You know, I guess, take care of each other. I think He would want us to take care of each other."[10] Although Sheila has been much maligned by theologians, sociologists, and journalists, in the years since *Habits* was published she has become the book's most enduring character, a symbol of religious change, individualistic spirituality, and the erosion of the American religious community.

Ellen is not Sheila. The spiritual journeys of both women began in a similar way—feeling the need to free themselves from constraining family religious patterns. According to Bellah, Sheila was "trying to find a center in herself after liberating herself from an oppressively conformist early family life."[11] After that, however, their spiritual journeys diverge. Sheila's major religious experiences included hearing her own voice as God's and seeing her own face as God's—both of which took place around health crises. Therapeutic mysticism shaped Sheila's path.

Unlike Sheila's, Ellen's journey is more externally driven; in it she makes considered religious choices based on theology and behavior. It would be easy to dismiss Ellen as a religious consumer, a "church shopper" who is never satisfied. If she is a shopper, Ellen is a remarkably serious one. She engaged the theology of each community she encountered, participated in its life over time, and evaluated the proclaimed messages of each church against the behaviors the church practiced. She asked questions about important issues, political concerns, and theology. In the end, Ellen weighed the churches against both Jesus's teaching and her own experience in regard to women, egalitarianism, service, and authority. She tried to find a church community where words and deeds matched and where the theology embodied a robust sense of God's love.

Ellen did not leave willingly. She did not drift away into individualism; she specifically chose to leave the church. Her conscience could no longer abide what she understood to be institutional hypocrisy—all of the denominations failed to practice what they preached. Indeed, Ellen criticized churches for being too inner-directed and institutionally absorbed. Religion, she contended, fails when it forgets the oppressed, the marginalized, the poor, and the dispirited. Although she eventually found herself on an individual spiritual path, Ellen is still reaching for connection. Even after leaving the church, she attempts to create some sort of new faith community through books, the Internet, charity, and her workplace. She has not invented her own new religion, "Ellenism," but she has, in effect, become pastor, theologian, moral authority, teacher, and spiritual director of her own postinstitutional church.

Ellen's and Anne Rice's stories are tales of trying hard to be a good church member and a good Christian. Ellen and Anne are not spiritual drifters. There is a qualitative difference between their testimonies and that of Sheila. They are smart women who gave themselves seriously to their faith communities and whose religious institutions failed them. They experienced a jarring disjunction between their understandings of God and Jesus and what their churches taught and proclaimed and how they acted. Unlike Sheila, neither Ellen nor Anne would be content with therapeutic mysticism, an undefined inner world of only the self and God. According to Anne and Ellen, churches, synagogues, and other religious organizations are broken and have made themselves irrelevant. Ellen and Anne quit because they are unwilling to live with hypocrisy and are trying to find a better way of being connected to God, Jesus, and the world—and they equate the failure of institutions with a failure of religion.

They might well go to church if they could find a community—or a Christianity—that embodied God's love and mercy in practical and meaningful ways. Put simply, Anne and Ellen were asking more of the church, rather than less; they were searching for a community that practiced what it preached. If Sheila represented an important aspect of American religion a quarter century ago, Ellen represents an equally significant change in religion today. People are fed up. They are unwilling to put up with religious business-as-usual. And, perhaps surprisingly, their unwillingness—the rejection of religion—is also hope for the future of faith communities.

## Revivals and Awakenings

Of course, religious institutions are not America's only struggling institutions, and the religious recession runs parallel to economic, political, and social recessions as well. In its December 6, 2010, issue, *Time* magazine published a decade retrospective: "What Really Happened, 2000–2010." The issue's lead article posed the question "The end of history?" Beginning with the apocalyptic speculation of Y2K, author Nancy Gibbs says:

> We thought we got a reprieve . . . as the lights stayed on, banks
> didn't fail, planes didn't fall from the sky, cities didn't tumble into
> the sea. At least, not right away. It took more time for the bubbles

to burst and markets to plunge and cities to drown, for faith in institutions to collapse—the banks, the court, the church, the intelligence community, the press and finally the government, which nearly 1 in 3 people now say they "almost never" trust to do the right thing.[12]

Each successive story covered failure: the political failure of the 2000 presidential election; the security failure of 9/11; the failure of international policy with the war in Iraq in 2003; the failure of traditional cultural gatekeepers such as publishers and journalists throughout the decade; the failure to control or contain natural disasters, as with Hurricane Katrina in 2005; and the failure of the American economy from 2007 onward. It is an unflinching portrait of a grim decade, a picture of a nation in decline.

A few weeks before the *Time* issue, comedian Jon Stewart reminded the crowd gathered at his "Rally to Restore Sanity" that "these are hard times, not the end times." Indeed, only two months earlier, radio and TV personality Glenn Beck had marshaled his audience at the Lincoln Memorial preaching the possible end of America, the end of Christian faith, and the end of the-world-as-folks-knew-it. Although few people ran for the hills to await the Lord's return, Beck surely ignited a bull market for survivalist gear. These are days of doubt and discontent, of wondering why everything has changed and the fear that ensues from loss. The anxiety is such that some may well think it the end times, or the time of endings.

In such a climate, Stewart's words acted as a reality check: this is not the end of days, only a time of very challenging days. Indeed, the *Time* editors concluded their gloomy issue with the suggestion that this is not the "end" of history, but "more like the start." Writer Michael Elliott even named the last ten years "The Sparkling Decade," a time of innovation and optimism pushing toward a renewed future based on the "twin forces of technological advancement and globalization."[13] The bigger picture, he insisted, is that of international transformation, of the birth of a new world of information sharing, education, creativity, and economic growth—with the United States, Canada, and Europe joined by China, India, Brazil, and some African nations to lift "hundreds of millions" out of poverty. The shift will continue to challenge established institutions and nations that once monopolized wealth, influence, and power. However, if you "change your vantage point," as Elliott suggested, things looked less like a decline and more like a rebirth.[14]

Although the *Time* issue may seem overly optimistic to some, the lesson is clear: endings are often beginnings. Recession is the gateway to renewal. Dressed in a secular guise, this is actually a core teaching of many faith traditions—notably the idea of resurrection in Christianity, but also reincarnation in some Eastern religions, death and birth in ancestor worship, and cycles of nature in tribal or pagan faiths. This spiritual pattern suggests the possibility for new things to emerge from the demise of the old, and religion itself is not exempt from this process. Indeed, over time, religious institutions—like all institutions—and the theologies, rituals, and practices associated with particular religious expressions are born, grow, mature, and die. From a particular vantage point, it might look like the end of religion, more specifically, the end of a particular set of patterns organizing church, theology, and religious life, if not the end of Christianity. These patterns are what Dietrich Bonhoeffer referred to as "religion," or the "garment" of Christianity. The old garment of faith is taken off—or falls to shreds—as something new emerges from beneath the worn cloth.

In North America, there is a name for such a religious process: awakening. The late Brown University professor William McLoughlin notes that the terms "revival" and "awakening" are often confused. However, he differentiates between the two. Revivals are essentially rituals of personal religious renewal that are often emotional and always involve a conversion of some sort. Revivals may stand on their own—as in the yearly revival meeting at a Baptist or Pentecostal church or a massive Billy Graham meeting—or they may be the subset of an awakening.

An awakening is a much larger event. Awakenings are movements of cultural revitalization that "eventuate in basic restructurings of our institutions and redefinitions of our social goals." As McLoughlin writes, "Revivals and awakenings occur in all cultures. They are essentially folk movements, the means by which a people or a nation reshapes its identity, transforms its patterns of thought and action, and sustains a healthy relationship with environmental and social change."[15] Awakenings begin when old systems break down, in "periods of cultural distortion and grave personal stress, when we lose faith in the legitimacy of our norms, the viability of our institutions, and the authority of our leaders in church and state."[16] A "critical disjunction" in how we perceive ourselves, God, and the world arises from the stress. The end of the old opens the way for the new.

Historians of American religion generally recognize three significant awakenings in the United States and Canada: the First Great Awakening, 1730–60; the Second Great Awakening, 1800–1830; and the Third Great Awakening, 1890–1920.[17] During each period, old patterns of religious life gave way to new ones and, eventually, spawned new forms of organizations and institutions that interwove with social, economic, and political change and revitalized national life.

The First Great Awakening marked the end of European styles of church organization and created an experiential, democratic, pan-Protestant community of faith called evangelicalism. The Second Great Awakening ended Calvinist theological dominance and initiated new understandings of free will that resulted in a voluntary system for church membership and benevolent work. And the Third Great Awakening had two distinctive manifestations: the social gospel movement, with its progressive politics, and the Pentecostal movement, with an emphasis on miraculous transformation.

Despite the theological differences between the two movements, each emphasized the shift away from personal sin toward the idea of communal transformation of the social order through an experience of God active in history. The Third Great Awakening inspired new forms of mission work, possessed a keen passion for lifting the poor and oppressed, and was broadly ecumenical in vision and practice. In each of these three awakenings, older forms of Christian faith— European, Calvinist, or Protestant evangelical—were revitalized, reoriented, remade, and sometimes replaced by more culturally resonant conceptions of the self, God, community, and service to the world. In the process, new forms of Christianity came into being, with profound spiritual and political consequences.

In his small but influential book *Revivals, Awakenings, and Reform,* William McLoughlin suggests that North American Christianity had entered into a new period of awakening, a Fourth Great Awakening, around 1960, which continues to the present. McLoughlin believed that, with the Fourth Great Awakening, Christian dominance of the United States would end, that more effusive, even romantic, forms of experiential, pluralistic religion would emerge, and that eventually new institutions would coalesce to carry the new spirit into a global, egalitarian ethic of environmentalism, community, and economic uplift.

Many writers in contemporary religion and spirituality are arguing that just that sort of new Christianity is coming into being. They speak of "postmodern," emerging (or emergent or emergence), or new-paradigm Christianity. Phyllis Tickle, former religion editor of *Publishers Weekly,* asserts that the church is undergoing historic transformation, the sort of change that happens only once every five hundred years or so. The esteemed Harvey Cox, recently retired from Harvard Divinity School, claims that Christianity is currently making a break from the "Age of Belief," a fifteen-hundred-year period of Western Christian dominance. Others, perhaps more modestly, say only that Christianity is moving out of a three-hundred-year cycle that began in the Enlightenment. Whatever the exact chronological schema, the message is mostly the same: We live in a time of momentous historical change that is both exhilarating and frightening. Christianity itself is becoming something different from what it was.

With a due sense of regard for these fine discussions, trying to discern three-hundred-, five-hundred-, or fifteen-hundred-year patterns in history makes me a wee bit nervous; sometimes the biggest picture is not really the most helpful picture. It is very hard to understand how an individual, church, or faith community or a specific neighborhood or town fits in such a vast historical transformation. Certainly, it gives our times a sort of spiritual weight and helps people know their place in the unfolding of human history. It may well be exciting to live during such important times. But it may also weigh on one like spiritual determinism, a kind of historical predestination—there is not much one can do to change things, make things different, or shape the future. History happens to us. Who am I or what can I do that makes any difference as time carries everything away?

We do live in a time of change; this is a time of endings. Instead of arguing for a worldwide paradigm shift, I argue here for something less grandiose and more historically discrete. Ours is a time of awakening, even a Great Awakening, in line with other such periodic awakenings in North American history, a time of cultural revitalization and reorientation rather than a time of religious apocalypse. Since awakenings are cyclical times of endings and new beginnings, events that occur with some regularity as spiritual seasons, then it is easier to participate in what is happening around us with a sense of awareness, purpose, hope, and creative possibility.

Awakenings take work, as human beings respond to the promptings of God's Spirit in the world, but they are not the last days. There is no need to abandon family, friends, and home to run for the hills. Some things will cease to work, no longer make sense, and fail to give comfort or provide guidance. Institutions struggle to maintain only themselves, concentrating on their own survival.

Political parties wither. Religions lose their power to inspire. But that only means we have work to do here and now—to find new paths of meaning, new ways to connect with God and neighbor, to form new communities, and to organize ways of making the world a better place. These are hard times, not the end times.

## A Pattern of Awakening

If we have been living for the past three or four decades in the Fourth Great Awakening, as McLoughlin proposed, why are we having such a hard time seeing it, and why is it apparently taking so long to come to fruition?

Some identify this awakening as solely an evangelical event, having begun with the Jesus movement in the 1960s. Others see the new awakening as the birth of Pentecostal fervor. Occasionally, a critic will identify a new awakening with the new spirit of Christian activism, such as the Vatican II renewal, the Protestant drive to ordain women, or the expansion of political and social egalitarianism. A few experience awakening in movements that reclaim ancient liturgy and spiritual practices. Still others see awakening in the growth of new religious movements and Eastern religions. Some proclaim the new awakening is not occurring in the old geographies of Western Christendom, but is solely an event of the Global South. Others think awakening is found in a rebirth of conservative or liberal politics. Most recently, young adults hope the Fourth Great Awakening is being born in a movement known as emergent or emerging church and in new virtual communities that exist only in cyberspace. Indeed, where some journalists, pollsters, and authors see the end of religion, others spot awakenings almost everywhere.

In short, there are almost too many candidates for the Fourth Great Awakening. Which of these many movements might shape the next phase of Western religious life and practice? Of course, pastors, teachers, preachers, and leaders of each group have much invested in making sure their candidate wins—that any spiritual awakening will be led by their church, their theology, and their political agenda. Thus, many of these movements contend with each other—trying to outmaneuver the others for the most adherents, the spiritual bully pulpit, a seat on the president's religious advisory council, or the cover of *Time* magazine. Spiritual awakening may well escape notice, because it looks like little other than religious chaos and division. The jumble obscures the transformation that is occurring in religion. A map—or spiritual GPS—would be helpful.

In 1956, anthropologist Anthony F. C. Wallace mapped awakenings as cultural change in his influential article "Revitalization Movements." Although his study examined religious and cultural change among the Seneca peoples, he believed that the pattern applied to Christianity, Islam, and Buddhism as well. In *Revivals, Awakenings, and Reform,* McLoughlin borrowed Wallace's framework to explore North American Christian awakenings. He mapped the shape of religious renewal movements in American history by examining five stages of change:

1. During a *crisis of legitimacy* individuals cannot "honestly sustain the common set of religious understandings by which they believe they should act." People wonder if they are the only ones who see the problems and experience the frustrations of the old ways. Thus, they begin to question conventional doctrines, practices, and their sense of identity.

2. People then experience *cultural distortion,* during which they conclude that their problems are not the result of personal failings, but rather "institutional malfunction," as they seek ways to change these structures or reject them.

3. Significant individuals or communities then begin to articulate a *new vision,* new understandings of human nature, God,

spiritual practices, ethical commitments, and hope for the future. New possibilities begin to coalesce that make more sense in the light of new experiences than did the old ones.

4. As a new vision unfolds, small groups of people who under-stand the necessity for change begin to *follow a new path;* they experiment, create, and innovate with religious, political, economic, and family structures in a search for a new way of life. They develop new practices to give life meaning and make the world different. They embody the new vision and invite others to do so as well.

5. *Institutional transformation* occurs when the innovators manage to "win over that large group of undecided folks" who finally "see the relevance" of the new path and embrace new prac-tices. When the undecideds "flip," institutional change can finally take place.[18]

In McLoughlin's map, the first two stages are stages of breakdown and decline; the second two are stages of imagination and possibil-ity; the last is a stage of reform of institutions and social change. In this terrain, changed minds and hearts—that is, what we think about ourselves, God, and the world—precede institutional change (which means, of course, that those people who seek to change minds by changing institutions are probably working backward). This is not necessarily a chronological map—that is, stage one does not entirely end when stage two begins, stage two may begin before stage one is completed, and so forth. Individuals may move through these stages at differing personal rates than large groups do, and the stages overlap in time and space. Finally, maps never describe every human experi-ence perfectly or predict the future with pinpoint accuracy. But these stages offer a way of seeing a pattern of religious and cultural change, helping us locate our larger communities and ourselves in this spiri-tual awakening and giving us a sense of future possibilities.

Given the limitations of any such pattern of human experience, Wallace's stages and McLoughlin's use of them can be very helpful. When many people feel lost, this can be a simple and empowering orienting device. Throughout these pages, I employ this framework of awakening to explore the endings and beginnings North Americans are currently experiencing in connection with religious faith and practice. My interest is primarily Christian, but not exclusively so, as the spiritual awakening in which the world finds itself is not only a Christian event. This book uses the five stages as a map through contemporary spiritual awakening.

Part I, "The End of Religion," outlines the breakdown of religion, especially in the past decade. This chapter, named "The End of the Beginning," presented the problem of religious decline and offered the possibility of awakening. Chapter 2 examines the "crisis of legitimacy" from the perspective of recent polling data in religion and focuses on the shifts of "believing, behaving, and belonging" (the three social markers for measuring religion and spirituality) roiling American faiths today. Chapter 3 explores the failure of institutional religion and looks at contemporary spiritual longings—the struggle to find new paths of meaning. Part II, "A New Vision," proposes that the search for a new vision is well under way in the form of experiential faith. Chapter 4 explores the new terrain of believing as experience; chapter 5, the new understandings of behaving as practice; and chapter 6, the new quest for belonging as relational and communal. Chapter 7 explores the connections between believing, behaving, and belonging.

The first two parts of this book largely cover what has already happened. The religious decline of Part I is clearly visible in polling data, surveys, statistics, and the news. The revisioning described in Part II is work that has been done by thought leaders, historians, social scientists, cultural critics, philosophers, scientists, and spiritual leaders in the past two or three decades in a number of fields. This section attempts to link much of that work in a clear, more concerted presentation and argues that there exists a need for more spiritual, social, and political communities (whether churches, congregations, or gatherings of friends) to embody this vision in both worship and work in the world. Part II envisions the shape that a new form of Christianity is taking.

Part III, "Awakening," turns toward what is happening now and what can happen as the awakening moves from vision to practice. Chapter 8 describes the Fourth Great Awakening as a "romantic" spiritual movement and delves into the tension between dogmatic and romantic forms of faith. Chapter 9 concludes with a call to action and offers what we can and should do as the necessary spiritual work of these times. Based on McLoughlin's map, I believe that most people are still struggling with the first two stages of breakdown and discontent; many see and have begun to embrace the third stage's new vision; and some have entered into the fourth stage of creating new practices and communities that embody the new vision. Only rare leaders have called for or ventured into the last stage of institutional renewal; that aspect of awakening still lies in the future, because some sort of consensus is necessary for the hard work of organizational change. We are not there yet. As a culture, the United States is struggling somewhere between the late second and early fourth stages, embroiled in significant tension over the direction of awakening.

Is it the end of Christian America? The end of Christianity? The end of religion? I think that the endings around us make a new beginning—a beginning that the Ellens of this world await as the old institutions fail. Ellen's story signals not *the* end, but *an* end, as she expresses her discontent by walking away from what was and asking new questions of religious traditions. Ellen is far from alone.

And the awakening? What will it look like? It entails waking up and seeing the world as it is, not as it was. Conventional, comforting Christianity has failed. It does not work. For the churches that insist on preaching it, the jig is up. We cannot go back, and we should not want to. Lot's wife turned to a pillar of salt when she looked back to catch one last glimpse of the past as her family fled to an unknown future (Gen. 19:26). Centuries later, Jesus reminded his followers, "No one who puts a hand to the plow and looks back is fit for the kingdom of God" (Luke 9:62).

But waking up is only the first step toward *awakening*. To awaken spiritually means that we develop a new awareness of God's energy in the world in order to discern what is needed to open the possibilities for human flourishing. Discernment leads to new understandings of self, neighbor, and God—a vision of what can and should be. Thus, awakening demands we act upon the new vision. Wake up, discern, imagine, and do. What will make a difference to the future is awakening to a faith that fully communicates God's love—a love that transforms how we believe, what we do, and who we are in the world.

# CHAPTER TWO

# Questioning the Old Gods

WHY ARE YOU GOING to Minneapolis?" asked my seatmate on a flight out of Chicago. He was a nicely dressed businessman.

"Speaking at a conference," I replied. I hesitated to say that I was speaking at a Lutheran synod meeting. Sometimes, especially on a short flight, I take my mother's advice that one should not talk about religion with strangers.

"What kind of conference?" he insisted.

"Lutherans," I replied. In the world of religious geography, I figured he would know about Lutherans. With Lutheran headquarters in Chicago and a huge Lutheran population in Minnesota, there is a high probability of sitting next to one on a Chicago–Minneapolis flight.

He looked at me, wondering as well if he should continue. "I used to be a Lutheran. I guess I still am, but I don't go to church anymore. I'm not mad at the church or anything—I appreciate what it gave me when I was young. Went every Sunday. My mother made me. Confirmation, youth group, the whole thing." He sighed. "But I just don't know where it fits anymore, and I just drifted away. My life is full without church; it seems kind of irrelevant. They don't care about my questions; there's no reason to go."

"What questions?" I asked.

"Oh, doubt, life, making the world a better place. You know, questions. They seem interested in things that don't really matter. Church is disconnected from real life."

"Do the questions bother you?"

"Sometimes," he said. "But mostly I'm just trying to figure them out with my wife and family—sort of making things up as I go along."

"What do you do on Sunday morning now?"

"Sleep in, mostly. Soccer with the kids. Read books. It's nice."

He put on his headphones. Another thirty minutes and the plane landed. We went down the jet bridge and he said good-bye. I watched as he walked toward the exit, home to his own post-Lutheran world.

## Choice

A generation ago, the Lutheran businessman would probably not have drifted away from church. His parents, family, and neighbors would have pressed him to attend to his religious obligations, and few other Sunday activities would have distracted him from church. But, like Ellen, he had the choice to attend another church, find another religion, or just not go. Neither of them felt religiously "obligated."

Some may shake their heads at this, wondering where character has gone or why young people are no longer loyal. But the loss of obligation is not only a religious phenomenon; it is a social phenomenon, as people now organize their lives by association and negotiation. By the mid-twentieth century, we developed a choice-based society, one driven by preference and desire instead of custom and obligation. Adulthood means picking—education, career, partner, location, goods, political party, causes, beliefs, and faith.

"I'll have a cup of coffee," the woman in front of me in line said to the clerk at a popular coffee shop.

"Just coffee? Decaf? Room for milk? House blend? Organic? Extra hot?"

"Just coffee. Black."

She laughed a little, shrugged her shoulders, and offered a "whatever" glance in my direction.

I replied to her gesture, saying, "You know, I go to Seattle for business quite a bit. Once, I had dinner with a coffee executive and asked him how many choices were possible in one of his stores. He said there were eighty-two thousand—give or take a few dozen—possibilities for a drink from the menu."

She did not look surprised. "Eighty-two thousand? That just makes my head hurt."

Americans, even those of modest means, exercise more choices in a single day than some of our ancestors did in a month or perhaps even a year. From the moment we awaken, we are bombarded with choices—from caffeinated or decaffeinated, to flipping on any one of a hundred television stations as we ready the children for school, to getting our news in print, online, or via a mobile device, to what sort of spinach to buy to go with dinner (local, organic, fresh, frozen, chopped, whole leaf, bagged, or bunched).

When my grandmother was a young woman, she had fewer choices. *If* she had a dime, she might order a cup of coffee at the local lunch counter. Or, *if* spinach happened to be in season, she would pick up a bunch at the greengrocer. She was born into a Roman Catholic family, but felt mistreated by some nuns who reneged on their promise to give her an education in exchange for scrubbing convent floors. When she and my grandfather eloped, she joined his Methodist church (I think she secretly worried she might be going to hell for being angry at the nuns and living in sin with a Protestant). Thus, my family carried on my grandfather's Methodism, as had every generation before them back into the mists of colonial history. Coffee, spinach, and the Methodists. Years ago, we did not choose any of these things. If we had money, if the grocer stocked the vegetable, or if we happened to be baptized in a Methodist family, we were simply obliged in relation to these particular things.

For most of Western history, the Christian religion did well as an obligatory religion. Family obligation maintained churches in local towns and villages over time. Obligations to God, like going to Mass or feeding hungry people, held people in the faith for fear of angering the divine. And theological obligations like believing in Jesus so that one would not rot in hell sufficiently filled Sunday services and revival meetings to support many thousands of congregations.

But what now? In a world of choice, obligatory religions are not faring well. How can a religion actually obligate anyone to come? What is a church to do? Threaten people with the eternal torments of hell? Only 59 percent of Americans actually believe in hell, a number down significantly in the last decade, and even fewer think either they or their neighbors will go there.[1] Damnation is a much less powerful motivator than in ages past. Refuse people the Mass? In that case, they will just become Episcopalian, Methodist, or Lutheran. Or maybe they will not go to church as all—as roughly 60 percent of Catholics no longer do. Refuse to baptize their children? No worries. Someone else will. Or maybe they just won't bother.

Of course, some people do not like choices; it makes their head hurt. Coffee, black. They always order the same thing. But when presented with new or different choices, many people take the chance and pick—in amazingly creative and innovative ways, which usually threaten those still following the old paths. In religious circles, choice is often viewed negatively as a violation of tradition, a break with custom, rebellion against God or the church, heresy: "We've never done it that way before." Critics assail religious choice as self-ish, individualistic, consumerist, narcissistic, navel-gazing, disloyal, thoughtless. But, if for a moment, you strip away all the judgmental religious language, it is just choice.

The economic, social, and political world in which we live has opened up the possibility for eighty-two thousand choices at the coffee shop and probably about ten times that many when it comes to worshipping God and loving your neighbor. Some will choose well, others badly. Some will choose thoughtfully, others not so much. Some choose something new, others choose what they have always known. In the end, however, everybody chooses. Contemporary spirituality is a little like that line at the coffee shop. Everybody makes a selection. Even if you only want black coffee.

## *1960 and 2010*

Anthony F. C. Wallace argued that awakenings begin when old norms—the guidelines and rules our parents, communities, and government once followed—no longer work, and people begin to make different choices about their daily lives. The old playbook ceases to function. Once upon a time, Americans had little choice regarding their spiritual lives. Religion was a "norm," an accepted pattern of life. Typically, Americans were Christians, and most were Protestants. There were a lot of Roman Catholics, and a few Orthodox. In Utah, being Mormon was the religious norm—but most other Christians did not consider them to actually be Christians. And there were Jews, a small group, but enough so that it was typical for many Protestants and Catholics to have a Jewish friend or two.

Until 1970, some 95 percent of Americans said they were certain God existed, and 99 percent believed in God. Two-thirds of all Americans were Protestants (including mainline Protestants, Anglicans, black Protestants, and evangelicals), 24 percent were

Roman Catholic, and approximately 2 percent were Jews. About 6 percent reported they were "other," including Buddhists, Muslims, Hindus—leaving around 2 percent of Americans to opt out of the question, perhaps because they were atheists or agnostics. Sociologist Will Herberg described the typical pattern of belief in 1960:

> What do Americans believe? Most emphatically, they "believe in God": 97 per cent according to one survey, 96 per cent according to another, 95 per cent according to a third. About 75 per cent of them, as we have seen, regard themselves as members of churches, and a sizable proportion attend divine services with some frequency and regularity. They believe in prayer: about 90 per cent say they pray on various occasions. They believe in life after death, even in heaven and hell. They think well of the church and of ministers. They hold the Bible to be an inspired book, the "word of God." By a large majority, they think children should be given religious instruction and raised as church members. By a large majority, too, they hold religion to be of very great importance. In all of these respects their attitudes are as religious as those of any people today, or, for that matter, as those of any Western people in recent history.[2]

Some fifty years ago, Americans were unwaveringly and overwhelmingly religious.

Herberg was quick, however, to point out that there existed certain "discrepancies" in the data. When pushed, more than half of Americans admitted that these views had no impact on their political or business practices, leading Herberg to conclude that belief in God might well have been social convention, a framework "providing them with some fundamental context of normativity and meaning."[3] In other words, these views were as much norms as they were committed beliefs—and perhaps they were more the former than the latter. These are the things that Americans said they believed, and somehow these ideas provided a communal sense of purpose, guidance, and authority. To say you believed differently, that is, to make different choices or question these particular beliefs, made you somehow un-American, outside the bounds of accepted behavior. How deep the beliefs were to individuals is hard to gauge, but on the face of it at least people went along with such claims, because these ideas helped order the world and gave them a sense of belonging to the American family. Good Americans were God-fearing ones. Piety and patriotism went hand in hand, at least as public obligation.

In 2008, Pew Research Center conducted a massive and thorough poll of American religion, questioning some thirty-five thousand people. One of the key questions: "Do you believe in God or a universal spirit?" The question is rather more vague than the 1960 question regarding belief in God (the 1960 interviewers did not add the "universal spirit" part) and yielded surprising results. Only 71 percent of Americans were "certain" that such a God or spirit existed (other surveys found this number to be 64 or 69 percent[4]); another 17 percent harbored some doubts; 4 percent claimed a lot of doubts; while 5 percent said no God existed, and 3 percent just did not know.[5] Thus, in the half century since 1960, the number of Americans claiming belief in God went from a "most emphatic" 97 percent to 71 percent—a 26 point drop. If you consider the softer, more inclusive term "universal spirit," you get the picture: American belief in the biblical Father God is surely not what it once was. In the last five decades, the choice not to believe has opened up—a choice that once did not really exist as a publicly accepted option.

From 1972 onward, new choices appear on religion surveys. In the 1970s, the General Social Surveys found that together Buddhists, Hindus, and Muslims accounted for approximately 0.4 percent of the population. Today, that number has at least quadrupled, to around 2 percent of the population (and that may well be a conservative figure). During the same period, the number of people claiming other religions (Unitarians, New Age religions, Native American traditions) has jumped from 0.4 percent to 1.2 percent. But the real indication of change in American religion is the category of "unaffiliated" or "none of the above," those who opt out of all the traditional labels for religious belief and practice. Indeed, many people in this category reject the term "religion" altogether. In 1960, these folks barely registered on polls; by 1972, they had risen to approximately 5 percent of the population. Now, depending on the survey used, some 16 to 20 percent of Americans are "nones" or "unaffiliated," making their numbers roughly equal to or slightly higher than the number of mainline Protestants (16 percent or 18 percent, depending on the poll), and slightly fewer than Roman Catholics (23 percent) and evangelicals (26 percent).[6]

And, to underscore the fact that Americans now have more choices in their spiritual and religious lives, young adults are far more likely to be "nones" than their more religiously obligated grandparents—somewhere between 25 and 30 percent of adults under thirty claim no religious affiliation. Although the United States still comprises many Christians and has a history of religious diversity, the percentage of Christians in the United States has clearly declined, and religious diversity is more obvious and widespread across the population than ever before. By 2010, in a stunning change, America's third largest religious group—and one of its youngest—is "unaffiliated," an independently minded group, with no single issue, theology, or view of God; the "nones" include atheists, agnostics, "nothing in particular," religiously oriented and secular unaffiliated people.[7] If these trends continue at the current pace, "nones" and other religions combined will outnumber Christians in the United States by about 2042.[8]

Choosing faith is now a bit like ordering off the menu at a high-end coffee shop—there are a host of possibilities, some simple, some complex, some already assembled, some seasonal, some regular, and some that people invent for themselves. When faced with such a wide array of ways to connect with God, to love one's neighbor, and to practice faith, we all now have to decide for ourselves. Choice in religion is just what is. There is no escaping it.

## *Three Big Questions*

A crisis of legitimacy begins when new choices present themselves and when the path ahead is not clear, but such a crisis is made manifest when large numbers of people question basic aspects of meaning and life. Certainly, there are a myriad of questions that are reshaping religion. However many specific questions can be imagined, most revolve around three much larger ones: *What do I believe? How should I act? Who am I?* These are the basic questions that every religion answers, that every great spiritual teacher preaches, that every church, synagogue, mosque, temple, or religious community must engage, that prompt most human spiritual stirrings. And the three questions suggest a process of choosing one's faith—they offer a framework in which to negotiate whether to stay within or leave a tradition.

Indeed, when people share their faith stories, they often start with "I don't think that the pope really speaks for God," "I can't recite the creed anymore because I just don't believe it," or "I can no longer say that Jesus is the only way to heaven." *Belief* questions prompt a reexamination of *behavior*. Actions change—like ignoring church teaching, standing silent during the creed, or avoiding the yearly revival meeting. Eventually, if a person ceases to act like a Roman Catholic, mainline Protestant, or evangelical, he or she will probably cease to *belong* to that church and no longer identify as a "good" member. Belief, behavior, and belonging are three intertwined strands of religious faith.

Sociologists refer to believing, behaving, and belonging as the three dimensions of religion: religious ideas, religious commitment, and religious affiliation. Surveys, polls, studies, observation, and research of all sorts try to measure and evaluate these three aspects of faith in the lives of individuals and communities in order to deepen human understanding of religion. By examining some of the recent studies in religion, it becomes clear that each one of these areas—believing, behaving, and belonging—is under stress in the early twenty-first century. Some might refer to this as a "decline," but it might be more fruitful to think of it as spiritual discontent. The old ways do not work, and there are few obvious new paths. Americans are not particularly happy with established religions right now, any more than they are happy with established political parties. Things are chaotic at the moment, and that sense of confusion is reflected both in polls and in the pews, revealing a profound lack of trust and confidence in conventional beliefs, practices, and organizations.

## Believing: What Do I Think?

What do you believe? When interviewers ask about beliefs, they want to know what people think about an idea, principle, or dogma. In religion, belief questions range from, "Do you believe in God or a universal spirit?" and "Do you believe in hell?" to "Do you believe prayer works?" and "Do you believe that the Bible is God's Word?" Belief questions concern how people conceptualize God, how they understand religious teachings, and what they think to be right and wrong.

At the beginning of the twentieth century, many scholars claimed that Western society would become increasingly secular, that science would erode belief in God. Religion would, accordingly, go away. As it happened, the twentieth century saw something of a rebirth of the sacred—and the once commanding secularization theory has largely fallen on academic hard times. Certainly, atheism is growing in most Western countries, and books like Richard

Dawkins's *The God Delusion* sell prodigiously. However, not all of the "nones" are atheists; in the United States only 1.6 percent of the population claims to be atheist. Indeed, Pew's 2008 study found that the "net" belief in God in the United States—adding together the 71 percent who are certain God exists with the 17 percent who hold some doubts and the 4 percent who have many doubts—is 92 percent of the population. And that number, 92 percent, is historically in line with belief levels in previous generations. So what's the big deal?

Although most Americans have not particularly stopped thinking there is—or might be—a God, they do appear to think differently about that God. Pushing beyond surface belief in God, Pew further probed toward what kind of God. Of adults, 60 percent claim that God is a person "with whom people can have a relationship," while 25 percent define God as an impersonal force. About 7 percent say that God exists, but it is impossible to know anything about that God. Broken down this way, somewhat more than half of Americans view God as "personal," and slightly less than half view God as a spirit, a vague entity, or nonexistent. In other words, belief in God is relatively soft in the United States, not nearly as robust as some commentators present.

Baylor University researchers further explored the specific views of God that Americans now hold. They too found that roughly 92 percent of Americans say they believe in God. However, the Baylor team also discovered that Americans actually believed in four different Gods! Not, however, the Christian God, the Jewish God, the Muslim God, and everyone else's God. Rather than dividing up according to religion, Baylor researchers discerned that Americans divide up according to how they perceive God's character. Thus, there are four American Gods: the Authoritarian God (31 percent of the population), the Benevolent God (23 percent), the Critical God (16 percent), and the Distant God (24 percent).[9] The Authoritarian God, a wrathful sin-hating deity, may come closest to beliefs about God that once dominated American Protestant-majority culture. But other images shape American belief in God as well—the Benevolent God, the forgiving friend of sinners, peacemaker, and caring healer; the Critical God, the bringer of justice who will make all right at the end; and the Distant God, the cosmic creative force behind and beyond the natural universe.

These surveys are like snapshots—how Americans view God in the early twenty-first century, with no way to compare views of God over time. It may well be that Americans have always believed in widely divergent Gods (as nineteenth-century American religious history suggests). Yet it can also be argued that there was a "normative" idea of God as Father, a belief in a deity drawn from the Bible and related to American values and identity that formed a cultural consensus in the recent past. Certainly, the Authoritarian God was the God of most Roman Catholic, Protestant, and evangelical Sunday schools in the mid-twentieth century. That view of God has been eroding, as the world Will Herberg so aptly described in 1960 disappears. Older Americans will certainly remember this stern normative God, having grown up with images of God as Father or God as Judge or God as King, an Old Man on a Heavenly Throne dominating churches of yesterday. A generation or two ago, it was assumed that the United States was one nation under this God, but that is no longer the case. It may well be more accurate to pledge to "one nation under Gods." Baylor sociologist Paul Froese claims that the stereotype of conservatives as religious and liberals as secular is "simply not true. Political liberals and conservatives are both religious. They just have different religious views."[10] The authors of the Pew study suggest that Americans are less dogmatic and more diverse than might be expected and that might be the case historically: "Most Americans have a non-dogmatic approach to faith."[11] God as Stern Father is going away and is being replaced by a multifaceted divinity open to invention and interpretation.

Pew found the same dynamic of "nondogmatic and diverse"

in relation to a variety of religious ideas. For example, Americans prefer to believe in a loving heaven (74 percent) rather than a judging hell (59 percent). Although large numbers of Americans believe in both heaven and hell, fewer believe in hell, and even fewer believe their neighbors or they (0.05 percent) will go there. Seventy percent believe that "many religions can lead to eternal life." The American God is far less interested, evidently, in theological purity and punishment than in inclusive acceptance. A 2010 Pew survey of religious knowledge found that atheists, agnostics, Mormons, and Jews know more about religion and traditional religious beliefs than do Protestants and Catholics—leading to the conclusion that most Christians hold flexible, fluid, or unformed views about doctrine. Religious ideas are in flux.[12]

American beliefs about the Bible, the book from which many people draw their conceptions of God, faith, and salvation, have changed considerably in recent decades. A survey of generational views of scripture found that 56 percent of younger Americans think that the Bible, the Qur'an, and the Book of Mormon "offer the same spiritual truths" as compared to only 33 percent of adults over sixty-four. Ninety percent of Americans who came of age in the 1960s consider the Bible to be sacred; while only 67 percent of America's youngest adults (those who are now eighteen to twenty-five) revere the Bible as holy. This study found that in contrast to fifty years ago, young Americans believe the Bible to be less sacred, less accurate, equal to other sacred texts, and more influenced by mistakes of human opinion and transmission—and they confess to reading the Bible less frequently than older adults.[13]

Against the backdrop of increasing religious diversity, American beliefs about God, traditional doctrines, and sacred texts are open to influences from a wider range of sources, experiences, relationships, and faith traditions. Thus, choice about belief takes place in a much broader context than in any other time in American history. It is a marked change from the commonly held public beliefs of fifty years ago when Will Herberg's civic faith of "Protestant, Catholic, Jew" shaped what was normative in religion. A Pew statistic from 2008 reveals much of the erosion of convention toward an open and often uncertain field of choice: 68 percent of us think "there is more than one true way to interpret the teachings of my religion," leaving the theological door wide open for personal interpretation and creative adaptation of what we think about God. A large majority of Americans believe that we are free to choose what we believe. The United States has not become more specifically secular; rather, Americans now speak of belief in a wide variety of sacred languages, voices, and accents.

## Behaving: How Should I Act?

Of course, "norms" include not only beliefs, but also behavior. How do you act in relation to what a religion teaches? How often do you attend religious services? How often do you pray? Questions of behaving ask what people do, how believers practice their faith.

No measure of American religious behavior is more controversial than the perennial question on weekly church—or "religious service"—attendance. Since 1960, approximately 40 to 45 percent of Americans say they attended a church, synagogue, or mosque in the previous seven days. This figure is nearly a given in any discussion of American religious life. Journalists, historians, and authors frequently use U.S. church attendance figures to prove that America is exceptionally religious, especially in contrast to other wealthy nations.[14] This "stable and strong" number leads sociologists Kirk Hadaway and P. L. Marler to claim: "If the poll data can be believed, three decades of otherwise corrosive social and cultural change has left American church attendance virtually untouched."[15] And the number undermines claims that American religious behavior has changed much in the past fifty years. As it happens, however, the "if" is a pretty big one.

In a cross-cultural study of church attendance and by employing a different data-collection methodology, researcher Philip Brenner, at the University of Michigan, has found that Americans overreported their attendance at religious services by anywhere from 10 to 18 points. Unlike Europeans, who answer the question more honestly, when a pollster asks Americans, "Did you attend church or another religious service in the past seven days?" slightly less than half will respond, "Yes." By examining actual behavior, however, Brenner identified a church attendance rate of around 24 percent over the past decade as well as considerably lower actual attendance rates since the 1970s. In 1974, for example, self-reported attendance was 44.9 percent, while actual attendance was 31.6 percent; in 1985, traditional surveys reported 44 percent church attendance, while actual attendance was 29.3 percent. Using Brenner's method, there is a steady decline of actual religious service attendance from 1975 to 2008, falling from 32 to 24 percent; at the same time, conventional surveys report stable church attendance in the mid-40s. By comparing this with numbers for Canada and European countries, Brenner concludes that, although the percentage of churchgoers is still relatively high when compared with other Western countries, America's overall pattern of religious decline parallels patterns found in Canada and Europe—with actual rates nearly identical to those of Italy and Slovenia. Does America act in exceptionally religious ways? Brenner concludes that America is exceptional in one way: only so far in that "unlike other countries . . . American behavior continues its consistent failure to match self-reported rates."[16]

Noted scholars Robert Putnam and David Campbell claim a more modest but still optimistic 32 percent church attendance figure, but note nevertheless that "society became slowly *less* observant" from 1970 to 2008.[17] Factoring in Brenner's 10–18 point difference between self-reported surveys and actual attendance rates,

Putnam and Campbell's figure of American weekly religious attendance may really be in the range of 14 to 22 percent of the population. Indeed, researchers Hadaway and Marler suggest that actual
attendance is half of reported attendance in the United States—
confirming (depending on the polls and data used) a real weekly
observance number of anywhere from 16 to 22 percent. Hadaway
and Marler also tracked denominational church attendance statistics
over time and found that from 1961 to 1996, actual church attendance fell by half, even while self-reported attendance remained the
same.[18] Put simply, Americans do not tell the truth to survey takers.
They want to be seen as good churchgoers, even if they do not go
to church.

Added to inflation of self-reporting is the genuinely new phenomenon of Americans attending multiple sorts of religious services. Fifty years ago, attending a weekly church service meant that
you went to your sort of church—whether that was Catholic or
Protestant. Now, however, 35 percent of all Americans say they
attend multiple places and most (24 percent overall) indicate that
they attend religious services of another religion![19] Confident headlines, such as Gallup's "Americans' Church Attendance Inches Up in
2010," are clearly based more on what Americans aspire to do rather
than their actual practice.[20] Actual practice has changed greatly in
the last five decades, as fewer and fewer people attend weekly worship services in any faith tradition, and more attend diverse services
than a single place.

If it is difficult to discern how often Americans participate in a
public religious practice, like going to church, it is even more difficult
to quantify changes in private religious behaviors like prayer. Robert
Putnam and David Campbell, in their book *American Grace,* say:

> In terms of private religious behavior one finds virtually the same
> rock-steady levels of religiosity. Polls covering the four decades
> between 1948 and 1990 found that nine of ten Americans pray

at least occasionally, a fraction that did not vary more than a few percentage points over these decades. The wording of a similar question in the General Social Survey between 1983 and 2008 differs slightly, but three quarters of Americans say they pray at least once a week, also a figure that has not varied more than a few percentage points from year to year throughout the last quarter century.[21]

To claim that prayer has remained a "rock-steady" indicator of religiosity between 1948 and 1990 begs a serious question: To whom and how were people praying?

If church attendance took place within a denominational setting in 1948, that is, most people were born, raised, and died in the same church, then it is to be expected that people prayed in denominational voices. Catholics said Hail Marys, prayed with rosary beads, and uttered prayers in Latin; Baptists prayed free-form. Episcopalians echoed Shakespeare while reading from their Book of Common Prayer. Methodists asked that their trespasses be forgiven, while Presbyterians pleaded for forgiveness for their debts. People prayed, but they prayed in languages, styles, and wordings that were written, approved, and taught by their churches and synagogues within certain traditional frameworks.

Today, prayer is a very different practice, as praying altered dramatically in the last two generations. For instance, at the beginning of the twentieth century, Catholics prayed primarily in their church buildings or at home altars, through formal liturgies, using written prayers, in acts of penance and confession, with devotions led by priests, monks, or nuns. Traditional authorities mediated Catholic prayers through established spiritual ranks. By the end of that century, Catholic prayer was far more likely to be ad hoc, lay-oriented, and outside the confines of a church building. Catholic historian James McCartin writes: "Increasingly, laypeople pursued devotional exercises without the help of leadership of ordained clerics, and many came to expand their notion of prayer to encompass a variety of practices, including even the routine activities of their everyday lives."[22]

Although American Catholics borrowed freely from more Protestant styles, including being influenced by practices like the Pentecostal speaking in tongues, American Protestants also discovered Catholic prayer practices. Methodists, Lutherans, Congregationalists, Episcopalians, Baptists, and others embraced the ancient practice of praying the Divine Office (a practice of prescribed hourly prayer) and experimented with prayer forms found in Catholic monastic orders, especially the Benedictines and Franciscans. In addition, American Protestants borrowed from the practice of praying with icons from the Eastern Orthodox and re-created prayer practices out of ancient Celtic, Nordic, and Native American traditions.[23] Both Catholics and Protestants borrow from other religions as well—especially true when it comes to meditation and bodily prayers such as yoga.[24] And the biggest change of all—people now pray with one another across denominational walls and religious barriers. Catholics pray with Protestants; evangelical Protestants pray with Jews; mainline Protestants pray with Muslims; Buddhists with Unitarians. A Methodist pastor recently sent me a T-shirt from his church's interfaith Thanksgiving service. Emblazoned across the front are the words "Prays Well with Others," with a Christian cross, a Star of David, the Sikh khanda, the Buddhist Dharmacakra, the Hindu Om, and the Muslim crescent and star.

On the surface, practicing prayer seems relatively stable over time. But the work of historians, theologians, and sociologists reveals that in just a few decades, the ways in which Americans pray have changed a great deal. When it comes to religious behavior, numbers do not tell the whole story. "Thinking about prayer requires the recognition that prayer is dynamic, not static, and that it changes over time," states one historian. "Both the form and content of prayer—the specifics of how people pray and what they experience in prayer—are conditioned by the circumstances in which those who pray find themselves."[25]

Both of these markers of behavior—churchgoing and praying—seem to indicate that American religion has not changed very much since 1960. However, underneath the relatively stable numbers, both practices are considerably different than they were a generation or two ago. People attend religious services less often (even if they want to present a public image that they are regular churchgoers), and when they do attend public worship, a significant number of people attend the service of a faith other than their own. And, in the case of prayer, the most widely held spiritual practice, blending, borrowing, and mixing forms are far more common than maintaining a single, church-approved rite, ritual, and style. When it comes to how Americans act out their faith, people still want to be seen as churchgoers and pray-ers, yet flux and fluidity in trying to figure out how to connect with God through practice rule the day.

## *Belonging: Who Am I?*

If religious belief is changing and religious practice is in flux, it only makes sense that people's sense of belonging is not particularly stable, as millions switch religious traditions seeking new communities of belief and practice, communities more congruent with the choices they are making. Belonging is an important aspect of religion. To which family of faith do you belong? What community will you join? What is your religious tribe? Do your people have a name? Where is your spiritual home? As with biological family, knowing one's religious family enables individuals to know who they are in the world, where they fit, and what their role in society might or should be. To belong is to be, for belonging is ultimately a question of identity: Who am I?

Through many generations in Western societies, people did not ask if their neighbors were Christians. They assumed they were. Americans and Europeans had a relatively secure sense of religious identity related to their long history and to the church. As Christianity split, people labeled themselves "Catholic" or "Protestant" or "Orthodox." Eventually, when they explained their religious identity, Christians appealed to their denominational traditions, "Episcopal" or "Methodist" or "Baptist," thus aligning themselves with particular doctrines, creeds, and practices.

In the late twentieth century, however, traditional religious labels began to take on negative meanings. Even the most general term, "Christian," was increasingly defined by its most narrow partisans and often used synonymously with "religious Right" or "conservative evangelical." Carol Howard Merritt, a young Presbyterian pastor in Washington, D.C., relates a story typical of her peers: "People in my congregation tell me that when the others know that they are going to church, they always have to qualify it by saying, 'But it's not like that.'" She continues:

> There are some assumptions in our culture about what kind of person a Christian is, or what kind of person goes to church and still has the nerve to talk about it, and it is frustrating to be lumped in together with them. I've noticed that people who are deeply committed to Christianity will identify themselves as a "Christ follower" or a "disciple of Jesus." You can almost see them stepping away from Christianity in their reply. It's their way of saying, "It's not what you think. I'm trying to do something different. I'm trying to be someone different."

Young adults sometimes lack words to label their identity. One thirty-something Christian said, "Facebook has places for 'religious views' and 'political views.' I never can seem to come to anything satisfactory to label myself in either category." But people are not necessarily ambivalent about practicing their faith or talking about a spiritual journey, even a spiritual journey associated with a particular tradition. Indeed, some Christians are very comfortable defining themselves as adherents to a way of life modeled by Jesus, rather than adherents to a particular doctrine or creed. "When someone asks me what kind of Christian I am," says Brent Bill, a Quaker writer, "I say I'm a bad one. . . . I see myself as a pilgrim—traveling the faith path to the destination of being a good Christian—and into the eternal presence of God."[26]

One of the most prominent trends is religious switching. Roughly 44 percent of Americans have left their childhood faith in favor of another denomination or religion or by dropping any religious affiliation at all, with the biggest gain of "adherents" in the "unaffiliated" category. As the authors of the *U.S. Religious Landscape Survey* write: "Sizeable numbers of those raised in all religions—from Catholicism to Protestantism to Judaism—are currently unaffiliated with any particular group," with the largest losses among Roman Catholics.[27]

Fifty years ago, people were born into a religion—a faith often passed down through many generations—and tended to stay with their childhood church. Inherited faith was an important dimension of personal identity, often intertwined with ethnicity or national origin: "I come from a Catholic family," "My people are Lutherans," or "We have always been and will always be Jews." Yet the connection between identity and family tradition is unraveling as people choose their own spiritual paths, embracing faiths that may once have been outside the realm of possibility for their ancestors. A Jew becomes a Buddhist? A Mormon, an Episcopalian? A Baptist, a Catholic? A Catholic, a Hindu? A Presbyterian, a Sikh? A Buddhist, an evangelical? A Methodist, a Muslim? Sure. With almost half the population switching, any journey is just as likely as another.

Although there appears to be no reliable survey data on the subject, a new phenomenon seems to be developing in the West—the possibility of multireligious identity. In the same way that some people are biracial or multiracial, others are describing themselves as multireligious. Recently, I spied an advertisement in a major American airport that read, "Who says you can't be devoted to more than one religion?" Even though the ad was for a luxury auto, it made a startling cultural point about multifaith identity.

In a focus group I conducted on religious commitment, several people claimed some sort of multiple or blended identity. A proud Methodist confessed that he was also a Roman Catholic. When he was a baby, his Catholic grandmother had him secretly baptized in her church against the wishes of his "pagan" parents. When his parents had their own religious experience, they also baptized him— this time in the Methodist church. "Had a joint identity ever since," he joked. "We're all church mutts these days."

An Asian American in the group interpreted his Christian faith through the lens of Japanese culture, which encourages "listening more than talking, being attentive, respecting the other, saving face, and appreciating beauty and simplicity." Likewise, a Chicano Christian who celebrates his Native American traditions claimed a multireligious heritage: "I've participated in many indigenous ceremonies, including sweat lodge, sacred pipe, and sun dance. For many Chicanos, including me, there is no contradiction between Christian practices and Native ceremonies. Both paths together complete our cultural makeup." About half of the people reported that they were fascinated by or borrowed practices from Buddhism; one described himself as a "Buddhist Baptist." One woman is both Christian and Muslim and participates fully in both communities and sets of practices. "Becoming a Muslim," she told me, "has made me a better Christian."

In recent years, in addition to these people, and more likely combinations of Catholic-Protestant, Christian-Jew, or multi-Protestant, I have conversed with people who call themselves Hindu-Unitarian, Jew-Hindu-Buddhist, Congregationalist-Sikh, and Disciples-Sufi.

One of the most well-known Christians to claim multireligious identity, the noted theologian Raimon Panikkar (1918–2010), born of a Spanish Catholic mother and Indian Hindu father, who lived in Europe, the United States, and India, said of his own identity: "I left Europe [for India] as a Christian, I discovered I was a Hindu and returned as a Buddhist without ever having ceased to be Christian."[28]

Not only is identity flux evident in the lives of individuals, but familial identity is also changing. Family faith was, up until recent times, one of the most "impermeable social and cultural boundaries." Churches and synagogues, parents and relatives enforced strict rules about marrying inside one's faith. About a century ago, almost three-quarters of Americans believed that shared religious beliefs were "very important" in making a successful marriage, and only 12 percent of American couples were in an interfaith marriage. Through the last century, attitudes toward shared religious beliefs softened and the number of interfaith marriages rose in every decade, reaching highs in the 30 to 33 percent range as the twentieth century closed, and "a bit fewer than *one-third* of all marriages remain mixed today."[29] Not only do couples participate in each other's faith practices, but their children carry multifaith identities. Children in such families do not choose to belong to multiple religious communities; they simply do by virtue of their birth. Their inheritance is diversity.

It might be easy to accuse these people of sloppy thinking or spiritual silliness, of participating in a thoughtless mélange of postmodern goofiness. But that would not be the case. Their spiritual lives reflect considered choices, and they well illustrate that religious identity—as well as religious belief and religious behavior—are not static. Religion, in all its dimensions—belief, behavior, and belonging—is in dynamic and dramatic states of transition away from what was once accepted and normal. New possibilities and questions have opened up for all of us.

## Norms and Deviations

While doing research, I stumbled across a website on religion statistics. The home page headline announced in large, bold print, with "Decline" in red: "Revealing Statistics: America in *Decline:* The Present Costs of the War Against God." The anonymous Baptist author used many of the same statistics I have given in this chapter to prove that "an undeclared war is being waged against God" and argued that poll data help "quantify the earthly expense" of this spiritual battle. Sound the alarm: only 20 percent of the population attend church each weekend! The number of Americans who do not attend church increased 92 percent since 1991! Christianity in America has suffered a loss of 9.7 percentage points in eleven years! The number of Islamic mosques in America has increased 25 percent since 1994! Adherents to Buddhism have increased 170 percent in a decade! The fastest growing religion is Wicca! Only 27 percent say the Bible represents the actual word of God! Surveys, the writer proclaims, demonstrate the full extent of America's decline, the church's failure, and the evidence that Jesus must surely be returning soon. The end is near.[30]

Although most Christians would eschew the anonymous Baptist's alarmism, there is a more subtle "end is near" feeling in many churches and not a few other traditional religious communities. What was is no longer. And the statistics do, indeed, feel disorienting if you are looking for familiar paths of faith. Depressing perhaps if you are a grandparent worried about your grandchildren's eternal salvation. Grim if you are a denominational leader, a pastor, or the president of your church board. Changes in belief, behavior, and belonging point to a discomforting conclusion for those who remember what once was. Religion has left normal.

In *Revivals, Awakenings, and Reform,* William McLoughlin states that awakenings begin with a "crisis of legitimacy" and "deviations from the old rules" whereby the old norms cease to make sense, as people "begin to doubt their sense and their sanity and to search about for new gods, new ways to perceive and comprehend the power that guides the universe."[31] The plethora of new survey data does not indicate either apocalypse or secularization. Instead, it points toward a different possibility: a turn away from the old gods in search of new ones. In such a situation, diversity is a given (since no new norm has arisen) and dogmatism is a problem (since there are so many options and no single option can claim to be the ultimate answer). Indeed, statistical research might prove that philosopher Robert Wright is more correct when he suggests that God is currently undergoing an "evolution" than Richard Dawkins is when he claims that God is a delusion.[32] Not an end, but a beginning? Are there signs of longing in the midst of the discontent? Are new answers arising as people question the old gods?

# CHAPTER THREE

# When Religion Fails

O NE SUNNY DAY IN spring 2010, I was driving around Virginia Beach, home to evangelist Pat Robertson's media empire, the Christian Broadcasting Network, and Regent University. Not surprisingly, the town has plenty of conservative evangelical churches and a conservative political reputation to match, something one might expect in the geographical headquarters of a major Christian Right organization.

A Prius with Virginia license plates was immediately ahead of me on the freeway; parking decals indicated that the driver was a local resident. It was not, however, the decals that caught my attention. Instead, I noticed the bumper stickers. On the right side was a bright blue "COEXIST" sign, the letters of which were symbols from major world religions. On the left bumper another sticker read: "Loving Kindness Is My Religion." I laughed reading this interfaith protest in a sea of Christian fundamentalism. The quote is from the Dalai Lama, about as theologically distant from Pat Robertson as one can get. I figured the driver would probably count herself among the "spiritual but not religious." They are everywhere these days. Even Virginia Beach.[1]

* * *

ABOUT TWO YEARS EARLIER, I had been invited to address a large gathering of mainline Protestant pastors, mostly folks who would consider themselves theologically moderate or liberal. Before starting my speech, I asked the crowd, "How many of you are Lutherans?" A large number raised their hands. "Episcopalians?" About as many as the Lutherans. "Methodists?" John Wesley's followers cheered for their team. "Presbyterians?" The Calvinists affirmed their identity. "Baptists?" Lots of hands went up. "Congregationalists, Disciples, Mennonites?" After I made my way through the list of labels, I asked, "Now, how many of you consider yourself 'spiritual but not religious'?" Scores of people shot their hands up (many of whom had raised them previously) and laughed, looking a little embarrassed by their admission. They hoped, I suspect, that their bishops or supervisors were not in the room.

In recent decades, religion pollsters in a number of countries have begun to ask a simple question: "Do you think of yourself as . . . spiritual but *not* religious, religious but *not* spiritual, religious *and* spiritual, or *not* spiritual and *not* religious?" The question is straightforward, not complicated or off-putting with denominational labels or theological precision. The results have been both surprising and steady. In the United States, some 30 percent of adults consider themselves "spiritual but not religious." One estimate says that 40 percent of Canadians refer to themselves by this phrase, approximately 25 percent of Australians use this description, and some surveys suggest as many as 51 percent of the British understand themselves in this way.[2] The World Values Survey, run out of the University of Michigan, has found that in many developed nations as high as 70 percent of the population self-define as "generalized" spirituality in contrast to traditional religions.[3] In 2009, Princeton Survey Research Associates found that only 9 percent of Americans consider themselves "religious but not spiritual," and some 48 percent try to combine the two into "religious and spiritual."[4] Whatever the exact number, the trend seems clear enough in a variety of polls across the post-Christian societies: the word "spiritual" is a far more appealing term than "religious."

I shared these numbers with some clergy hoping to engender a discussion about what this meant for churches and religious leaders. Instead of thoughtful engagement, however, the pastors criticized the sociologists who gather such data: they complained that without definitions of the terms "religious" and "spiritual," all those questioned would have their own individual interpretations. Despite this unspiritual and prickly sort of defensiveness displayed by my friends—many professional clergy—they have a point: What do the words "religious" and "spiritual" mean? Why are people rejecting the word "religious" in favor of the word "spirituality"?

For much of Western history, the words "religious" and "spiritual" meant roughly the same thing, how human beings related to or connected with God in rites, rituals, practices, and communal worship. People did not generally separate the two terms. Historian Robert Fuller points out, however, the popular definitions of the words diverged throughout the twentieth century: "The word *spiritual* gradually came to be associated with the private realm of thought and experience, while the word *religious* came to be connected with the public realm of membership in religious institutions, participation in formal ritual, and adherence to official denominational doctrines."[5] Not only did the words come to signify different aspects of faith by the early twenty-first century, but the terms "spiritual" and "religious" have become laden with emotional connotations. In general, "spirituality" is taken as a positive term, whereas "religion" is often negative; spirituality is understood as somehow more authentic, religion as having "a somewhat cynical orientation." Indeed, one British researcher found that Americans, Canadians, and British who identified as spiritual were more "socially desirable" than those who defined themselves as religious—that is, they were more appealing life partners![6]

The language of "spirituality" is certainly different from the language for God and faith that many Christians used as children (or the language their parents used). Because it is a new language, it fosters misunderstanding. Religious people sometimes dismiss "spirituality" as vacuous or vague, too closely related to "spiritualism" (the practice of communicating with the dead), Wicca, or some other New Age faith. Others tag spirituality as consumerist or individualistic, lacking intellectual content or any sense of commitment, a fad, "Oprah religion."

But spirituality is neither vague nor meaningless. Despite a certain linguistic fuzziness, the word "spiritual" is both a critique of institutional religion and a longing for meaningful connection. In a wide variety of guises and forms, spirituality represents an important stage of awakening: the search for new gods. As the old gods (and the institutions that preached, preserved, and protected the old gods) lose credibility, people begin to cast about for new gods—and new stories, new paths, and new understandings to make sense of their new realities. In the process, the old language fails, and people reach for new words to describe the terrain of their experience. "Spirituality" is one such word, an ancient word, to be sure, but a word that is taking on fresh dimensions of meaning in a fluid and pluralistic religious context. To say that one is "spiritual but not religious" or "spiritual and religious" is often a way of saying, "I am dissatisfied with the way things are, and I want to find a new way of connecting with God, my neighbor, and my own life." It might not be a thoughtless mantra at all—in many cases, it may well be a considered commentary on religious institutions, doctrine, and piety.

## Word Association

What do you think of when you hear the word "spiritual"? When you hear the word "religious"? In a very unscientific experiment over the course of a year and a half, I asked groups with whom I was working to play a word association game with me. On a whiteboard, I drew two columns, one headed with "Spirituality," the other with "Religion," and had them list in each column words they associated with that term. I worked with groups in Texas and Toronto, New Jersey and Newport Beach, Colorado and Columbus, Sydney and Seattle. Interestingly enough, they all came up with almost the same lists:

| *Spirituality* | *Religion* |
| --- | --- |
| experience | institution |
| connection | organization |
| transcendence | rules |
| searching | order |
| intuition | dogma |
| prayer | authority |
| meditation | beliefs |
| nature | buildings |
| energy | structure |
| open | defined |
| wisdom | principles |
| inner life | hierarchy |
| 12-steps | orthodoxy |
| inclusive | boundaries |
| doubt | certainty |

Depending upon the gathering, the words showed up in different order and with different emotional content. Groups in Seattle, Toronto, and Newport Beach quickly and energetically filled out the "spirituality" column, offering testimonies to the power of nature, prayer, and meditation in their lives, whereas New Jersey Presbyterians were skeptical of "spirituality" and warmly described "order," "structure," "orthodoxy," and "beliefs" in the "religion" column. Many groups included these words and went beyond them, filling flip charts and whiteboards with related terms. In addition to positive words, there were negative terms as well. Some described "spirituality" as "individualistic," "selfish," "lacking an ethical compass," and "self-centered" and accused those who talk about spirituality of contributing to the decline of the church or of turning their backs on social justice. But "religion" got the worst of it: "cold," "outdated," "rigid," "hurtful," "narrow," "controlling," "embarrassing," and "mean." And those words came from people who were church members! No matter the region or denomination, all of the groups associated spirituality with experience and religion with institutions.

Wendy, a fifty-eight-year-old Texas Episcopalian, summed up the exercise by saying, "Religion is the organized affiliation one identifies with; spirituality is the practicing, intimate relationship that resides within." Others agreed: "Religion means organization, doctrine, and hierarchy; spirituality is a path of inner transformation." "Religion is belief in God and the principles of a religion, engaging in the practice of worship; spirituality is rooted in faith in a Higher Being, a Creator, and belief in the Holy Spirit." "Religion is believing and following church doctrine," a Presbyterian remarked, "but being spiritual means feeling God's Spirit guiding my daily life." Jonathan, a layman in his early fifties, shared: "Religion is a set of beliefs about God, words used to describe a particular understanding of the divine. Spirituality is an experience, based sometimes in religion (but not necessarily so) that shapes my view of the world and my place in it." He continued, "It develops over time and is transformative."

A word association game is not a controlled study. Rather, it is a quick way to gauge popular ideas and sentiments. Participants had little time to nuance their responses and simply reacted by sharing terms and ideas. Yet in these gatherings, made up of many clergy, church leaders, and church members, "spirituality" and "religion" were defined as distinct but overlapping concepts, with the former leaning toward experience and the latter toward institutions.[7] But no matter how hard they tried, most found it difficult to get very excited about religion. They have essentially substituted the word "religion" for institutional religion and "spirituality" for lively faith. As one leading psychologist notes, religion as "this newly defined construct is contrasted with the spiritual, which refers to the personal, the affective, the experiential, and the thoughtful."[8]

## The Business of Religion

Not long ago, a Presbyterian minister drove me through the streets of Saginaw, Michigan, once a manufacturing center for the automotive industry, especially General Motors. Facing crisis and collapse, General Motors pulled out of the town. Deserted factories now line wide commercial boulevards; empty churches and abandoned houses checker once middle-class neighborhoods. "I don't know what we can do," the pastor said. "How do you turn all this around? What use is there for all these empty plants?" At one time, it was a thriving city. But dependent on the old model, Saginaw is half the size it was in 1960, left in a state of postindustrial decline. "I can't even say that young people should move here," she said. "There's nothing here to do. Everything has ended."

Clearly articulated or not, even religious leaders know that the old church institutions are unsustainable and are failing. And that probably should not surprise anyone, since American churches were organized on the same principles and structures as were twentieth-century American corporations. Beginning around 1890, denominations built massive bureaucratic structures, modeling themselves after American businesses, complete with corporate headquarters, program divisions, professional development and marketing departments, franchises (parish churches), training centers, and career tracks. Other than the fact that denominations offered religion as the product, they differed little from other corporations that dominated America in the last century. As a Presbyterian elder once sighed to me, "Our church is like GM, only we sell faith." And if the Presbyterian Church—or any denomination, for that matter—is like GM, that is not a good thing.

Like the corporations that once brought life to cities like Saginaw but now struggle to stay in business and face difficult economic times, so too organized religion is facing a tough spiritual climate. The religious model that once worked so well serving to educate, spiritually enliven, and socially elevate so many does not accomplish those goals as well any longer. As with other corporations of the same vintage, church executives became too distanced from the regular folks; managers (i.e., pastors) grumbled about pay, benefits, and working conditions; creativity was strangled by red tape; expenses began to outrun income; and huge facilities needed to be maintained. Faith increasingly became a commodity and membership roles and money the measures of success. The business of the church replaced the mission of the church. Slowly, then more quickly, customers became disgruntled. Resources declined. Brand loyalty eroded. Former successes blinded those in charge to increasing discontent in the pews, thinking that the system only needed to be tinkered with, tweaked, or somehow fixed and everything would be fine once again. It did not seem to occur to the folks in charge that collapse was possible or that their brand might be permanently tarnished.

At first, people simply switched religious companies—rather like changing from a Pontiac to a Toyota. If the old mainline churches were unresponsive to their spiritual needs, the faithful would go elsewhere. The "elsewhere" that some (but certainly not all) people went was to evangelical churches and denominations. At the time, most evangelical churches were small, flexible, devotional, and local spiritual communities. But evangelical churches grew and became successful, resembling the mainline churches of the 1950s they had displaced, and they started to embody some of the same problems of distance, careerism, and institutionalization of the older churches. By 1980, they had become even bigger business than most mainline denominations, with their own radio and television stations, political action committees, and lobbying groups. As a result, corporate evangelicalism has been suffering losses since the mid-1990s—even the mighty Southern Baptist Convention is seeing record decline.[9]

Even some independent megachurches have followed the pattern of business success and subsequent decline. The original megachurch, the Crystal Cathedral, is bankrupt and facing sale! Willow Creek Community Church, one of America's most famous megachurches, has suffered membership stagnation and a lack of enthusiasm among the faithful. Pastor Bill Hybels confesses that although Willow Creek is successful at some things, it has failed to meet the congregation's deepest spiritual needs.[10] A quarter of Willow Creek's core members described themselves as spiritually "stalled" or "dissatisfied" with the role of the church in their spiritual growth. Church leaders found that 25 percent of the "stalled" segment and 63 percent of the church's "dissatisfied" segment contemplated leaving the church.[11] A good business model brought thousands to Willow Creek. But did it work as a community of deepening connection to God and others? Maybe not.

Americans forget that religion was not always organized in the same way it is now. Until the Civil War, religion was typically the matter of small-town or village dynamics led by itinerant preachers and settled pastors who formed little congregations based on styles of prayer or preaching or liturgy. Denominations were ad hoc, messy affairs consisting of people bound by ethnicity, language, prayer practices, confession, or theological tradition. Most churches did not even think of themselves as part of "denominations" until well into the nineteenth century. Religious faith was not centralized; there were no national headquarters. Faith life was organized locally and regionally, with slow communication between clusters of Presbyterians, Methodists, Baptists, Episcopalians, or Catholics.

There were few seminaries, and most of the clergy did not have formal theological education, having been trained instead in a local church with a senior pastor who was likewise self-educated. Clergy tended to be entrepreneurial, often starting new congregations and new styles of worship (even under the banner of traditional labels) and easily adapting inherited forms of theology and prayer to personal and communal preferences and customs. In such a system, denominations tended to be held together by written material, prayer books and newspapers, more than by authoritative leaders or church decree. The written directives of faith—creeds, rule books, prayers, and theologies—tended to be interpreted through local tastes and cultures. Faith was a matter of devotion, piety, family tradition, and communal needs.

Because of the lack of trained clergy and the long distances people sometimes had to travel to even get to a church building, parents acted as the arbiters and authorities of a faith tradition, teaching their children the Bible, Christian ethics, and even liturgy in their own homes. Mothers and midwives often baptized infants, especially those in distress. Homes often served as ritual space, as most baptisms, marriages, and funerals happened in the family parlor. The ad hoc nature of early American religion helps explain much of its creativity—and much of its diversity—as people interpreted faith and created spiritual practices that worked for them. When interpreting existing religion failed to meet their needs, they invented their own faiths. The result? American Christianity emerged as a myriad of different interpretations and local customs, along with a dizzying array of new denominations.

As the United States became more urban, educated, and business-oriented after the Civil War, it faced increased social pressures through immigration, mobility, economic recessions, and technological change. The religious nonorganization of the early republic no longer worked, and it began to make sense to think about religion in business terms. By centralizing and regularizing religious work, more poor people could be fed, more churches could be built, and more schools and colleges could be supported. Standardized education would raise theological literacy and increase Christian virtue. Trained clergy could teach from a common curriculum and model shared practices of piety. Pooling money and effort strengthened the nation's charitable resources, creating a large and successful interdenominational system whereby the faithful could solve social problems. Denominations erected massive churches, established seminaries, built impressive headquarters, regularized education, and instituted rigorous training standards for clergy, musicians, and professional Christian educators. It was a massive, expensive, and successful effort to restructure religion.

And it worked. Other countries, both Protestant and Catholic, followed similar patterns of religious organization. The Vatican, for example, organized its first bank in 1887 under Pope Leo XIII, hoping to accomplish the same sorts of charitable ends as the Protestant benevolent empire. All churches mobilized massive missionary forces in an effort to market their brand to new religious consumers around the world. By the mid-twentieth century, religion was a big business, having embarked on a "period of unprecedented institutionalization" in the United States and elsewhere.[12] If North Americans and Europeans perceive "religion" as "institutional religion," it may be because the denominations did this to themselves. The perception is largely correct. Churches may have a more altruistic product line than General Motors, but the history of big business and the big business of faith are intertwined.

And it is not only regular folks who are frustrated with institutional religion. I frequently meet clergy who either publicly or privately confess to discontent, anger, and doubt with the organizations they serve. Although they often like their local congregations, they wonder if their denominations can change or even survive.

One day, a note arrived through my website from Paul, a pastor whom I had never met. He shared a story that well expresses the discontent of those who have been "inside" religious institutions for a long time:

> After over 20 years of parish ministry I am leaving it. My wife, who has been a faithful companion in this journey, is also leaving the church. I have resigned from all my denominational roles, and no one has said a word. . . . Yet, we are sad to leave, because of what it means. It means to us the church has become irrelevant to us. We care about spiritual disciplines of study, worship, confession and forgiveness, discernment, fellowship, and mission. In the church, I spent more time discussing the replacement of the church roof than on discerning our purpose as a church. We miss the liturgy and the relationships, but I do not miss the constant bickering over meaningless garbage, evening meetings and working every weekend.

Even some of those in charge are dissatisfied. Indeed, several studies reveal that pastors leave church ministry at surprisingly high rates, reporting that they feel "blocked or frustrated" in their attempts to "bring new life" to congregations.[13] Disillusionment, discouragement, and discontent are driving even leaders away from institutional religion. As the old forms of economic organization fail, so too the old forms of religious organization that paralleled them are failing.

## 2000–2010: The "Horrible Decade"

As it happened, the first decade of the twenty-first century was not particularly good for religion as a whole—not just particular congregations or denominations. Indeed, that may well be the understatement of the century. The first dozen years of the new millennium have been downright horrible for religion, leading to a sort of "participation crash" in churches of all sorts as the new millennium dawned.[14] In particular, five major events revealed the ugly side of organized religion, challenging even the faithful to wonder if defending religion is worth the effort, and creating an environment that can rightly be called a religious recession.

*2001: The September 11 terrorist attacks.* Following the terrorist attacks in New York and Washington, D.C., many Americans turned to church for answers and comfort. President Bush called for a National Day of Prayer on September 14, 2001, and delivered a presidential sermon from the Washington National Cathedral. For about a month, maybe two, clergy reported full pews and pitched interest in issues of the soul. Then, without much fanfare, attendance started to drop; people stopped coming to church. Everything went back to normal—until normal got worse.

As time passed, the media, politicians, columnists, and pundits began to blame religion for the attacks, calling the terrorists things like religious fanatics, fundamentalist zealots, medieval crusaders, and holy warriors. Of course, at the beginning, everyone understood that these pundits meant "Islam" when they said "religion." This, of course, was bad enough—most especially for Muslims—but the more politicians blamed Islam, the more religion in general looked bad.

It did not help that some religious leaders, like Pat Robertson, Jerry Falwell, and Franklin Graham, blamed American infidelity for the attacks, saying we had been too tolerant of homosexuals and feminists. Many churches called for retribution, not peace or understanding. Pastors felt threatened by their flocks when they urged churchgoers to pray for their enemies. The more religiously conservative individuals were, the more likely they were to back the wars in Afghanistan and Iraq.[15] It became hard to discriminate between healthy, life-giving religion and violent, life-ending religion, inspiring journalist Christopher Hitchens to write: "People of faith are in their different ways planning your and my destruction, and the destruction of all the hard-won human attainments [art, literature, philosophy, ethics, and science]. *Religion poisons everything.*"[16] As the war on terror descended into a morass of duplicity, immoral tactics, national division, and exploding debt, churches looked pretty bad for going along with the whole misadventure in the first place. Anti-Islamic prejudice and unthinking hyperpatriotism worked as a double-edged sword of religious self-injury throughout the decade.

*2002: The Roman Catholic sex abuse scandal.* In early 2002, the *Boston Globe* began a series of reports on five Roman Catholic priests accused of sexually abusing children in their care. As the news unfolded, it grew into an international story involving thousands of priests in scores of dioceses with tens of thousands of victims across the globe. Since the 1960s, the Catholic Church had systematically covered up cases of sexual abuse by priests, protected predators, broken civil laws regarding rape and sexual abuse, ignored victims' pleas for redress, and used church money to defend these secrets, often rewarding bishops and archbishops who hid the crimes with higher ecclesial positions. The scandal stretched across the Catholic Church; some of the worst cases were in the United States, Ireland, Australia, New Zealand, and Canada.

The Roman Catholic Church has a long history of difficulties in the United States, yet the Catholic population had grown steadily through the past three centuries. In 2008, however, Pew reported that one-third of Americans who were raised Catholic no longer describe themselves as Catholic—a statistic that translates as "roughly 10 percent of all Americans are former Catholics," a defection from that church on an astonishing scale.[17] Those numbers do not include lapsed Catholics or those who are nominally Catholic. The statistics include only those who have intentionally left the church in some formal or informal way. At this point, the Catholic Church in the United States maintains membership mostly through Hispanic immigration.

The Catholic problems have no doubt contributed as well to an erosion of overall respect for the clergy. In 2010, only 53 percent of Americans said that ministers had "high or very high" ethical standards—they trusted grade-school teachers, police officers, doctors, and military leaders more than ministers of the church—a percentage down almost 14 points since the scandal broke. Clergy ranked with bankers (post–Wall Street crisis) as the profession seeing the greatest decline over the decade.[18]

*2003: Protestant conflict over homosexuality.* In 2003, the Episcopal Diocese of New Hampshire elected V. Gene Robinson, an openly gay priest with a long-term partner, to become its next bishop. Although mainline Protestants had been arguing over homosexuality, church leadership, and theology for several decades, this event pushed the conflict into public consciousness as never before—and raised denominational stakes to the point of global schism. Newspapers, cable television, and a new cadre of bloggers reported on every threat of division, elevating ecclesiastical dirty laundry and theological meanness to a point not witnessed since the pamphlet wars of the Protestant Reformation, when the leaders of the new churches regularly lambasted the pope as Satan and worse.

Although some Christians surely felt theologically and morally uncomfortable with the idea of a gay bishop, many more were appalled by the nastiness of the controversy, the obvious politicization of their denominations, the low spiritual tone of the discussion, and the scandal of churches suing their mother denominations over property. It is not entirely clear how many people left the Episcopal Church in the wake of the fight, and whether people may have left because they disagreed with the decision or because they were weary of the argument. But internal membership decline is not really the point. Mainline churches have been struggling with membership losses for four decades, but they have remained among the most "likeable" and respected religious groups in the United States.[19] The public brawl over homosexuality undermined this reputation, however, serving to remind the general public that even the most tolerant and genial Christians can get riled up to the point of inquisition. The Episcopal conflict over Gene Robinson's vocation only underscored the new narrative—Christianity is mean, bigoted, and makes people behave badly.

*2004: The religious Right wins the battle, but loses the war.* The second election of George W. Bush in 2004 may well be the greatest victory of conservative evangelical religion in the last four decades. Journalists crowned evangelicals as the most powerful and successful religious group in the United States. Following the 2004 election, *Time* magazine featured a cover story on the twenty-five most in-fluential evangelical leaders, the folks reshaping American religion and politics. Yet what appeared on the surface to be a success may have, in fact, signaled a deeper failure. In their recent book *American Grace,* Robert Putnam and David Campbell cautiously suggest that the real victory of the religious Right has been to alienate an entire generation of young people.[20]

All was not well in the Bible Belt. Unnoticed by elite observers, the conservative evangelical admixture of faith and politics was at odds with the cultural and spiritual values of younger Americans—particularly with regard to views of women, same-sex relationships, the environment, issues of global poverty, and legalization of mari-juana. Young evangelicals tired of their parents' political and social agenda, leading them to wonder if the Bible and theology they had been taught were true. When major leaders, like Ted Haggard, were caught in major sex and money scandals, the religious Right became the butt of late-night comedians' jokes and Internet gossip, adding fuel to the smoldering discontent of young evangelicals, who increasingly suspected that their churches and leaders were just as guilty of doctrinal and moral misconduct as the Roman Catholics.[21]

During the decade, many young evangelical Christians opted out of their parents' churches in favor of starting their own con-gregations in loose associations that became known as the emergent or emerging church. Not a formal denomination, the emergent church attracted wide attention in 2004 with the publication of Brian McLaren's *A Generous Orthodoxy,* a book that critiqued the established religious Right and offered a new, more open version of Christian faith to a generation of young evangelical discontents. That book, combined with progressive evangelical leader Jim Wallis's stinging assault on conservative Christian politics in a campaign claiming that "God is not a Republican," empowered dissent in the evangelical ranks.

There was ample evidence that young adults—even evangelical ones—now understood "Christian" to be coterminous with "religious Right" and were leaving churches because of it.[22] In 1985, 26 percent of young adults under twenty-nine claimed to be evangelicals; that number now hovers around 15 percent, while the number of "nones" under twenty-nine has risen from 12 percent to nearly 30 percent. Indeed, most evangelical loss stems from the defection of young people, who increasingly identify Christianity (not just evangelical religion, but Christianity as a whole) as antihomosexual, judgmental, hypocritical, out of touch with reality, overly politicized, insensitive, exclusive, and dull.[23] The old religious Right may have won some cherished political battles, but in the war over the hearts of their youth they surely lost more than they gained. And for American public opinion, conservative evangelical politics may have been the worst marketing campaign for the word "Christian" since the Salem witch trials.

*2007: The Great Religious Recession.* The first years of the twenty-first century marked a swift and shocking reversal of the religious mood of the late 1990s. Before the millennium, American religion went through a period of optimism, growth, and wealth. Indeed, from 1990 to 2000, Americans expressed increasing confidence in religious institutions and religious leaders. At that time, evangelicals expanded their base and coalesced cultural power in politics and media, Roman Catholics experienced visionary leadership of spiritual heroes like Pope John Paul II and Mother Teresa, and even beleaguered mainline Protestant churches slowed or stopped their membership declines, posting modest gains in Sunday attendance and renewed interest in Christian education, theology, and church planting.

But the events of the early 2000s ended all such enthusiasm for conventional religion. Since 2000, General Social Survey data shows as much as a 12 point drop in public trust in religious institutions, with only about 20 percent of Americans saying they have a "great deal" of confidence in "organized religion."[24] The American public places more confidence (in order) in the scientific community, medicine, the U.S. Supreme Court, and education. The religious favorable rating now hovers around the confidence rank of Wall Street and major corporations. When the economic recession hit in 2007, religious institutions were already struggling under the weight of the psychological, spiritual, and moral shocks that were already pressing on their communities. Although political leaders looked to faith-based organizations to help alleviate the suffering of the poor and unemployed when the stock and housing markets collapsed, churches were already woefully short on resources. The economic recession arrived at a moment when churches and denominations were already in a religious recession. The national economic crisis served to weaken embattled religious organizations, further marginalizing conventional faith institutions in a chaotic cultural environment. The economic crisis did not drive people to religion; instead, it drove religion farther into irrelevance. Sociologist Mark Chaves sees, if not a connection between the economic loss of confidence and a religious one, then the same magnitude of institutional failure in the two realms, representing "real change," not just trend fluctuation.[25] As the Great Depression of the early twentieth century paralleled a religious depression, so too the Great Recession has twinned with a great religious recession.[26]

In the introduction, I shared Ellen's story. Born a mainline Protestant pastor's daughter, she left church when she went to college. After marriage, she returned to a mainline church, but was turned off by the fight over women's ordination. Seeking a community of social justice and service, she became a Catholic. But authoritarian hierarchy eventually soured her on participation. She joined an evangelical church, where she had run-ins with the pastor over politics and theology. "I knew when I left," she said, "that I wouldn't be going anywhere else for a time." Ellen ran out of choices. She had nowhere else to go. No wonder. All three of America's great Christian traditions—Catholic, mainline Protestant, and evangelical have bungled the faith pretty badly in the last decade, at a time when religions were swimming across a historic tide of doubt. All of these larger institutional failures are evident in Ellen's story.

Between business-as-usual church, internal stresses, external scandals, and rank hypocrisy, finally compounded by economic crisis, American Christianity is in a mess. When it comes to "elsewheres," Americans are running out of choices. Although many people still express a level of satisfaction with their local congregations, the undercurrents of discontent are strong. Some 42 percent of churchgoers confess they are only moderately satisfied or dissatisfied with their churches, leaving open the "possibility of considering other options."[27] Are we all in the process of becoming Ellen?

## Holy Discontent

On the final day of 2010, a friend sent me a New Year's greeting wishing me the gift of "discontent" and enclosed this prayer:

> O God, make me discontented with things the way they are in the world and in my own life. Make me notice the stains when people get spilled on. Make me care about the slum child downtown, the misfit at work, the people crammed into the mental

hospital, the men, women and youth behind bars. Jar my com-
placence, expose my excuses, get me involved in the life of my
city and world. Give me integrity once more, O God, as we seek
to be changed and transformed, with a new understanding and
awareness of our common humanity.[28]

Not many people think of discontent as a gift. As the prayer
points out, however, discontent is the beginning of change. Only
by noticing what is wrong, seeing the systems and structures that
do not foster health and happiness, can we ever make things different. If people were satisfied, there would be no reason to reach for
more, no motivation for creativity and innovation. Discontent is
one short step from the longing for a better life, a better society, and
a better world; and longing is another short step from doing something about what is wrong. Indeed, restlessness possesses a spiritual
quality: "Blessed are the poor in spirit," said Jesus, "for theirs is the
kingdom of heaven" (Matt. 5:3).

In the last decade, Americans have witnessed the power of
discontent—especially in politics. In 1990, approximately one in ten
voters considered themselves "independents"; in 2010, that had risen
to nearly four in ten. "Unaffiliated" became the largest political
party in the United States, with both Democrats and Republicans
lagging behind. One *Politics Daily* article proclaimed "Independent
Voters Fed Up with Entire Political System," citing voter discontent
with the structure of two-party politics.[29] Such discontent contributed to the rise of the Tea Party, but the Tea Party did not corner
the market on political restlessness. In 2006, discontent led to the
election of a Democratic House; in 2008, to the nomination and
election of Barack Obama. And in 2010, political progressives, envi-
ronmentalists, Christian conservatives, and other groups articulated
equal—but not nearly as well organized as the Tea Party's—anxiety,
discontent, and anger with the way things are.

Of course, discontent can easily become rage. Rage is frightening, especially when it is combined with fear, lies, or violence. But it is also a sign that on a vast scale people want change. From politics to business to education, people are longing for new structures that resonate with and respond to their day-to-day experience, giving them a sense of participation and voice and a real stake in the future. "Everybody has an agenda for themselves and not for the people," said Tim Tennis, a forty-five-year-old factory worker from Ohio, to writer Linda Killian. "The people are not being heard. The politicians are doing what they want and getting away with it."[30] But rage only results from discontent when restlessness is unfocused or its longings remain unfulfilled. When channeled wisely and fueled by a hopeful vision for the future, discontent can be the beginning of genuine social transformation by inspiring courageous action.

The rise of political unaffiliateds parallels the rise of religious unaffiliateds, as discontent has led to defections from most major religious groups. The two movements are not identical, but they share in the same spirit of frustration about institutions, authority, and leadership. As the old two-party system of American politics has become bogged down in issues, styles, and practices of the past, so too is American religion stuck in issues, styles, and practices of the past. American religion has been much more diverse than American politics, of course, giving people a wider range of choices than politics. But even denominations can roughly be grouped into liberal and conservative "parties," a reality that has led some scholars to suggest that American religion is essentially a two-party system.[31]

Even more nuanced renderings, however, made American faith into a tripartite world—liberals, conservatives, and the "middle." Or Protestants, Catholics, and Jews. Or liberal Protestants, evangelical Protestants, and Catholics. The addition of "other" for Buddhists, Hindus, and Muslims stretched the world of religious parties. But even that seems less than adequate. In the same way that political independents feel that labels and parties have failed them, so religious people feel the same—opting out of the system because of anger, boredom, sadness, a sense of disconnection, lack of control, or whatever. In a very real sense, those who describe themselves as "spiritual" are a protest vote against churches of all sorts—mainline Protestant, Catholic, and evangelical. Or perhaps the "spiritual" are swing voters of the faith world, unsure as to where they might land.

If you are the one being voted against, it does not feel very good—especially if you or your congregation is doing the hard work of listening to the needs of the world and trying to respond in hopeful and imaginative ways. But even satisfied believers and congregations can learn from discontent. When people leave, or even when they drift, they are saying, "This idea, group, or path no longer makes sense. The organizations that once enabled me to live well in the world no longer help. There must be a different way."

The religious unaffiliateds are primarily young adults. In the United States, somewhere in the range of 25 to 30 percent of the population under thirty neither attend religious services nor have any religious preference, although about half of the unaffiliated group still say that they believe in God or understand themselves to be spiritual.[32] Whatever else may be said of them, they are profoundly disappointed in religion, religious ideologies, and organizations as those things currently exist. In a 2004 survey, the Barna organization found that young adults who are outside of church hold intensely negative views of Christianity: 91 percent think that Christianity is "antihomosexual," 87 percent say Christians are "judgmental," 85 percent accuse churchgoers of being "hypocritical," and 72 percent say Christianity is "out of touch with reality." Only 41 percent think that Christianity seems "genuine or real" or "makes sense," while only 30 percent think that it is "relevant to your life."[33]

Those numbers are sobering, especially to Christians who find meaning in their congregations, have worked for social justice for LGBT (lesbian, gay, bisexual, or transgender) persons in their churches, or who practice their faith in loving ways. Because such statistics are hard to hear, they are easy to dismiss as the ignorance of youth or a lack of maturity: "Ah! The discontent of youth! I once felt the same. But when they grow up and have children, they will see things differently!" However, in a roundabout way, their criticism actually demonstrates authentic spiritual longing. Somewhere these young adults have evidently heard that Christianity is supposed to be a religion about love, forgiveness, and practicing what Jesus preached and that faith should give meaning to real life. They are judging Christianity on its own teachings and believe that American churches come up short. Thus, their discontent about what is may reflect a deeper longing for a better sort of Christianity, one that embodies Jesus's teaching and life in a way that makes a real difference in the world.

Paul, the pastor who e-mailed to tell me he quit church, left because he was longing for something better. Tired of trying to maintain an institution and quelling quarrels, Paul still loved much of what faith was about; he cared about the "spiritual disciplines of study, worship, confession and forgiveness, discernment, fellowship, and mission." Despite the fact that he thought the church had become "irrelevant," he clearly dreamed of being part of a community that embodied these spiritual practices. He desired a different sort of church, a robust community that connected people to God and to one another. For two decades, he had worked to create such a church and failed. He said he was watching his denomination "self-destruct." But the undertow of longing still pulses through his note. His frustration and sadness are matched by the wish for a fuller life of faith and a better church. Paul's story is one of leaving and longing, just like Ellen's. They both left, but still long to find a community where a more just and loving form of Christian faith is enacted.

During a lecture to a group in California, I stated that about 30 percent of Americans consider themselves "spiritual but not religious." A man in the audience shouted out, "That's the state slogan of California!" The phrase "spiritual but not religious" is the contemporary way of trying to explain some sort of connection to God, separate from, in tension with, or in opposition to religious institutions. The same polls that find religion on the wane also find this thing called "spirituality" on the upswing; Americans are showing intense fascination for everything from new sorts of communal gatherings for worship to individual mystical experiences, to classical prayer and meditation practices. At first, many religious leaders hoped such experimentation was a passing fad—a spiritual search on the part of a restless baby-boom generation. Now that half a century has gone by and the baby boomers' grandchildren are even more discontent than their elders, it is increasingly difficult to dismiss spirituality as a sort of cultural phase. To speak of "spirituality" simultaneously signals discontent with religious institutions and longing for a new, different, and deeper connection with God, one's neighbor, and oneself.

## Outbursts

Religious discontent is indistinguishable from the history of spiritual renewal and awakening. Religion is often characterized as contentment, the idea that faith and faithfulness offer peace, security, and certainty. In this mode, God is depicted in kindly ways, the church as an escape from the cares and stresses of the world, and religious leaders as pastors, the spiritual caretakers of the flock. Although most faith traditions do offer such surety to believers, religion has another guise as well—the prophetic tradition. In the prophetic mode, faith discomforts the members of a community, opens their eyes and hearts to the shortcomings of their own lives and injustice in the world, and presses for human society to more fully embody God's dream of healing and love for all peoples.

Religious faiths struggle between the pastoral and the prophetic, comfort and agitation. In a very real way, institutions are inherently pastoral—they seek to maintain those things that give comfort by baptizing shared values and virtues of a community. They reinforce the way things are (or were) through appeals to divine or super-natural order. They are always slow to change. Institutions resist prophets. Prophets question. They push for things to be different. They push people to behave better toward one another. They want change.

The history of Christianity can be told as a story of the tension between order and prophecy.[34] Jesus came as a prophet, one who challenged and transformed Judaism. A charismatic community grew up around his teachings and eventually formed into the church. The church organized, and then became an institution. The institution provided guidance and meaning for many millions. And then it became guarded, protective of the power and wealth it garnered, the influence it wielded, and salvation it alone provided.

Many of the people in the church did not seem to notice, but some did. What the church taught seemed at odds with their experience of life or God. They became increasingly disenchanted with what the church offered. Discontent grew. They questioned the way things were done. They experimented with new ideas and spiritual practices. They met on the sly, singing subversive songs and praying to their favorite (and often unapproved) saints, and served people the institution overlooked or oppressed. They bent the rules and often broke them. The established church typically ignored them, sometimes tolerated them, often branded them heretics, tried to control them, and occasionally killed them. When enough people joined the ranks of the discontented, the institutional church had to pay attention. In the process, and sometimes unintentionally, the church opened itself up for genuine change and renewal.

Today, the movements of the discontent are remembered by names many people revere: the Benedictine renewal, the Franciscan movement, the Brethren of the Common Life, the Protestant Reformation, the Anabaptist community, the Methodist and evangelical revival, the Great Awakening, the Oxford movement, the Pentecostal revival. Others, I suspect, are remembered by no grand title.

In my own search for family history, I discovered one such small movement. During the 1920s, some of my ancestors—who were most likely Lutherans—left their traditional church for the passion of Pentecostal experience. They rejected the faith of the old world in favor of embracing the fervor of the Spirit and leaving behind a contented existence of roasting coffee, delivering ice, and being carpenters, praised by those who knew them for their "fine Christian character." They became spirit-filled preachers and church planters, and one relative was a singing evangelist who helped spark a revival on Maryland's eastern shore. They refused to attend more respectable churches, and women stood up to authoritarian husbands in a quest to pray in tongues. Their memory is not recorded in any scholarly book. Instead, from the seeds of spiritual discontent, they changed themselves, their households, their neighborhoods, and their families' future. That single spiritual outburst, my ancestors' wild, abandoned leap into Pentecostal fervor, still reverberates in my life almost a century later. They changed history, not as grand leaders who started a new church, but in little bits at a time.

No historian can even guess how many small movements of individuals or congregations have existed in the past, movements made up of those who experienced God in new ways that remade their lives and communities without much notice or credit. Some movements lasted only a short time and were local events; others lasted decades or centuries and spread throughout Christendom. Such things are part of the long historical process of renewing faith. How would any religious tradition stay alive over hundreds or thousands of years if not for the questions of discontent and the creativity brought forth by longing?

Robert Jones, director of Public Religion Research, remarks of this history: "There's a sense in which the spiritual, experiential elements are always overflowing the bounds of the official reli-

gious channels. . . . Much of religious history is about the institutions trying to catch up with and channel those outbursts."[35] Organized religion fears such outbursts; but spiritual outbursts almost
always precede real reform. Might spiritual discontent be today's
prophetic edge, needling institutions to listen, to change, to be
more responsive and relevant? Are the outbursts signs of some new
form of faith?

## The Energy of And

In Newport Beach, California, a group of Presbyterians engaged
in the "religion" and "spirituality" exercise could not decide to
which category they should assign "worship." One woman argued
for "spirituality," because for her worship was an experience that
connected her to God, but, she said, "not all worship, of course, just
*good* worship."

A minister countered, insisting that "worship" was in the category of "religion": "It is the work of a church, follows certain forms,
and is organized." He paused. "Believe me, it is organized—I spend
half my week figuring out how to organize it!"

The discussion emboldened one young woman to challenge my
whiteboard categories altogether. "I don't think these things can
be so neatly divided," she said tersely. "The spiritual and the religious are often connected." The group started to call out words that
overlapped the categories: singing, liturgy, tradition, community,
providing charity, doing social justice. People argued about how
the terms related to one another, how both fluidity and order were
needed to accomplish certain things.

Afterward, one pastor said to me: "I want both—spirituality
and religion. The problem is that the Presbyterian Church has emphasized too much of the religion side without the spiritual side.
I don't want to give up religion. I want better religion, one that's

more open, more in tune with the Spirit. But the denomination is afraid of spirituality. If we don't have both, we will die."

Of the people who participated in my word association exercise, 72 percent considered themselves "spiritual and religious" (all in this category claimed affiliation with a denomination); 20 percent said that they were "spiritual but not religious"; 6 percent self-identified as "religious only"; and 2 percent declined to respond. Although the percentage of "spiritual and religious" people in my audiences was higher than the national average, they are not unusual in their desire to relate the two words with an *and*. According to sociologists P. L. Marler and Kirk Hadaway, "The most significant finding about the relationship between 'being religious' and 'being spiritual' is that most Americans see themselves as both."[36]

That has not always been the case. In 1999, before the "horrible decade," Gallup polled Americans asking whether people understood themselves to be spiritual or religious. At that time, people answered as follows:[37]

| | |
|---|---|
| Spiritual only: | 30 percent |
| Religious only: | 54 percent |
| Both spiritual and religious: | 6 percent |
| Neither spiritual nor religious: | 9 percent |

In 2009, *Newsweek,* through Princeton Survey Research, asked whether respondents considered themselves spiritual or religious. Their results—just ten years after the Gallup poll—are a bit startling, but not perhaps in the way one might guess. In 2009, people responded:[38]

| | |
|---|---|
| Spiritual only: | 30 percent |
| Religious only: | 9 percent |
| Both spiritual and religious: | 48 percent |
| Neither spiritual nor religious: | 9 percent |

Notice the shift. From 1999 to 2009, the number of people who claimed to be spiritual but not religious remained the same at 30 percent, as did the number of people who said they were neither at 9 percent. The big shift was in the number of people who claimed to be "religious only," falling from more than half of the population to a mere 9 percent; while the number of people identifying themselves as spiritual *and* religious rose from 6 percent to a whopping 48 percent of Americans.[39]

Any number of factors might account for this shift. There may have been some difference in the wording of the survey questions. There was certainly a demographic shift during the decade—an older generation, more likely to say they were "religious only," was replaced by a younger one, more likely to respond with a blended answer. It could be that many people still hold relatively similar views to those of a decade ago, but that the language has changed. In the 1990s, the word "spiritual" may have been more closely associated with New Age religion; now it has a broader and more inclusive meaning. And, of course, other people may have just changed their views.

The key to the shift is the horrible decade. In ten short years, the positive image of religion significantly decreased in public perception. In the midst of it all, "religion" became a less acceptable word, and people searched about for new ways to articulate their faith. As a Presbyterian lay leader said to me recently, "It was almost as if we woke up one morning and everything had changed. I was ashamed to tell my secular friends that I was religious. Instead, I began to tell them that I was spiritual, but I still went to church." Another person told me that she now tells people that she prays, sings, and serves others, saying, "I explain my faith through my practices rather than my church membership."

Both of these people attend the same mainline church, one that proclaims on its website: "Our mission is to grow spiritually as disciples of Jesus Christ through worship, fellowship, mission, learning, and prayer." Notice there is no mention of denomination or even the fact that it is a church! Instead, the emphasis is on a purposeful community learning to become like Jesus through spiritual practices. The whole religion business is displaced by renewed attention to experiential Christian life. The people still do religious things, like worship services and mission trips, but they do them to connect more deeply with God, one another, and their community. That particular church is exploring the territory of the *and*.

Whether this is a shift in survey taking, generations, language, attitude, or some combination of them all, the numbers indicate a change in how people choose to describe their lives and spiritual understandings. And it is surprising. When journalists assess religious change in the early twenty-first century, they talk about the growth of the "spiritual but not religious" and the new atheists. However, the numbers of Americans claiming those labels have been relatively stable in the last decade. The real switch has been among those people who once understood themselves to be "religious only" and who now are heading toward a new self-understanding and public expression—a longing, perhaps—to be "spiritual *and* religious." In a simple shift of phrase, many Americans are articulating their discontent with organized religion and their hope that somehow "religion" might regain its true bearings in the spirit. Sometimes, much is communicated in a word—institutional failure and longing. One of the most significant religion stories of the decade can be found in the overlooked conjunction *and*.

## The Great (Re)Turning

In *The Great Turning,* an influential book about contemporary prospects for human community, David Korten asks: "By what name will our children and our children's children call our time? Will they speak in anger and frustration of the time of the Great Unraveling? . . . Or will they look back in joyful celebration on the noble time of the Great Turning, when their forebears turned crisis into opportunity . . . and brought forth a new era of human possibility?"[40]

The questions are good ones that point to the fact that we must make some choices in our day. Korten contrasts the old order, "empire," with the emerging one, "earth community." "Empire" can no longer be sustained; "earth community" is the way forward; human beings must turn away from the former to create the latter. But the Great Turning is not inevitable. As Korten says, "We must each be clear that every individual and collective choice we make is a vote for the future."[41] The Great Turning is an awakening—a movement to reorient human culture toward connectedness, economic equality, democracy, creation, and spirituality. The Great Turning awakens us to becoming "fully human."[42]

An awakening is holy geography. Awakenings imply new awareness, inner transformation, a change of heart and mind, and a reordering of priorities, commitments, and behavior. Korten claims that spirituality will play a key role in the Great Turning. But what of religion? Will the early twenty-first century be remembered as the Great Unraveling of Christianity? The time when religion was part of the old order, the things that went wrong, when church organized the gods on behalf of the collapsing empire? When it all fell apart?

Insofar as religion was guardian, pastor, and priest of the old order, it will have to give way and is already doing so. Western Christendom has ended; a "Christian America" survives as mythic memory and political slogan. Some suggest that a new Christendom is found in Africa, Latin America, or Asia. But that is merely placing old imperial dreams on new geographies of faith—and the whole vision of some new Global South Christendom does not really mesh with historical, economic, or political realities of the contemporary world. If not a new Christendom, then what? In some places, like

Europe and Australia, perhaps, religion will give way to the secular; in others, it will give way to an eclectic and generalized sort of spirituality.

But there is another choice as well, the longing sounded by those who place hope in the *and*—that religion may be transformed and renewed by spirituality. This can happen in Christianity, even in worn-out, ennui-filled Western Christianity, for it has happened time and time again in the last two millennia. And it can happen in Islam, Hinduism, Judaism, and other religions as well. Indeed, if the Great Turning is about global community, then religion—with churches, buildings, and doctrines—is an essential component of global renewal.

According to the World Values Survey, the vast majority of the world's people believe in God and say that religion plays an important role in their lives. World Values Survey data prove two distinct and seemingly contradictory theses: one, that religion declines as societies become more successful; and two, that the role and importance of religion are increasing worldwide.[43] In other words, in a global context, religion cannot simply be dismissed when searching out paths of human happiness and meaning. No matter how fractious, wounded, irksome, hypocritical, or potentially destructive it can be, religion makes a difference, especially in the lives of the disadvantaged, the oppressed, and the poor. Even Christopher Hitchens admits that religion will never die out, "at least not until we get over our fear of death, and of the dark, and of the unknown, and of each other."[44] What the world needs is better religion, *new forms* of old faiths, religion reborn on the basis of deep spiritual connection—these things need to be explored instead of ditching religion completely. We need religion imbued with the spirit of shared humanity and hope, not religions that divide and further fracture the future.

One way of turning toward the future is by looking back. Fifty years ago, Wilfred Cantwell Smith, a professor of comparative religion at Harvard, pointed out that the end of religion was neither unexpected nor necessarily a bad thing. In his 1962 book *The Meaning and End of Religion,* he drew a distinction between the modern word "religion" and its Latin root, *religio.* He showed that the contemporary concept of "religion" was a relatively recent invention in European history. Christian writers began using the word "religion" more frequently during the seventeenth century to signify a system of ideas or beliefs about God. Throughout the following centuries, Smith says, "in pamphlet after pamphlet, treatise after treatise, decade after decade, the notion was driven home that religion is something that one believes or does not believe, something whose propositions are true or are not true, something whose *locus* is in the realm of the intelligible, is up for inspection before the speculative mind."[45] In modern times, religion became indistinguishable from systematizing ideas about God, religious institutions, and human beings; it categorized, organized, objectified, and divided people into exclusive worlds of right versus wrong, true versus false, "us" versus "them."

But the modern definition of "religion," according to Smith, is not close to the original meaning of *religio.* Unlike religion as system of belief, *religio* meant faith—living, subjective experience including love, veneration, devotion, awe, worship, transcendence, trust, a way of life, an attitude toward the divine or nature, or, as Smith describes, a "particular way of seeing and feeling the world." Accordingly, "the archaic meaning of *religio* [w]as that awe that men felt in the presence of an uncanny and dreadful power of the unknown. . . . That *religio* is something within men's hearts."[46] When it comes to religion, the Great Turning is less of a turn toward something completely new and unknown; it is more of a Great Returning to an ancient understanding, of finding a forgotten path of wonder and awe through the wilderness of human chaos and change.

The only thing that needs to end is the modern Western definition of religion. It is already ending. For a generation or more, many people in the West have been reaching toward *religio*—only they call it "spirituality," because no other English word communicates their longings—as a replacement for what needs to change. We have been returning to a time before our time for wisdom and were not even aware that we were retracing ancient ways of insight. People intuit that the modern conceptualization of religion as an ideology or institution is bankrupt and has already, in some significant ways, failed. The world cannot afford the sort of religion that we have had for the last two or three centuries. People are searching for something new. That something new, as Wilfred Cantwell Smith said a half century ago, is actually something quite old: *faith,* the profoundly personal response to "the terror and splendor and living concern of God."[47]

Although the ancient definition of *religio* emphasized "a warm, reverberating and sustained affirmation of a personal relation to [a] transcendent God,"[48] the actual etymology of the word *religio* is equally helpful. Modern scholars argue that the word itself comes to us from *ligare,* meaning "to bind or connect." Hence *re-ligare,* or *religio,* means to "reconnect." By its very nature, its ancient definitions and meanings, *religio* is the territory of the *and,* of reconnecting, and of the longing to bind ourselves to God and others. *Religio* enfolds rituals and theologies with experience and wonder. It enlivens the heart, opening the soul to others and to creation.

According to surveys, studies, polls, and stories, many millions of people in the old territories of Christendom are longing for *religio,* to reconnect. Not all, of course. Plenty of North Americans and Europeans are satisfied with being secular or agnostic or atheist; plenty more are satisfied with spirituality alone; a minority will hold on to their conventional religion and be happy. The discontent, however, is in the middle ground, where large numbers of people seek some sort of connection between religion and spirituality, or, as I have suggested here, *religio.* How might that connection be rewoven? Where is the *and* to be discovered?

In earlier American awakenings, preachers extolled "old-time religion" as the answer to questions about God, morality, and existence. This awakening is different. Yes, *religio* is "old-time religion," but it is not about sawdust trials, mortification of sin, and being washed in the blood of the Lamb. The awakening going on around us is not an evangelical revival; it is not returning to the faith of our fathers or re-creating our grandparents' church. Instead, it is a Great Returning to ancient understandings of the human quest for the divine. Christianity of the Great Returning is the oldest-time religion—reclaiming a faith where belief is not quite the same thing as an answer, where behavior is not following a list of dos and don'ts, and where belonging to Christian community is less like joining an exclusive club and more of a relationship with God and others. *Religio* is never satisfied with old answers, codified dogmas, institutionalized practices, or invested power. *Religio* invites every generation to experience God—to return to the basic questions of believing, behaving, and belonging—and explore each anew with an open heart.

# PART II

# *A New Vision*

There is a need for spiritual vitality. What protection is
there against the danger of organization? . . . Our relationship to God [is] not a religious relationship to a supreme Being, absolute in power and goodness, which is a
spurious conception of transcendence, but a new life for
others, through participation in the Being of God.

DIETRICH BONHOEFFER
*Letters and Papers from Prison*

# CHAPTER FOUR

# *Believing*

THE GYM WAS PACKED for the baccalaureate service, not only with people, but also with anticipation, because a respected Christian scholar would be preaching on this happy academic occasion. Like everyone else, I looked forward to hearing his words of wisdom. Glancing through the program, I read the scripture passage chosen for the occasion:

> *Let the same mind be in you that was in Christ Jesus,*
> *who, though he was in the form of God,*
> > *did not regard equality with God*
> > *as something to be exploited,*
> *but emptied himself,*
> > *taking the form of a slave,*
> > *being born of human likeness,*
> *And being found in human form,*
> > *he humbled himself*
> > *and became obedient to the point of death—*
> > *even death on a cross.*
> *Therefore God also highly exalted him*

*and gave him the name*
*that is above every name,*
*so that at the name of Jesus*
*every knee should bend,*
*in heaven and on earth and under the earth,*
*and every tongue should confess*
*that Jesus Christ is Lord,*
*to the glory of God the Father.*

The sermon text is from the New Testament book of Philippians, ascribed to the apostle Paul (2:5–11). The unusual arrangement of the words indicates that the author is quoting a hymn, one most likely used in early Christian worship. It is an ancient and beautiful text.

It is also a rich theological passage. These words form the basis of the doctrine of *kenosis,* or the "emptying" of Christ. Jesus surrendered aspects of divinity in order to become human. Although there are many theological complexities regarding this idea, the spiritual intent of the passage moves from the humility of God toward a triumphant Jesus lifted up in glory.

The preacher mounted the pulpit dressed in the scarlet regalia conferred upon him by a prestigious university, thus reminding the audience of his authority to interpret the Bible's deeper meanings. As expected, he spoke of *kenosis* and humility. But then his tone changed. He told us that the word "Lord" used in the passage was the same word used for Caesar in the Roman Empire. Hence, "Jesus Christ is Lord" was to say "Jesus Christ is Caesar." This, of course, is true. He, however, proclaimed that one day Jesus—like Caesar of old—would exert his imperial will across the world and "force every living thing to its knees" to confess his name. At the end of time, God would make everyone worship him, just as everyone subject to Caesar had to pay homage to the Roman emperor—crawling backward to the imperial throne.

He continued likening Jesus to an imperialist warlord whose triumph over recalcitrant sinners, doubters, discontents, and rebels was assured. Emphasizing Jesus's regal glorification, he turned God into a vengeful king out to get those who had killed his son. Oddly enough, his tone was not that of a hellfire-and-brimstone evangelist. Instead, the entire lecture was delivered with stern intellectual certainty and detached professorial authority. "You will confess Jesus is Lord someday," he stated coolly. "Believe and confess this now."

I wanted to run out of the gym. Instead, I quietly slipped from my seat and stood shaking outside on the balcony. A friend, who was equally as distraught, joined me.

"How could he do that?" I exclaimed. "He turned Jesus into Caesar, a hierarchical and tyrannical monster!"

My friend draped her arm around my shoulder and said, "I think that's what he honestly believes. That's what many people believe."

I looked at her and replied hopelessly, "How could I believe that Jesus is like Caesar? That's not my God, and if that's what Christianity is, I don't want any part of it."

## The Belief Gap

That sermon marked the moment in which I fell into the belief gap. I may have been walking near the edge for some time, but this sermon pushed me over. What once made sense no longer did. It was not a case of rejecting everything; rather, it was more like seeing from some angle you never imagined. Like slipping off a wet rock and finding yourself in the river rather than above it. There are lots of questions when you slip. Will I stop falling? Will I regain my footing? Will I reach solid ground? Where will the current take me?

That baccalaureate service was twenty years ago. I admit that through the haze of middle-age memory, I cannot recall the preacher's words verbatim. But I remember the increasing alarm I felt as he preached, and I wondered, "Is this what Christians really believe?" At an earlier time in my own life, I would have approved of the professor's sermon. On that evening, however, I heard Jesus presented in a deeply discomforting way, a way that made me understand why others might not like Jesus, embrace Christianity, or want to go to church. Up until then, I could not fathom the hurtful side of Christian faith. It was the first (but it would not be the last) time that I felt horrified by a presentation of Christian doctrine. A gap of belief opened before me. I knew that Christians believed as the professor did, but I just could not believe it anymore myself.

A few months later, I was preaching in a small, rural Lutheran church. The church was charming and old-fashioned, mostly older people with only a few young families; their weekly bulletin announced a quilting bee and plans for members to pave the parking lot the next Saturday. About seventy people gathered for church in a cozy sanctuary where we listened to the Bible being read and sang hymns together. After my sermon, we all shared a potluck lunch. A young woman sat next to me and shared her story of being in the belief gap.

She was a student at the nearby university, one of the only young and single members of the church. "I love this congregation," she said. "The people have become my family." She paused, and her voice dropped to a confessional whisper. "But I don't know what to say to my classmates when they ask me what I believe. Whenever I say 'I believe in Christianity,' they look at me as if I'm crazy. Besides, I don't even know if I believe 'in' Christianity or Lutheran doctrine or anything like that. I just experience how to love God and how God loves me through these people, by learning how to quilt and singing these hymns. I don't know what to call it, but it is less about believing and more about living. Does that still count as being Christian?"

Her confession remained with me, because it was one of the first gap stories that anyone shared with me. In the two decades since, the gap has widened, and the confessional whisper is gone. The gap is everywhere, and people are not afraid to share the news. On November 9, 2010, I was sitting at O'Hare airport and opened *USA Today*. A large advertisement trumpeted the gap:

> What some believe: "A woman should learn in quietness and full submission. I do not permit a woman to teach or to have authority over a man; she must be silent" (1 Timothy 2). What humanists think: "The rights of men and women should be equal and sacred" (Robert Ingersoll).

It was an ad for an atheist group. Between the time of the student's confession and that November day, hundreds of people have trusted me with their stories of not believing—not believing that wives must submit to their husbands, not believing in the virgin birth, not believing in an inerrant Bible, not believing in hell, not believing that Jesus is the only way to salvation, not believing that only one religion is true, not believing that the institutional church is important, not believing in Jesus, not believing in the resurrection, not believing that God cares or heals or loves, not believing that God exists. They don't believe in Christianity anymore. When many people slip from believing into not believing, they find it difficult to regain their footing. Maybe because they are trying to climb back on the same rock. Or maybe because they know they cannot go back to the path that landed them in the drink in the first place.

Despite the differences of detail in testimonies, almost all of them share an important assumption about belief. "Belief" is the intellectual content of faith. Typically, belief entails some sort of list—a rehearsal of ideas about God, Jesus, salvation, and the church. What to believe? If I am slipping, do I hold on tighter or let go? If I no longer believe, am I still a Christian? Am I spiritual, but not religious? An agnostic? An atheist?

Belief, especially Christian belief, has entered a critical stage in Western society. Masses of people now reject belief. For many centuries, Christians have equated faith with belief. Being faithful meant that one accepted certain ideas about God and Jesus, especially as articulated in creedal statements. Denominations specified what adherents must believe about the sacraments, salvation, and authority. Confirmation in faith entailed memorization and recitation of doctrine or facts about the Bible. Some groups even insisted that true Christians must further believe particular ideas about drinking, women, science, the end times, or politics. Layers of beliefs, stacked through the centuries from the apostles to our own times. Alongside this weighty pile of beliefs, it often seems as if Christians actually live their beliefs less—beliefs like "God is love" or "Blessed are the peacemakers" or "Love your neighbor as yourself"—thus leading to often heard charges of hypocrisy.

With this accretion of beliefs, a corresponding incredulity spread through Western culture, leading to doctrinal boredom, skepticism, agnosticism, and atheism. As science, history, and psychology offered ever more sophisticated understandings of the universe and human experience, some Christians became increasingly hostile to secular knowledge, building museums to creationism, proclaiming that America is a Christian nation, and excommunicating those who would question the existence of hell. Put simply, as they reacted to unbelief, certain Christians asked for more belief about increasingly unbelievable things.

Meanwhile, other Christians began to wonder if belief was even the point. At the college where the professor who delivered the baccalaureate sermon taught, for example, the majority of younger faculty signed the institution's doctrinal statement with crossed fingers and a knowing wink to their friends, telling sympathetic souls that they "agreed in spirit" with the statement, even if the exact words rang hollow. Eventually, they revised their statement of faith to be more open and inclusive. It is not only the case that the Western world has grown weary of doctrine, but that Christianity itself is changing—shifting away from being a belief-centered religion toward an experiential faith.

Many philosophers, scholars, and theologians have explored the shift in Western culture away from beliefs toward experience, a move from rationalism toward practice. Harvey Cox proposed that Christianity reflects this broader transformation regarding human knowledge and experience by dividing church history into three ages: the Age of Faith, the Age of Belief, and the Age of the Spirit. During the first period, roughly from the time of Jesus to 400 CE, Christianity was understood as a way of life based upon faith (i.e., trust) *in* Jesus. Or, as Cox states, "To be a Christian meant to live in his Spirit, embrace his hope, and to follow him in the work that he had begun." Between 300 and 400, however, this dynamic sense of living in Jesus was displaced by an increasing emphasis on creeds and beliefs, leading Professor Cox to claim that this tendency increased until nascent beliefs "thickened into catechisms, replacing faith *in* Jesus with tenets *about* him. . . . From an energetic movement of faith [Christianity] coagulated into a phalanx of required beliefs."[1] Cox argues that the Age of Belief lasted some fifteen centuries and began to give way around 1900, its demise increasing in speed and urgency through the twentieth century. We have now entered into a new phase of Christian history, which he calls the Age of the Spirit.

If the Age of Faith was a time of "faith *in* Jesus" and the Age of Belief a period of "belief *about* Christ," the Age of the Spirit is best understood as a Christianity based in an "experience *of* Jesus." The Age of the Spirit is nondogmatic, noninstitutional, and nonhierarchical Christianity, based on a person's connection to the "volatile expression" of God's Spirit through mystery, wonder, and awe. "Faith is resurgent," Cox claims, "while dogma is dying. The spiritual, communal, and justice-seeking dimensions of Christianity are now its leading edge. . . . A religion based on subscribing to mandatory beliefs is no longer viable."[2] When questioned by an interviewer about his thesis, Cox further explained:

> What I see, and what a lot of others see too, is that people frequently want to refer to themselves now as not really "religious," but "spiritual." I used to be very suspicious of that. But I began asking questions and finding out what the dimensions of the term are. . . . What I think it really means is that people want to have access to the sacred without going through institutional and doctrinal scaffolding. They want a more direct experience of God and Spirit. And I don't think it's really going to go away. This is an increasing tendency across the board.[3]

Accordingly, Christianity is moving from being a religion *about* God to being an experience *of* God. In a real sense, both the baccalaureate speaker and the student questioning her faith at the Lutheran church I preached at were right. The professor's world of "belief about" God was eroding, leading him to reassert ideas he believed necessary to faith; and the student's intuition regarding an experiential future has been coming to pass, leading her to question the older definitions of "Christian." Although I have no idea what happened to the young woman, the professor has called for a new fundamentalism, writing books that few people read, arguing that what is old is better, and defending narrow understandings of belief and piety, something clearly evident in his sermon two decades ago. If one believes that Christianity is about belief, taking refuge in fundamentalism is logical. On the face of things, it sometimes seems as if fundamentalism may be the only vibrant form of faith. As Harvey Cox argues, however, "Fundamentalisms, with their insistence on obligatory belief systems, their nostalgia for a mythical uncorrupted past, their claims to an exclusive grasp on truth . . . are turning out to be rearguard attempts to stem a more sweeping tidal change."[4]

The professor's "Jesus/Caesar" was like Romulus Augustus, the last ruler of a collapsing Roman Empire.

## The Religious Question: What Do I Believe?

Despite such obvious changes, most religious institutions act as if the gap does not exist and that the questions have not substantially changed in recent decades. Conservative or liberal, evangelical or mainline, Protestant or Catholic, denominations and churches still provide answers to questions *about* God. Most assume that dogma and doctrine are the right approach to holy matters, differing only on the details of their preferred answers. Religion answers *what* questions: What should one believe? What do Christians believe?

This is bad news for Christianity. The *what* questions are the very questions causing people to slip into the gap. Doctrine is seen as not only divisive, but as contrary to the message Jesus himself taught. Many people stumble on the creeds, thinking them to be a sort of doctrinal test for church membership, and are unable to recite them in full or even part. As a pastor asked me, "Can we stop reciting the creed now? I'm tired of it driving people away from church." Theologian Dwight Friesen puts it bluntly—and speaks for many—when he says that Jesus had no interest in orthodoxy, but rather offered his followers "a full and flourishing human life."[5] At an event I was leading recently, an Episcopal priest inquired, with a sense of hopeful anticipation, "Isn't it true that belief-oriented faith is disappearing?" His colleague chimed in, "My generation doesn't really care about doctrine; that's just not the way we think." Indeed, even among Christians, there is a sense of mild relief, maybe even quiet jubilation, that the Age of Belief is giving way to something else.

The erosion of belief has occasioned many a new jeremiad from those who, like the professor, feel threatened by the current situation. The college faculty who fudge the truth about the doctrinal statement or the clergy who wish they could get rid of creeds are, both in my experience and as surveys seem to point out, fairly typical. Yet they fear someone finding out—that they might lose their jobs in religious institutions that continue to mark their boundaries with such beliefs *about* God. It is not only loss of employment or community that they fear, but the cultural ridicule that comes upon people pondering such questions. The media scorn them as "cafeteria Christians" and "spiritual consumers" who pick and choose what they like about faith, while conservative pastors accuse them of vacuity and spiritual shallowness and use them as scapegoats for all that is wrong in religion.

It may be easy to dismiss anxiety about belief as anti-intellectualism or as a theological problem associated with Western religious decline. But something else is at work. On the face of it, *what* questions should be benign. After all, *what* is a fairly objective question, a request that seeks information. "What time is it?" "What color is the sky?" "What day does school start?" "What would you like for dinner tonight?" Even more philosophical questions, like "What is art?" or "What do you want to do with your life?" assume a well-formed opinion, if not a conclusive answer.

During the last few centuries, to ask "What do you believe?" in the religious realm was to demand intellectual answers about things that cannot be comprehended entirely by the mind. Thus masked as objective truth, religion increasingly became a matter of opinion, personal taste, individual interpretation, and wishful thinking. People became quite militant about the answers they liked the best. The *what* questions often divided families and neighbors into rival churches, started theological quarrels, initiated inquisitions, fueled political and social conflict, and led, on occasion, to one losing one's head.

It's time to face up to the truth: an increasingly large number of people are experiencing the *what* questions in profoundly negative ways. In the minds of many, dogma deserves to die.

SPIRITUAL QUESTION 1:

## *How Do I Believe?*

"You're a Christian?" quizzed my acquaintance. "How do you believe in that? I don't know how I could ever believe that."

Belief is not going to disappear, and it will not become a relic of the religious past. Rather, as religion gives way to spirituality, the question of belief shifts from *what* to *how*. People generally assume that they know the *what* of religion. For example, they may know that Christians believe that Jesus died and was raised, that Jews believe that Moses freed the slaves from Egypt, or that Buddhists believe that the Buddha achieved Enlightenment. Indeed, in many years of discussing faith in public few have ever asked me, "What do Christians believe?" *What* is not the issue—the world of religion is a world full of *what*. Instead, they have asked *how*. Belief questions have become, "How do you believe?" "How could I ever believe?" "How does this make sense?" "How would believing this make my life different?" or "How would this change the world?"

*How* differs from *what*. "How do I get to your house?" "How would that move change my family's life?" "How do I love?" *How* is the interrogator of direction, of doing, of curiosity, of process, of learning, of living. When we ask *how*, we are not asking for a fact, conclusion, or opinion. Rather, we are seeking a hands-on deeper knowledge of the thing—a neighborhood or city, a craft or recipe, an open possibility, an idea, a sense of ourselves or of a relationship. *How* moves us around in the question. Instead of being above the information, giving an expert opinion about something, *how* weaves our lives with the information as we receive, review, reflect, and act upon what we sought. *How* provides actionable information; we can choose to act upon the answer or not, and we choose the extent of our action.

*How* is a question of meaning and purpose that pushes people into a deeper engagement in the world, rather than memorizing facts. Parker Palmer refers to the shift from *what* to *how* as part of the "inner search" that enables individuals to develop the "habits of the heart" necessary to forming both a grounded moral life and a caring community. He asserts that inner-life questions are the sort of questions Americans ask most regularly, and the *how* questions are the ones our schools and churches often fail to address. Institutions cannot "dictate" answers to *how* questions. Instead, spiritual communities must open space to engage the inner search: *"How can I connect with something larger than my own ego?"* This, Palmer insists, involves going "beyond teaching the *what* of things into the labor-intensive process of teaching the *how* of things."[6]

From *what* to *how* is a shift from information *about* to experience *of*. *What* is a conventional religious question, one of dogma and doctrine; *how* is an emerging spiritual question, one of experience and connection. We have lived through many generations of *what* and have nearly exhausted ourselves by doing so. But *how* opens the question of belief anew: How do I believe? How do we believe? How does belief make a difference? How is the world transformed by believing? Belief will not entirely go away. Rather, "believing *about*" appears to be going away. Belief itself is being enfolded into a new spiritual awareness as belief questions morph from *what* to *how*, from seeking information *about* God to nurturing experience *of* the divine.

SPIRITUAL QUESTION 2:
## Who Do I Believe?

Several years ago, I asked students in a seminary class a question: "To whom do you turn when you have an ethical or spiritual concern?" One quickly said, "I ask my friends." Another laughed, saying, "I ask Google." For the next few minutes, they came up with a variety of answers, mostly those involving personal relationships, the media, or the Internet. Interestingly enough, none of these future pastors said that they asked a bishop, priest, or seminary professor about their religious questions, much less read a book of canon law or turned to a creed.

The question is, of course, a question of religious authority. Who provides trustworthy answers to difficult questions? Once upon a time, Americans would have deferred to the clergy, a teacher, or a parent on issues of belief. When it comes to questions of meaning and purpose, however, it no longer seems adequate to say, "The church teaches," "Christians have always believed," or "the Bible said it, so I believe it." External authorities do not carry the weight they once did. Thus, questions of belief have not only morphed from *what* to *how,* but they necessarily include the secondary dimension of *who.* My seminary students did not look to conventional institutional authorities for answers. Instead, they looked to relationships and online sources and social networks. Who is trustworthy in the search for meaning?

As the question of *how* is experiential, so is the question of *who.* In the early twenty-first century, trustworthiness is not simply a matter of an expert who holds a degree or a certain role in an institution. Rather, authority springs from two sources: one, relationship, and two, authenticity. People trust those with whom they are friends or feel they could be friends—thus the presidential election question, "With which candidate would you rather have a beer?" Authority comes through connection, personal investment, and communal accountability, rather than submission to systems or structures of expertise. Related closely to friendship is the test of authenticity. Something is true and trustworthy because it springs from good motives and praiseworthy intentions, with results that prove to increase happiness and make peoples' lives better. Practicing what one preaches is a mark of spiritual truth, and humanity and humility foster trust. Although certain people will always hanker for authoritarian or charismatic leaders, there is a much broader longing for authentic leaders in these times—those whose message and actions validate their deepest beliefs. In the emerging spiritual culture, *what* matters much less than *who* is sharing the news, and the messenger has become the message.

This is a very interesting development in terms of faith. After all, Christians, Jews, and Muslims consider God to be personal and truthful, the Messenger of Good News to humankind. Thus, religious organizations, ordained leaders, and conventional creeds recede in importance as mediators in favor of direct friendship with God through prayer and discernment as means to spiritual understanding. Friendship with God can be mystical and individual, but it is also communal and corporate—every major faith asserts that friendship with God is strengthened through friendship with our neighbor. Ultimately, spiritual authority rests in the voice of God, the voices of community, and in our own voices. It is a harder path to hear answers than to ask someone to give us an answer, but it is the path that many people have embarked upon.

## Spiritual Insight: Belief as Experience

As demonstrated in the polling data, about 9 percent of Americans understand themselves as "religious" only. They are probably still greatly concerned with the *what* of faith. About a third of Americans describe themselves as "spiritual" only. They have embarked on a quest of *how* to relate to transcendent things. But half of all Americans claim to be "spiritual and religious." For them, *what* is not necessarily being replaced by *how;* the *what* of religion is being redefined by the *how.* When belief springs from and is rewoven with experience, we arrive at the territory of being spiritual *and* religious: experiential belief.

Understanding belief-as-experience is not a new concept. Actually, it is much closer to the original definition of believing than the popular definitions we have inherited from more recent centuries.

In his essay "Believing: An Historical Perspective" (first published in 1977), Wilfred Cantwell Smith argues for a distinction between "faith" and "belief" based upon the etymologies of the terms. Although the words overlapped at one time, he says, the "English word 'believe' has, in usage, connotation, and denotation, undergone an arresting transformation" in recent centuries—one that has had an unprecedented negative impact on Western religious life.[7]

"To believe" in Latin (the shaping language for much of Western theological thought) is *opinor, opinari,* meaning "opinion," which was not typically a religious word. Instead, Latin used *credo,* "I set my heart upon" or "I give my loyalty to," as the word to describe religious "believing," that is, "faith." In medieval English, the concept of *credo* was translated as "believe," meaning roughly the same thing as its German cousin *belieben,* "to prize, treasure, or hold dear," which comes from the root word *Liebe,* "love."[8] Thus, in early English, to "believe" was to "belove" something or someone as an act or trust or loyalty. Belief was not an intellectual opinion. As Smith says:

> The affirmation "I believe in God" used to mean: "Given the reality of God as a fact of the universe, I hereby pledge to Him my heart and soul. I committedly opt to live in loyalty to Him.". . . Today the statement may be taken by some as meaning: "Given the uncertainty as to whether there be a God or not, as a fact of modern life, I announce that my opinion is 'yes.' I judge God to be existent."[9]

In previous centuries, belief had nothing to do with one's weighing of evidence or intellectual choice. Belief was not a doctrinal test. Instead, belief was more like a marriage vow—"I do" as a pledge of faithfulness and loving service to and with the other. Indeed, in early English usage, you could not hold, claim, or possess a belief about God, but you could cherish, love, trust in, or devote yourself to God.

From a historical perspective, the misidentification of faith-as-experience and belief-as-opinion also involved the translation of the Bible from Greek (the other theology-shaping language of Christian thought) into English. In Greek, there is a verb for the experience of beloving God: "to faith" (i.e., *pist-*). In English, however, "faith" is a noun and not a verb. With no equivalent active word, English translators rendered the Greek verb "to faith" in English as "to believe." The verb "to believe" (meaning "to belove, prize, or treasure," as explained above) appears frequently in the English Bible. It typically occurs without a direct object, in the forms "I believe" or "I believe you" (or "him," "her," or "God"). This reinforces its original meaning of "belove" as a general confession of trust or a specific disposition of trusting someone—it is a personal and relational action initiated by love. In only 12 percent of scriptural cases does "to believe" appear as "I believe that . . . ," an impersonal affirmation about something.

To read the Bible with this understanding orients our attention away from cognitive speculation about God toward the state and direction of our hearts. For example, John 3:16 might be the most well-known Bible verse across North America as a result of signs held up by evangelistically minded Christians at sporting events: "For God so loved the world that he gave his only Son, so that everyone who believes in him won't perish, but will have eternal life" (CEB). If we think that "believe" means doctrinal truth, then the verse means "everyone who agrees that Jesus is the Son of God won't perish" or "everyone who thinks that Jesus is the Second Person of the Trinity won't perish." According to its more ancient rendering, however, the verse would better read, "everyone who trusts in Jesus" or "everyone who directs his or her heart toward Jesus" will not perish. You may or not may want to trust in or incline your love toward Jesus, but it is an entirely different, and more spiritually compelling, invitation than an offer of debate about Jesus. And it is a fresh way of understanding a widely misused text.

Smith demonstrates how belief shifted away from "trusting the beloved" toward being a word that is "increasingly technocratic and thing-oriented," outside the realm of personal relationships.[10] The shift occurred gradually in the eighteenth century, mostly through the work of the influential philosopher David Hume. When people use the word "believe" today, it is often for factually erroneous opinions, disconnected from any aspect of interpersonal trust or love: "I believe that dinosaurs walked the earth at the same time as human beings," or "I don't believe in global warming." No wonder people can no longer "believe" in Christianity. For masses of contemporary people, to believe in Christianity is like believing in aliens or that President Obama was born in Kenya, since "the word [belief] denotes doubt, and connotes falsehood."[11] Thus, Smith claims, "The idea that believing is religiously important turns out to be a modern idea. . . . [A] great modern heresy of the Church is the heresy of believing. Not of believing this or that, but of believing as such."[12] Christianity was never intended to be a system or structure of belief in the modern sense; it originated as a disposition of the heart.

From an ancient perspective—whether of Latin or Greek, of the creeds or the Christian scriptures—the words "belief" and "believing" implicitly carried within them relational and lived dimensions. Accordingly, you cannot "believe" distinct from trust, loyalty, and love. Wilfred Cantwell Smith, analyzing this history some forty years ago, had a dim view of the future of belief. He writes:

> The English "belief," which used to be the verbal sign designating allegiance, loyalty, integrity, love, commitment, trust, and entrusting, and the capacity to perceive and to respond to transcendent qualities in oneself and one's environment—in short, faith; the Christian form of God's most momentous gift to each person—has come to be the term by which we designate rather a series of dubious, or at best problematic, propositions.[13]

Smith clearly wished this were not the case, but held little hope that it might change.

A surprising thing has happened, however. In those same forty years, in some quarters at least, there has been a return to the older understanding of belief-as-trust. Half of the American population now claims to have had "a mystical experience," a statistic that suggests we are in the process of returning to the idea of faith as an encounter with God. As religion in the modern sense fails, we appear to be busily restitching the ancient fabric of belief. It seems we may have entered a new (or perhaps very old) theological door, the way of experiential belief.

## Spiritual and Religious: Experiential Belief

*The Priority of Experience.* I spend most of my work time with mainline, liberal, and progressive Protestants, religious groups with high educational attainments and little patience for faith without reason. They are doubters and skeptics (that is, indeed, their spiritual gift) and downright skittish regarding experience. Despite the fact that many of them share the cultural anxiety about the creeds (worrying that the creeds are not factually true), they are not entirely comfortable with the shift toward experiential faith either. Put the words "experiential" and "belief" in the same sentence, and you are asking for trouble.

At a United Church of Christ clergy education day, I explained Harvey Cox's chronology, saying: "Professor Cox argues that the 'Age of the Spirit' began around the turn of the twentieth century with the modern Pentecostalism movement. That was the first expression of the turn toward experience." Silence filled the room.

Then one pastor said, "You mean we're all going to become Pentecostals? My congregation would rather die first! Faith isn't about feelings. It has to have intellectual content."

Her reaction is not unique. When Americans think about religious experience, the first thing that often comes to mind is some form of religious enthusiasm—a fulminating revivalist, a frenzied faith healer, or a fainting congregant. A significant tension in American religious identity is shaped by two enduring images—one, the orderly parish church, and the other, the exuberant tent meeting. Since the First Great Awakening, Americans have often felt forced to choose: the pew or the anxious bench, the prayer book or the praise chorus, restraint or revival, mind or heart? Or, as one of my Facebook correspondents bemoaned, "Why is it that the choice among churches always seems to be the choice between intelligence on ice and ignorance on fire?"

Religious experience and the Spirit are often associated with Pentecostalism, the global form of Christianity that emphasizes the work of the Holy Spirit in and through religious ecstasy, miraculous gifts, and healing. In the 1880s and 1890s, an intense and radical form of evangelical religion took hold in the form of healing revivals and holiness meetings emphasizing the power of the "Holy Ghost baptism." On January 1, 1901, Agnes Ozman, a Topeka Bible school student, prayed to receive the gift of the Holy Spirit. After her friends laid hands on her to pray, she began to speak in tongues—thus began the modern Pentecostal movement.

An African-American evangelist named William Seymour heard Agnes's story and embraced the new teaching. He moved in 1906 from the American heartland to Los Angeles, where his preaching sparked the Azusa Street revival and thence spread around the world.[14] For Pentecostals, the experience of speaking in tongues validated and confirmed true faith and empowered believers to do God's will. For them, faith, feeling, action, and experience were a tightly woven cloth of Christian life, the threads of which could not be pulled apart. This experiential rendering of faith made sense to the poor, the deprived, working-class people, and rising middle-class folks, many of whom felt marginalized by liberal elites and their restrained religion. In Pentecostalism, many outsiders discovered a new sense of self and God and a sort of spiritual land of opportunity. By the end of the century, Pentecostalism had given birth to scores of new denominations, claiming hundreds of millions of adherents in nearly every country on earth.

Pentecostalism developed, however, within a larger historical context—one increasingly fascinated with the territory of human and divine experience. Grant Wacker, a leading expert on Pentecostal history, points out the similarities between Pentecostalism, Protestant liberalism, and Roman Catholicism at the turn of the twentieth century. Despite the "vast gulf" between Pentecostals and liberals, Wacker suggests that both traditions emphasize "the nearness and salvific power of God's Spirit in history," while Roman Catholics "evince unprecedented interest in the Holy Spirit's sanctifying presence."[15] As the "Age of the Spirit" dawned, radical evangelicals, liberal Protestants, and Roman Catholics alike were caught up in a quest for transforming religious experience—they wanted to know how God's Spirit made a difference in their lives and the world around them.

This was certainly fostered by a more general, and even secular, impulse toward understanding the nature of human behavior—how experiences molded human personality, thought, and action and how personality, thought, and action were shaped by experience. As the Pentecostal movement began in the early years of the twentieth century, Sigmund Freud published the first of his books exploring the connection between conscious and unconscious experience and its relationship to human development.

With enthusiastic Pentecostals on one side and secular Freud on the other, liberal Protestants also opened up issues of religious experience as a way to protest spiritual ennui in organized religion. The most influential of these was American Transcendentalism, a movement that appeared some fifty years before Pentecostalism and Freud, replete with its rejection of church in favor of nature mysticism, poetry, and spiritual solitude. Although not every Protestant embraced Transcendentalism, the movement created a yeasty spiritual environment in which experiential religion could eventually grow. By the time Protestant liberalism emerged in the late 1800s, its most thoughtful proponents argued that experience was central to vital faith.

The insight regarding experience was partly the result of the American religious environment and partly the result of the theological influence of the first liberal Protestant theologian, Friedrich Schleiermacher, who wrote:

> Religion is the outcome neither of the fear of death, nor of the fear of God. It answers a deep need in man. It is neither a metaphysic, nor a morality, but above all and essentially an intuition and a feeling. . . . Dogmas are not, properly speaking, part of religion: rather it is that they are derived from it. Religion is the miracle of direct relationship with the infinite; and dogmas are the reflection of this miracle.[16]

There are many ways to criticize Schleiermacher, but if you read these words simply and directly, you intuit that there is something to them. Religion is not its accretions of dogma; rather, faith is a divine encounter. Experience needed to be the starting place to engage a skeptical, dogma-weary world. Belief is "derived" from a "direct relationship with the infinite." Beliefs gain credibility insofar as they spring from rightly directed human experience.

William James wrote of this impulse in his *Varieties of Religious Experience* in 1902, an essay on the "feelings, acts, and experiences of individual men in their solitude, so far as they apprehend themselves to stand in relation to whatever they may consider the divine."[17] James discussed saints and mysticism and philosophy. In the end, James concluded that religious experience is useful even if not provable. Experiences connect human beings with an "altogether other dimension of existence" and enable people to live more meaningful lives.[18]

Thus, at the beginning of the twentieth century, Pentecostalism and liberal Protestantism—as well as various streams of mystical Catholicism—came together in a quest for an experience of God. The Age of the Spirit dawned not only with Pentecostal fervor, but experiential faith also arrived with the reflections of William James at Harvard and in the candle-lit prayer of Roman Catholics to their saints. And it was not only Christians exploring the realm of the Spirit—restless seekers appeared across the landscape with new spiritual practices and formed new communities.[19] These groups competed with each other, to be sure, and often did not think the adherents of other ways would find salvation. But they all shared the traits of experiential belief—a practical spirituality that transformed beliefs about God into a living relationship with the divine. The impulse toward experience grew, developed, and deepened throughout the twentieth century, leading to increasing awareness that the nature of Christianity itself was changing. Mysticism and religious experience were no longer limited to a spiritual elite in a monastery or a forest cabin. As once predicted by the ancient Hebrew prophet Joel, the Spirit was poured out on all flesh (2:28).

*The Need for Reason.* "But anyone can have a religious experience," protested a minister during a question-and-answer discussion. "The members of the Taliban have religious experiences; Hitler might have had mystical experiences. Experience can't be the basis for religion, because you can't say what counts as a valid experience. Creeds and doctrine have to be the test."

Experiential religion is not a new phenomenon; it is an ancient one. And the question as to the validity of religious experience is about as ancient as the experiences themselves. Although many people in a tribe may have had spiritual experiences, only one arose as the shaman or wise woman. Thus, even primitive people recognized that some religious experiences were more profound than others and set up authorities to help others achieve certain kinds of experiences. People adjudicated between experiences, discerning which ones nurtured the tribe and which ones might not foster group prosperity. Meaningful religious experiences were shared through story and ritual in an attempt to enable other people to participate in a sense of the divine. Occasionally, an independent mystic would challenge the authority of established religious leaders or rituals by claiming a new experience, leading the tribe to either accept the new insights or reject the messenger. History is rife with accounts of experiential religious figures facing the wrath of institutional doubters—Jesus, Joan of Arc, and Oscar Romero, to name only a very few.

Although Western Christianity turned toward the rational and away from the mystical in the seventeenth and eighteenth centuries, the question of religious experience actually remained important. In the 1740s, a group of religious protesters called "evangelicals" argued against established Christians by claiming that an experience of being "born again" was necessary to faith. Their experiential religion wreaked havoc in English and colonial churches, where revivalists interrupted worship services, led people to psychological breakdowns, and undermined the social order. Women preachers and unlettered male evangelists roamed the land and stirred up the religious rabble, inciting everyone to believe that their experiences of God were equal to any theological insight proclaimed by the educated clergy. In the midst of revival fervor, Jonathan Edwards, a philosopher and pastor deeply shaped by an experience of God, tried to discern true religious affections from delusion.

Edwards condemned both intellectualism and emotionalism in religion, arguing instead that "true religion, in great part, consists in holy affections." Although some of his learned colleagues said that "affections" were "inferior animal passions," Edwards oriented true religion toward what he called "the heart," a unitary faculty of will and love. "The Holy Scriptures do everywhere place religion very much in the affections," he wrote, "such as fear, hope, love, hatred, desire, joy, sorrow, gratitude, compassion and zeal."[20] Affections were not only emotions, however. Affections were the capacity of the heart willing and acting upon that which was good or generous or lovely. How is one's will directed toward beauty? Edwards insisted that true religious experience emanated from a divine source that opened human beings to sensing the unity of God's love and beauty in all things. Put simply, human beings apprehend the spiritual dimension of the universe from beyond themselves through a transformative experience of what Edwards called "a divine and supernatural light."

The experience of divine light reshaped men and women in the virtues of humility, mercy, and justice. An experience of the divine leads people toward greater "tenderness of spirit . . . and a readiness to esteem others better than themselves."[21] True religious experience manifested itself in "beautiful symmetry and proportion" in one's character. Edwards argued that this culminated in a well-ordered and disciplined life: "Gracious and holy affections have their exercise and fruit in Christian practice."[22]

Of his own argument, Edwards claimed, "As that is called experimental philosophy, which brings opinion and notions to the test of fact; so is that properly called experimental religion, which bring religious affections and intentions to like test."[23] Edwards may sound like a rationalist here, as if he needed a scientific experiment to prove the goodness of religious experience. What counted as evidence for Edwards? The quality of one's life. Quite simply, truthful religious experience started with the affections and deepened one's character, one's love of God, and service to neighbor; it unified and balanced head and heart. In turn, the movement toward love served as the test for valid religious experience. Spiritual experience initiates the well-lived life; the well-lived life confirms the nature of one's spiritual experience.

Jonathan Edwards was both a mystic and a philosopher. At the time he lived, it was fashionable to speak of the "beauty of reason." For vast numbers of Christians, reason was an experience, and it was a powerful, life-changing one at that. Although difficult to remember now, *reason* had not yet hardened into *rationalism*. Reason was a capacity of deep understanding, not a set of opinions; it was a journey, a practice, and an inner adventure of soul, not a finished philosophical or theological product.

European Christianity was just moving out of a time when religious passion had resulted in schism, excommunications, exile, witch hunts, inquisitions, and wars of religion. Critical thought provided welcome relief from religious excess; reason, thankfully, muted the fervor of theological hubris and wild spiritual speculations. Reason was the gift of individuals to think for themselves, the ability to judge rightly, to make good choices. Reason sowed seeds of freedom and human rights. It was the philosophical twin of political democracy and the economic engine of an emerging middle class.

Reason did not oppose religion or religious experience. Rather, reason softened religion's sharp edges by providing balance, harmony, and order in a supernatural world too often ruled by a seemingly capricious God. Reason was beautiful. And it was mystical. Literature is full of accounts of people transformed by words, ideas, and books—as a growing industry of popular novels taught both men and women that logic and literacy opened the way to full humanity. Priests and professors wore the same garb; the church and the college embraced a common mission. In early modern depictions of reason, angels often accompany reason, crowning it with laurels of wisdom and justice. Often personified as a god or goddess, reason bestowed divine gifts on humankind. Indeed, people were tempted to worship reason as she had opened for them a new way of understanding themselves and ordering society.

Our own age has conflicted views of reason, because we understand its limits, feel its inhumane touch, and doubt the power of pure reason to solve our problems (indeed, we have witnessed how it has created quite a few). Long gone are the angels casting crowns; we now speak of the overly rational as "cold and calculating," possessed of "unyielding logic," people who "follow their ideas to the bitter end." As a result, education is devalued, and anti-intellectualism has taken hold. Experts are eyed with suspicion. Those who care about facts are derided as part of a "reality-based community." People make decisions "from their gut" or opine that something "just felt right" as they appeal to experience as the arbiter of personal, professional, and political choices. As our own age turns toward the authority of experience, it is good to remember that reason is not bad. Reason is part of human experience, often considered a reflection of God's image in humankind. To be spiritual *and* religious is to call for a new wholeness of experience and reason, to restitch experience with human wisdom and to renew reason through an experience of awe. Thus, the path of Christian faith in a postreligious age must be that of experiential belief in which the heart takes the lead in believing. As Parker Palmer writes,

> "Heart" comes from the Latin *cor* and points not merely to our emotions but to the core of the self, that center place where all of our ways of knowing converge—intellectual, emotional, sensory, intuitive, imaginative, experiential, relational, and bodily, among others. The heart is where we integrate what we know in our minds with what we know in our bones, the place where our knowledge can become more fully human.[24]

Experiential belief is integrated belief, that which brings back together capacities of knowing that modernity ripped apart. It is only in the territory of the heart where faith makes sense.

## The Creed Revisited

More than a decade ago, I was part of an Episcopal congregation that loved asking questions. Indeed, many people made their way to that particular church because the community valued questions. We felt free to question everything—the creeds, the prayers, the scriptures. A member once moaned to me, "I just wish we could get everyone together on this monotheism thing."

On another occasion, we were having an argument about the resurrection, whether or not it had happened and whether or not it could be proved. One of my friends shared the story of how she had asked a liberal bishop if he actually believed in the resurrection. "Believe it?" he answered incredulously. "I've seen it too many times not to!"

The question "Do you believe in the resurrection?" often results in long, often tedious, explanations of creeds and councils, of texts and evidence, of arguments about historic and scientific facts and in disputes between liberals and conservatives. Few, however, stop and ask what the real question might be. The question is not "What do you believe about the resurrection?" The question is simpler and more profound: "Do you trust in the resurrection?" The bishop was not interested in a doctrinal test, proving a historical event that happened many years ago. He believed—that is, he trusted and was loyal to—the resurrection, because he had witnessed it himself. "Do you trust in the resurrection?" is a much harder question than "Do you believe that Jesus was historically and scientifically raised from the dead?"

The bishop was pointing toward the same sort of belief that Jonathan Edwards suggested in the eighteenth century. He pushed the question out of the realm of scientific speculation toward experiential validation: How does the resurrection make things different in a discernable, practical way here and now in our lives, in our communities? Anyone can believe that a resurrection happened; the real question is whether one trusts the resurrection. The test for the bishop, as for Edwards, was a transformed heart and ethical action.

The bishop, however, pushed it one step farther than Edwards. Edwards was attempting to validate spiritual experience by appealing to the affections, but the bishop was trying to explain a theological idea, a classical Christian belief appealing to the heart. Edwards would have thought the resurrection a fact of history, one that needed little or no validation or explanation. It simply was. The bishop, however, lived in radically different times—when only a few question spiritual experience, but many question Christian doctrine. Although the two made the same links between Christian faith, character, and experience, the historical situation is inverted. The bishop needed to validate the central Christian idea of resurrection with an appeal to experiential belief.

Although some spiritual experiences appear as random insights or miraculous encounters, most are shaped by prayer. In stories, memoirs, and testimonies, saints, mystics, and ordinary people recount how speaking with God opened the way for an experience of God. It is in words, and in the territory immediately beyond our words, that human beings meet the divine. As John the Evangelist says, "In the beginning was the Word, and the Word was with God, and the Word was God" (1:1). The Jewish philosopher Martin Buber suggests that spirituality—a deep encounter with God—begins with trust-filled conversation. Prayer is not talking about God "in the third person," rather prayer means speaking to God as "You," a subjective person with the capacity for relationship. Buber claims that "in true prayer, cult and faith are unified and purified into living relation."[25] Prayer transforms religion, doctrine, and dogma into vital spirituality.

The ancient Christian tradition *Lex orandi, lex credendi,* or "The law of prayer is the law of belief," means that praying shapes believing. The first Christians prayed and worshipped for several generations before they had a written creed, and they prayed for several hundred years before they had a canon of scripture. The liturgy of the Jesus communities and the prayers early followers uttered nurtured Christian theology, doctrine, and creeds.

"I don't want to be part of your church, because I don't believe in the Nicene Creed" is a common objection of those considering Christianity—or those considering leaving Christianity. But Christians do not worship a creed. The Nicene Creed was written some three centuries after Jesus taught his followers to love God and their neighbors. For the first three hundred years of church history the followers of Jesus worshipped God, served others, preached, taught, baptized, and evangelized the world without the benefit of a formal, universal doctrinal statement. The creeds developed in the context of a living, transformative, prayer-filled, risky, and active spiritual life—not the other way around. Indeed, a creed is considered a "symbol" of faith, not the faith itself. The words function as an icon, a linguistic picture of a divine reality beyond the ideas and concepts, a window into the world beyond words. Creeds are not unimportant; they are important only in the right order.

Creeds are essentially prayers of devotion that express a community's experience of encountering God. Indeed, the first creeds emerged from the Jewish experience of Jesus. The earliest Christians were Jews, men and women raised in a strictly monotheistic faith: "Hear, O Israel: The Lord is our God, the Lord alone" (Deut. 6:4) and "You shall have no other gods before me" (Exod. 20:3). Yet these same Jews worshipped Jesus as God, functionally making them bi-theists. Their experience of Jesus led them to rethink their understanding of God the Father and God's relationship to Jesus the Christ. The "rethinking" in context of experience took a very long time and eventuated in what we now know as creeds.

The experiential nature of the creeds can be seen in the Apostles' Creed (ca. 390), which begins with the words *Credo in Deum patrem,* translated into English as "I believe in God the Father." For those who read this through the modern lens of "belief," it seems as if this is an idea *about* God to which one must assent in order to join a Christian group—a question to answer correctly for entrance into heaven. But, if we grasp that the ancient sense of "believe" means "trust" or "devotion," the creed might be better translated thus:

> *I trust in God the Father Almighty, Maker of*
> *heaven and earth. And [I trust] in Jesus Christ,*
> *his only Son, our Lord, who was conceived*
> *by the Holy Ghost, born of the Virgin Mary,*
> *suffered under Pontius Pilate, was crucified, died,*
> *and was buried. He descended into hell; the third*
> *day he rose again from the dead. He ascended*
> *into heaven, and sitteth on the right hand of*
> *God the Father Almighty. From thence he shall*
> *come to judge the quick and the dead. I trust in*
> *the Holy Ghost, the holy catholic church, the*
> *communion of saints, the forgiveness of sins, the*
> *resurrection of the body, and the life everlasting.*
> *Amen.*

Notice that when we insert ourselves as the ones who must trust, the tone changes and the Apostles' Creed takes on the quality of a prayer. Instead of factual certainty, the creed evokes humility, hope, and a bit of faithful supplication. It moves the action of the creed from the brain to the heart. Changing a single word, "believe," to its original sense of "trust" transforms the text from a statement of dogma to an experience of God.

Since all creeds derive from the spiritual experience of the community, it is occasionally necessary and appropriate to rewrite them. Using the experiential language of belief, the Apostles' Creed could be rendered:

> I give my heart to God the all-powerful One, who created the
> universe, and Jesus Christ, God's Son, the Christ, who through
> the power of the Holy Spirit was born of the Virgin Mary. . . .
> And I give my heart to the Holy Spirit, devoting myself to the
> church and the communion of saints, trusting in the forgiveness
> of sins, the resurrection of the body, and life everlasting. Amen.

Notice that not all the intellectual problems of Christian doctrine
are solved here—the language remains sexist and hierarchical, and
we are still stuck with a virgin birth and a sin-filled church. You
and your skeptical friends may not want to devote yourselves to this
particular God.

But the emotional thrust is different from the one in the creeds
recited in church. This no longer expresses philosophical ideas *about*
God; rather, these words turn the affections toward what the early
Christians experienced. They had found God, the One they called
Father, Son, and Holy Spirit, to be the trustworthy Creator, Savior,
and Sustainer of the universe, the beloved of their hearts. Through
these words, contemporary followers continually remind themselves
of the early Christian experience of God and Jesus, humbly dedicat-
ing themselves to a path of devotion and of beloving their God.

For people who have long recited the traditional creeds of the
church, it can be hard to think of reinterpreting them or rewriting
them. However, as Christianity expanded in the twentieth century,
new believers found it necessary to rewrite the creeds in words and
images that meshed with their cultures and their own experiences
of God. In 1960, the Maasai people of East Africa, aided by Catholic
missionaries, revised the creed in light of their encounter with Jesus:

> We believe in the one High God, who out of love created the
> beautiful world and everything good in it. He created Man and
> wanted Man to be happy in the world. God loves the world and
> every nation and tribe on the Earth. We have known this High

God in darkness, and now we know Him in the light. God promised in the book of His word, the Bible, that He would save the
world and all the nations and tribes.

We believe that God made good His promise by sending His
Son, Jesus Christ, a man in the flesh, a Jew by tribe, born poor in
a little village, who left His home and was always on safari doing
good, curing people by the power of God, teaching about God
and man, showing the meaning of religion is love. He was rejected by his people, tortured and nailed hands and feet to a cross,
and died. He lay buried in the grave, but the hyenas did not touch
him, and on the third day, He rose from the grave. He ascended
to the skies. He is the Lord.

We believe that all our sins are forgiven through Him. All
who have faith in Him must be sorry for their sins, be baptized in
the Holy Spirit of God, live the rules of love and share the bread
together in love, to announce the Good News to others until
Jesus comes again. We are waiting for Him. He is alive. He lives.
This we believe. Amen.

The Maasai creed invites us to go on a safari with Jesus. These are
not just words about God; rather, these words welcome us into a
story of God's hope for human happiness and healing.

Indeed, the word "doctrine," a word fallen on hard times in
contemporary culture, actually means a "healing teaching," from
the French word for "doctor." The creeds, as doctrinal statements,
were intended as healing instruments, life-giving words that would
draw God's people into a deeper engagement with divine things.
When creeds become fences to mark the borders of heresy, they lose
their spiritual energy. Doctrine is to be the balm of a healing experience of God, not a theological scalpel to wound and exclude people.

Rowan Williams, the Archbishop of Canterbury, pointed out
in a recent book that the Christian creeds are similar to the Three
Jewels of Buddhism, the vows that shape a Buddhist way of life: "I
take refuge in the Buddha; I take refuge in the Dharma (Teach-

ing); I take refuge in Sangha (Community)." The creed reminds us that Christians *take refuge* in God the Creator, *take refuge* in Jesus's teaching (forgiveness, love, and justice), *take refuge* in the life-giving Spirit, and *take refuge* in the church (the community). A vow. A prayer. An invitation. A living experience. Spiritual and religious. The heart of faith.

# CHAPTER FIVE

# *Behaving*

WHEN I FEEL STRESSED or sad, I often buy flowers, one of those colorful mixed bouquets—the kind wrapped in plastic and held together by rubber bands. I bring them home, take them to the sink, snip the packaging, clean the stems, and arrange them. As I pick up each flower, I examine its freshness and height and the size of its bud and place it exactly where I want it in the vase. Arranging is like painting with flowers and greens—a fleeting piece of art, unique in the composition of living things, a creation that exists only once in time and space. I attend to the task with great seriousness and thought, honoring each flower as it is giving its life for the purpose of beauty. The work cheers me, taking my mind off of whatever has bothered or irked me and replacing anxiety with a quiet sense of deliberate artistry. Creating something with my hands makes me feel different, better.

A few of my friends know that I arrange flowers. Occasionally, I have joined a church flower guild, offered my skill for a fund-raiser, or made bouquets for a wedding.

"I wish I could arrange flowers," an acquaintance will say after learning of my secret talent. "Will you teach me?"

I laugh and reply, "If only I could! I have no idea how to teach anyone to arrange flowers. It took me years to learn."

I did not choose this particular craft as my hobby. Instead, I inherited it. My father was a florist, as was his father and his father before him. When I was small, I would go to work with my dad and play or read at his table. Season after season, year after year, I watched him create wedding bouquets, altar arrangements, Mother's Day corsages, and casket sprays. He would pick up each stem as if he were picking up a paintbrush, eye color and placement carefully, and flower by flower make the most beautiful things. When I was about seven, he asked, "Would you like to try?" I felt nervous, knowing that I could never arrange anything as well as he could. But he directed my hands, teaching me about space and shape and size. And I learned.

One day, when I was only ten or so, he gave me an entire order of corsages to make by myself—it took me hours. How much more quickly he could have done it! Before I knew it, however, I was filling orders for bridesmaids' bouquets and table arrangements. My aunts said I had the "gene." Then, one day, he handed me an entire wedding order to do on my own. Working with the roses and daisies and baby's breath and greens, I lovingly made it all for a bride at the local Methodist church. "You did it," he beamed. "And it is beautiful." I was sixteen, and I was a florist.

In the language of the Old World, my father had apprenticed me. I started at the shop by playing, then by sweeping and cleaning up and by sorting flowers for the designers, always watching dad create. When I was old enough, he invited me to stand beside him as a learner, teaching me through doing by repeating his actions and guiding my hands. It took a long time and many of my creations wound up in the large trash bins behind the shop. After about six years, however, I was ready to work on my own, a journeywoman of the florist trade. I had done more than learn how to arrange flowers; I had become a florist. And I have no idea how to teach flower arranging (although I know that there are people who do teach such things), anymore than I would know how to teach someone to breathe. For me, arranging flowers embodies a way of life passed hand to hand down through the generations.

Religion used to be shared in much the same way. Inheriting faith meant standing—or kneeling—beside one's parents and learning the practices that composed a spiritual way of life. Not only did I learn to be a florist as a child, but I also learned to be a Methodist by observing my mother and by participating in the community. I grew up in the church building, learning not only in the sanctuary, but in the kitchen, the parish hall, the basement, the classrooms, and the hallways. Slowly, I learned how to be Christian. I learned about reading the Bible, singing, listening to sermons, feeding hungry people, gathering used clothing for those in need, saintliness (and sinfulness too). Faith was inherited, but it was also a craft, joining together skills and a community.[1] In the not too distant past, people became what their parents were through this process of teaching and transmission. Bakers who were Baptists; carpenters who were Catholics; pastors who were Presbyterian. Grandparents to parents to children, callings and crafts moved through generations.

## The Practice Gap

In 1986, following the death of my grandfather, the family florist shop went out of business. My uncle tried to run it for a short time, but he was not very good at it. My family had moved to Arizona, and my father did not want to go back east. None of the grandchildren—me included—wanted to run a florist shop. So it closed. Last time I checked, the building that once sheltered the family trade was an office supply store.

Somewhere, deep in my soul, I suppose I still am a florist and a Methodist. But I work as a writer and a teacher, and I am an Episcopalian. Although I learned a way of life passed on to me by my parents, I eventually chose a different path of both vocation and faith. On the new path, I have had to learn new practices of work and worship. My daughter never stood where I once stood and learned a family craft; I never guided her hands as she arranged a bouquet. We go to church, but she is not learning how to be a Methodist. I am teaching her different things. I cut the tether of family tradition. Because I chose my own way, she will not inherit what I once inherited.

I am not alone in breaking with family patterns. Although I do not know how many people opt out of family businesses, I do know that 45 percent of Americans have opted out of family faith. Almost half of us have chosen a way different from the one our parents gave us.

I have often wondered, "Why did I switch? Why am I not a florist or a Methodist? Did my parents fail?" I do not think so. They did what their parents had done before them, sharing their work and worship with the next generation. They were good workers and good church people who taught their children how to act and pray. What, then, was missing? They taught me *how,* but they did not teach me *what* was compelling about it or *why* I should devote my life to these traditions. Indeed, I learned how to be a florist, but not what was important about it or why I should be one. My father offered no compelling reason to walk the familial path other than "we've always done it" or "someone must take over after me." Sadly, family dynamics—complete with a German authoritarian patriarch and maddeningly eccentric uncles and aunts—suggested to keen young observers that leaving the flower shop might well be better for one's health and well-being than staying with it. No one told me that they were florists for the sake of beauty or service or joy. It was an obligation, often an onerous one at that.

The same was true for the Methodists. I learned *how* to be a Methodist. By observing and participating, I learned how to pray, sing, organize Sunday school, give an offering, and plan a church potluck. But no one ever shared *what* was significant about being Methodist or *why* I should be one. When I asked questions like "Why do Methodists eat meat on Fridays unlike the Catholics?" a sister congregant would inevitably reply, "That's the way we've always done it." No one told me about Wesley's protest against established religion, about his insistence that faith was a matter of the awakened heart, or that Methodism was a path of spiritual transformation and social justice. They simply said, "That's how we've always done it." That was the reason for everything. The clear implication of this was "Because we've always done it, you should as well." Another obligation.

In the post–World War II period, Western societies underwent what philosopher Charles Taylor calls "an expressivist revolution," whereby obligatory group identity—whether of nation, family, or church—was replaced with a new sense of individual authenticity and the "right of choice" based in personal fulfillment. External authorities gave way to internal ones, as we moved away from conformity to social structures toward the authentic self in society. Whether the switch is good or bad is beside the point. This revolution has happened, "releasing people . . . into the fractured culture" of consumerism, making everything from clothes and career to loves and faith a matter of choice. Thus, questions of meaning and purpose have become supremely important. Citizens of a "fractured" world must have reasons to choose if they are to choose well.[2]

Our grandparents and parents may have been very good at the doing of religion, the *how* of faith, but, in their world, there was no need to engage the interior questions of meaning, the *what* and *why* of faith. Maybe their parents forgot to share the *what* and *why* with them. In an inherited familial culture, the *what* was assumed and the *why* was unnecessary. In a fractured individualist culture, there exist no compelling reasons to reenact familial vocations in work and prayer and many compelling reasons to depart from old ways.

Since this cultural shift, three entire generations have been born into a world where the threads of memory have been cut and where life has to be woven anew by each of us. It is up to each one of us to stitch a new fabric of authenticity, meaning, and purpose.

When *how* became an end in itself, people began to ask *what*. If I am not going to be a florist, what now? If I no longer embrace Methodism, what faith will I embrace? When it comes to behavior (in contrast to belief), *what* emerges as the driving spiritual question. *What* always leads to *why*—the compelling reason to choose a particular path of *what*. Whereas religious behavior was largely a matter of *how,* spiritual practice entails the inner experience of *what* and *why* as people must intentionally choose their actions and vocations. After a choice is made, then we craft a new way of faith, the *how* follows the *what* and *why*. Choice, meaning, and practice interlace to open us to purposeful ways of being in the world.

## *The Religious Question: How Do I Do That?*

The room was full of Presbyterian pastors, meeting in a church in New Jersey. I asked them to fill out the "spirituality" and "religion" word association chart.

"What side would you like to fill in first?" I asked. They studied the whiteboard. Many were graduates of nearby Princeton Theological Seminary, a school rightly noted for its intellectual rigor.

"Religion," one answered. Heads bobbed in consensus.

"Okay. Religion it is." I moved to that side of the board, held my blue marker in anticipation. "What word comes to mind first when you think of 'religion'?"

Someone called out, *"Robert's Rules of Order,"* the guide to parliamentary procedure much cherished by Presbyterians.

I turned around, half expecting that the pastor was kidding. He was not. He was smiling, beaming, really. As if he had seen the beatific vision. I wrote *Robert's Rules of Order* on the board as I thought, "This is going to be a long day."

No matter the group or the city, the words on the "religion" side of the board were always about external things: *institutions, organizations, buildings, dogma, rules, hierarchy, order,* and *authority.* Indeed, the world of church has become, in many people's minds, coterminous with the world of religion, an external world of inherited rules, the enthusiasm of the Presbyterian pastor aside, the space of what William James once termed "dull habit."

Although this may be a mistaken understanding of religion—after all, religion derives from *religio,* a powerful experience of God—dull habit nevertheless describes popular sense of the word "religion" in today's culture, even among many clergy and churchgoers. That is bad news for religious denominations and churches. In William James's day, people tolerated "dull habit" as an acceptable form of faith, and churches could get away with offering conventional religion to their members. But no longer. Those on a search for personal authenticity, for expressive faith, will not abide "dull habit" as a substitute for meaningful spiritual experience.

When religion focuses on externals, the primary question becomes *how.* How to organize a church? How to manage an institution? How to run a meeting? How to train volunteers? How to teach Sunday school? How to create a budget? Ask *how* at a church meeting and someone will point you toward "how to" in a policy manual, a denominational handbook, canon law, or a business book. Ask a banker or a lawyer. Hire a consultant, engage a marketing company. Institutions and organizations demand technical expertise, trained managers, program specialists, and strategic planners. In the pursuit of expertise, religious communities lose their sense of being sacred locales for spiritual experience.

When I was small, learning *how* was a matter of being an apprentice, a communal and intuitive way of mastery based in the local community and family. Increasingly, as the church was externally defined as a national entity and a corporation, learning *how* meant being trained in how to: the professional and programmatic techniques to become an expert. "How to" meant following the rules or steps, mostly in business, management, or therapy, in order to fix problems. The *how* question in religion tracked developments in the corporate world—as the old family businesses gave way to larger corporations, *how* morphed from hands-on instruction into programs of technical expertise. This shift hastened the erosion of religion by decreasing the sense of participation, insight, and purpose that regular believers could bring to being part of a faith community and their own spiritual journeys.

Ironically, at the same time that religious institutions sought greater technical expertise, they also verbalized a theological vision of the church as God's people. This created an expectation gap between the way they conducted business and their stated mission, between the externals of religion and the internal quests of a new spiritual generation. As a friend of mine recently quipped, "You have to worship where upper management does not want you to get ahead." That is the gap of hypocrisy, or the practice gap, of doing one thing and saying another. When it comes to religion, the practice gap is the worst gap of all—it angers participants and alienates seekers. Asking *how* before you ask *what* and *why* is the road that leads right into this gap.

The practice gap is the opposite yet corresponding danger of the belief gap. It is as if Christians are standing on a hilltop. On one side, questions of belief threaten to push them into doubt. On the other side, incongruous behavior—where words and actions conflict and collide—threatens to push them into despair. To have a vibrant faith life, one must spiritually navigate the Scylla and Charybdis of both dull understanding and dull habit.

## What Do I Do? The Art of Intention

A few years ago, I was working with focus groups in churches. The first question asked to those gathered was always the same: "What is it that you do here in this congregation, in the last five to ten years, that has changed your life and the life of your church?" People paused to reflect on their experience.

Once, someone replied, "What do you mean, what do we *do*?"

I answered, "Oh, you know. The stuff that Christian people do."

"You mean like prayer?"

"Well, that's something that Christian people do. Tell me about it."

Although the word "practice" may be new to some, it is a familiar concept in most religious traditions. Practice is the doing of faith. Jews often refer to themselves as practicing Jews; serious Catholics who distinguish themselves from their lapsed brothers and sisters use the term "practicing Catholic"; committed Muslims devote themselves to five practices of faith; and Buddhism is a way of life composed of practice. Although they do not often use the language of practice, Protestants of all sorts—Methodists, Presbyterians, Episcopalians, Baptists, Mennonites—have specific practices that make up a distinctive way of life. Explaining the concept of spiritual practices, contemporary writer Brian McLaren says, "They are actions within our power that help us narrow the gap" between who we are and who we are becoming. Practices form character. He writes: "Spiritual practices could be called life practices or humane practices, because they help us practice being alive, and humanely so. They develop not just character but also aliveness, alertness, wakefulness, and humanity."[3] Practices are things we do that shape who we are as they awaken us to God and others.

Theologians Dorothy Bass and Craig Dykstra push toward a

specific definition of Christian practice as the "things that Christian people do together over time in response to and in the light of God's active presence for the life of the world."[4] Practices weave together a way of life, they shape character, create connections between people, order our choices, and deepen our wisdom about living in the world. Much of the contemporary interest in spirituality is a renewed attention to spiritual practices. As Bass and Dykstra relate:

> [Cultural] shifts have set many people on spiritual journeys, in search of solid ground. But here too, change complicates matters, for now a dazzling array of religious and therapeutic options is available. It is hard to know what is of value, and harder still to settle into a steady way. So great is the need for insight that people look for it in many places—sometimes, indeed, in many places all at once. What will it be? Eastern meditation or Western psycho-therapy, twelve-step groups or self-help books, spiritual retreats or private prayer?"[5]

As Bass and Dykstra note, the first step in a life of practice is engaging the *what* question. What practices will I engage?

The question is the same whether one has inherited and stayed with a religious tradition or if one is a spiritual explorer. For the comfortable: "What practices have I been given that shape my life in meaningful ways?" For the explorers: "What practices draw my spiritual attention?" But both sorts of folks ask: "What kind of person might I become if I seriously devote myself to learning these particular practices?" A choice must be made—to become more intentional about your actions, whether you are a lifelong Roman Catholic or Jew or Methodist, or if you claim the label "spiritual but not religious" or "none of the above." What do you do that has changed your life in the last five to ten years and has moved you toward God and your neighbor? What might you do?

Many spiritual practices are shared across religious traditions—

such as praying at fixed hours, giving to the poor, keeping a day of rest, fasting, and offering hospitality to strangers. Thus, it is possible to speak of practices in general religious terms and point toward interreligious commonalities. But we do not learn practices in a generic way; practices are embedded in and relate to specific traditions, and practices emerge from particular cultures, histories, and languages.

Many religions share fixed-hour prayer, hourly prayers that remind believers of God's presence throughout the day: traditional Jewish prayer takes place at three distinct hours; Muslims pray five times daily; and Christian fixed-hour prayer runs on a three-hour cycle through the entire day and night. Despite the similarity of the practice, Jews, Muslims, and Christians engage it in different ways. They practice different schedules of prayer, prepare differently for prayer, read different texts in prayer, and pray with different words, in different postures, and in different places. Some pray holding a book, kneeling on a rug, fingering beads, lifting up open hands, or scrolling through a text on a smart phone app. Some pray in Hebrew, others in Arabic, not a few in Latin, while millions pray in their local languages.

Fixed-hour prayer is an ancient and shared practice, but those who participate in such prayer learn it in particular ways because of their parents, a venerated teacher, or the simple happenstance of where they were born—prayer is never generic. It becomes embodied in our lives in the Jewish way, the Islamic way, the Buddhist way, the Hindu way, the Lakota way, the Catholic way, the Protestant way. Even those who self-conscientiously blend practices do so in the full awareness that they are blending elements from a variety of traditions. In the process, they are creating new—and very particular—expressions of ancient practice.

What practices frame our lives? Some religions, such as Islam, are very specific about the practices that compose their faith. Other religions, like Christianity, have looser clusters of practice. In Christian tradition, practices fall under two large categories, "love of God" (practices of devotion) and "love of neighbor" (practices of ethics). As such, Christian practice is highly malleable and culturally adaptable. In spite of variation, the tradition still insists that a faithful spiritual life consists of practices of both devotion and ethics, and it is through such practices that one will, as Jesus promised, experience "eternal life."

Christian devotional practices are the things that Christian people do to deepen their awareness of God and strengthen the inner life. These practices include prayers of all varieties: fixed-hour prayer, intercessory prayer, contemplative prayer, repetitive prayer (like the Jesus prayer or rosary prayers), prayers of praise, and extemporaneous prayer. Devotional practices also include reading and reflecting on holy texts, Bible study, scripture memorization, learning the lives of the saints, and concentrated study of and reflection upon theology and history. Christian practice also includes fasting on special days (such as Ash Wednesday and Good Friday) or as part of an intensive prayer ritual; a calendar of feasts and holy days that stretch through the year to mark "holy time"; meditation and silence; and keeping the Sabbath, primarily through public worship on Sunday.

But devotional practices are not the entirety of the Christian way of life. Indeed, inner practices of devotion lead to an active life in the world whereby Christians serve their neighbors and enact God's love toward all. Indeed, some of the devotional practices naturally extend into the world (certain forms of prayer and public worship, for example). Christian ethical practices derive from Jesus's teaching in the Sermon on the Mount (Matt. 5–7), an exposition of Jewish law. From these words, Christians have developed practices of serving the poor; caring for the sick, oppressed, and needy; humility; peacemaking; forgiveness and reconciliation; giving freely from one's resources; honoring the body; truthfulness; hospitality; healing; and discernment.

Although Western Christianity would eventually be defined as a belief system about God, throughout its first five centuries people understood it primarily as spiritual practices that offered a meaningful way of life in this world—not as a neat set of doctrines, an esoteric belief, or the promise of heaven. By practicing Jesus's teachings, followers of the way discovered that their lives were made better on a practical spiritual path. Indeed, early Christianity was not called "Christianity" at all. Rather, it was called "the Way," and its followers were called "the People of the Way." Members of the community were not held accountable for their opinions about God or Jesus; rather, the community measured faithfulness by how well its members practiced loving God and neighbor. Not offering hospitality was a much greater failure than not believing that Jesus was "truly God and truly human." Early Christians judged ethical failings as the most serious breach of community, even as they accepted a significant amount of theological diversity in their midst.

Today, people borrow practices from a wide number of sources. A recent Pew study found that more than a third of Americans attend multiple religious communities and freely mix spiritual practices from several sources.[6] Critics deride this as "cafeteria" religion, an eclectic faith constructed on the basis of personal taste and consumerism. But I think something more may be afoot. When religions are in the process of reformation or renewal, adherents frequently borrow and blend practices from other sources. From a historical perspective, borrowing simply means that conventional religious institutions—marked by "us" versus "them" attitudes—do not have adequate resources to respond to contemporary questions. Although there may be some comfort in what is familiar, millions of people intuit that familiar paths are somehow too restrictive in relation to their deepest concerns.

For example, when Christianity was forming, it posed a challenge to both Roman imperial religion and Judaism—the religions from which most of the early Christians came. The new adherents found the old ways moribund, somehow lacking the energy and inspiration to meet the challenges of the world around them. Yet they did not reject the old completely. Instead, the early Christians wove together their new way of life and the new stories of Jesus with practices they borrowed from other religions. In the process, they filled old practices with new meanings. Early churches were Christianized versions of ancient synagogues and built to resemble Roman basilicas; Easter borrowed elements from both Passover and pagan rites of spring; Christian theologians worked with Hebrew scripture and Greek philosophy. When ancient believers wed these elements to Jesus's teaching, they actually stitched a new religion—Christianity—a form of faith, belief, and practice that spoke to the needs of their own souls and the world with great insight and spiritual vitality.

Faith mixing signals a decline of the old ways. It simultaneously signifies a renewal of spiritual imagination and creativity. Blending, borrowing, mixing, and adapting often signal religious reform, as new patterns of faith and practice emerge in relation to new cultural challenges. The French have a word for this process of mixing practices: *bricolage*. The word means "to fiddle with or tinker with" or "to make creative use of whatever is at hand." In English, *bricolage* is often translated as "do it yourself." In the West, as religious institutions are struggling, people are engaging in spiritual *bricolage;* they are "doing it themselves," as they pick up fragments of practice from various sources at hand and construct new sorts of Christianity, Judaism, Islam, and other religions.

There can be dangers in blending. First and foremost, conventional religious institutions do not typically approve of such mixing, especially among clergy and theologians. *Bricolage* makes things messy, hard for the top people to maintain order and orthodoxy in such a situation. In recent years, there have been several cases of pastors who mixed practices from Christianity, Islam, and Buddhism who have run afoul of religious authorities in their denominations.

A Missouri Synod Lutheran pastor was suspended for participating in a post-9/11 interfaith prayer service with "pagan clerics." An Episcopal priest was prohibited from the priesthood for embracing Islamic spiritual practices. And the consecration of an elected Episcopal bishop was disallowed (among other issues) because he engaged in Buddhist meditation.

Second, and perhaps more troubling, not every practice is an appropriate candidate for mixing with another religious tradition. Is something lost in the process of adaptation? Much of the Christian New Testament is an argument about whether spiritual practices from other religions or cultural practices relate to the message of Jesus. Does, for example, the Roman practice of exposing unwanted children contradict Jesus's invitation for little children to come to him? Early believers came to see these two practices as contradictory and rejected exposure. In another case, early Christians permitted women to speak, preach, and prophesy in their churches. Their practice went against Roman customs, which did not allow women such public freedoms. Eventually, the church adjusted its practice in relation to Roman gender expectations and surrendered early liberation for cultural conformity. In nearly every New Testament book, there are arguments about blending faiths—from intermarriage to circumcision, to what sort of food to eat, to the role of women in public worship, to the political and religious status of slaves, and to the relationship between faith and politics.

Such arguments were not theological minutiae. Instead, they are at the heart of a vibrant, emerging faith. What should we do? For Christians, the question should be, as clearly and sharply as possible: What practices embody the teaching and compassion of Jesus?

Although Christianity itself is a blended faith—a combination of first-century spiritual experiences of Jesus, rabbinic Judaism, Greek philosophy, Gnosticism, and Roman paganism—Christian tradition has typically urged thoughtfulness (not caution exactly, but thoughtfulness) when mixing practices. Thus, Christianity actually has a discipline that enables people to choose among practices and answer the *what* question. It is called discernment, the wise choosing of a spiritual path. As the early Christians believed, although many practices may be permitted, not all practices are necessarily helpful in building character, knowing God, or serving one's neighbor. Wisdom, then, in the form of discernment, points the way toward answering the question, "What do we do?" Discernment is a relatively simple practice. It entails praying for guidance, asking questions, listening to the insights of others, and making considered choices. For Christians, discernment is the practice behind the practices.

At retreats and conferences, I often distribute a list of spiritual practices, describe a few of them, and engage people in a conversation about practices in their lives and their churches. "We want to become a congregation that practices our faith more intentionally. I'd like us to be 'practicing Presbyterians,'" a woman proclaimed at one retreat. "But where do we start? What do we do?"

As a Socratic sort of teacher, I don't really like giving specific answers. "What do you feel called to do?" I replied. "Pray more fervently? Work on behalf of outcasts? Make room for strangers in your community? Understand the Bible more deeply?"

"All of it, really. I don't know what to do," she said sadly. "We don't know where to begin."

"Pick one—one activity that tugs at your heart," I suggested. "Start there. Just one thing. Not all of them. Do one thing well, with passion, with depth, with openness and understanding. Engage it intentionally, pay attention to the practice. See where it takes you."

What spiritual practices give you a powerful sense of freedom and direction, of mastery and maturity, of purpose in life?[7] Do those things—that's what.

SPIRITUAL QUESTION 2:

## Why Do I Do It? The Art of Imitation

"Would you like to join the altar guild?" asked an older woman, a member of a church where I was a member. "After all, you like to arrange flowers."

She was a nice person, diligent in her service to the church. Most every week, she showed up early on Sunday morning to set up the altar. She ironed the altar cloths, shined the silver chalices, and laid everything out. Sounded like holy housework to me.

Instead of saying yes or no, I responded, "Why?"

"Because I've been doing it for thirty-five years," she said impatiently, "and I'm really tired. It is time for someone else to do it instead."

Not exactly an appealing invitation. I turned the offer down.

I suspect that the woman had a rich faith life. I always wondered what might have happened if she had answered the question this way:

You know, I've been serving on the altar guild for thirty-five years. Every Sunday, I awake before dawn and come down here to the church. It is so quiet. I come into the building and unlock the sacristy. I open the drawers and take out the altar cloths and laces, so beautifully embroidered with all the colors of the seasons. I unfold them, iron them, and drape them on the altar. Then I go to the closet and take out the silver, making sure it is cleaned and polished. I pour water and wine. While I set the table for the Lord's Supper, I've often wondered what it would have been like to set the table for Jesus and his friends. I've meditated on what it must have been like to be there with him. I've considered what it will be like when we eat with him in heaven. And I've learned a thing or two about service and beauty and community. You know, I'd like to share that with you. I'd like you to learn that too.

I know how I would have responded: "Sign me up."

The difference between what happened and what might have happened clarifies an important dimension of contemporary spirituality. In the first case, she asked me to take on an obligation—one that had worn her down and become rote. In the second, she would have been inviting me into an experience—and a powerful one at that. Had she answered the *why* question in the second way, she would have asked me to participate both in the practice of the church's women who had learned such wisdom over many decades and in the tradition of Jesus's last meal with his followers. To know *why* provides a sense of purpose to our actions. If we know why we engage in a particular activity, we experience deeper spiritual connections in our work. *Why* is the meaning behind any sort of work, craft, or practice.

A few years ago, a fad appeared in some churches—wearing bracelets bearing the letters WWJD, for "What Would Jesus Do?," thus popularizing the *what* question. But WWJD also points to the *why* question as well. Christians do things because Jesus did them first. As he said to his disciples in the Gospel of John, "For I have set you an example, that you also should do as I have done to you" (13:15). The primary *why* for any Christian practice is that the action, in some way, imitates Jesus. The meaning of Christian activity is found in being like Jesus and experiencing Jesus's presence in all that we do.[8]

The New Testament is rife with stories of imitating Jesus—from welcoming strangers to how one prays, from forgiving one another to accepting those who are different, from feeding hungry people to laying down one's life for one's friends. Indeed, Jesus's refrain to his followers is insistent: "Go and do likewise." Christian spirituality is grounded in the principle of imitation, as Paul reminds his readers, "Therefore be imitators of God, as beloved children, and live in love, as Christ loved us and gave himself up for us, a fragrant offering and sacrifice to God" (Eph. 5:1–2). To imitate Christ is a total way of life based in love, as we pattern our practices after his actions, to the point of the cross.

Christians also pattern their actions after other valiant followers. Not only do Christians attempt to do what Jesus did, but Christians also seek to imitate Paul, Peter, Mary, and Mary Magdalene; biblical heroes; early Christian martyrs; faithful kings and queens; self-giving saints; thoughtful theologians; mystical pray-ers; poets and hymn writers; missionaries and artists; and the humble devout who serve the poor. The witness and practices of those who went before are called tradition. This is not some stultifying form of habit or custom, the "we've always done it that way" path of conventional faith. Rather, this is what Yale church historian Jaroslav Pelikan once called "the living faith of the dead." The New Testament book of Hebrews calls these faithful followers "the great cloud of witnesses"; Catholics, Orthodox Christians, and Anglicans refer to them as the communion of saints; and others simply remember them as the Body of Christ or the invisible church.

The *why* for Christians is therefore deceptively simple: Christians do certain things seeking to imitate Jesus and Jesus's followers who went before. This is not a set of rules, a prescribed piety, a list of dos and don'ts, or convention. Rather, following Jesus and our forebears involves encountering the same God they encountered through prayers, study, and worship; imitating Jesus and the saints means enacting God's love in the world by feeding the hungry, comforting the sorrowful, standing for the oppressed, caring for the poor, healing the sick, and making peace. Jesus and the saints serve as models and mentors in the way of practice. Indeed, Jesus promised his friends that they would not only do the extraordinary things that he had done, but would do "greater works than these" (John 14:12).

Imitation is a powerful way to learn spiritual practices. As is the case with many people, my mother was a formative influence on my faith. When I was young, she used to tell me, "Do unto others as you would have them do unto you." Later, she shared with me the story of the day her high school was desegregated in 1956. Appalled by the court ruling opening white schools to African-American students, her friends arranged a student strike, refusing to attend school on the first day of integration. They invited her to join in. My mother, however, felt torn between her friends and what she knew to be right. She always believed that racial prejudice was wrong. Defying her friends, she went to school. And she decided to meet the bus and greet her new classmates.

I asked, "Mom, why did you do that?"

She replied, "Well, I realized that if I were a stranger at a new school, I'd want someone to be at the bus to welcome me."

From that day on, "do unto others" was more than mother's moralism. It was a heroic act of hospitality, one that echoed Jesus's own words, "I was a stranger and you welcomed me" (Matt. 25:35), and an action that I seek to imitate in my own life.

Most significant human learning happens through imitation, whether by story or observation. A mother tells a story of her life to her child as a way to inspire good choices. Or she holds her baby and smiles. The baby watches her face and, eventually, smiles back. The mother smiles and laughs with joy. The baby watches, sees her mother's response, and learns to laugh. Sitting, speaking, walking, running—all these things are practices we learned through imitation. Imitation takes us out of the realm of obligation and requirement toward the realm of relationship and discovery. Imitation connects us to others as it opens the door to self-awareness and mastery. We are part of a great guild of human activity, apprentices to the art of being truly human.

But imitation must be linked to intentionality. It is very possible to imitate without thinking, without choosing, and without understanding. If you imitate without making a choice toward health, goodness, justice, or kindness, you may wind up imitating a drunk, a liar, a criminal, or an ax murderer. Maybe, once upon a time, people could assume that those whom they imitated were safe, honest, or insightful. Maybe, as was my case at the florist shop, you did not even think about the process of imitation. Maybe you just did it. In a fractured culture, however, you must choose what you wish to imitate, consciously understand why some actions are surer than others, and determine who is worthy of imitation.

Ultimately, the *what* and *why* of behavior, of practice, leads back to the *how*. As philosopher Charles Taylor has noted: "One joins a denomination because it seems right to one. And indeed, it now comes to seem that there is no way of being in the 'church' except through such a choice."[9] And what follows that intentional choice is imitating the practices of others already on the same path—whether that is the imitation of the founder or those who have, in some measure, mastered the craft of living faith. What leads to participation is a community of people who know *how* to do it.

## Spiritual Insight: The Reign of God and the Art of Anticipation

"But church isn't supposed to be about spiritual practices, about finding ourselves and getting our needs met," protested a United Church of Christ pastor. "That's all navel-gazing, consumerist spirituality. Church is supposed to be about God's reign—the kingdom and justice."[10]

I have heard that objection many times. It is right to worry that spiritual practices exacerbate individualism and a church-shopping mentality. However, the divide between practices and the kingdom, between spirituality and social justice, is a false one.

Practices done in imitation of Jesus naturally extend to the kingdom that Jesus preached. From the beginning to the end of his ministry, Jesus proclaimed that God's reign of love, peace, mercy, and justice was at hand and invited all who heard him to recognize and participate in that kingdom. When his first followers heard this, they imagined that the end of the world was near, that Jesus had initiated the longed-for rule of the Jewish messiah who would overthrow Caesar and all oppressors. Even after Jesus died, early Christians lived in the apocalyptic expectation that Jesus would return in their own lifetime to fulfill this ancient promise.

When Jesus did not return and things got politically worse, Christians redefined the kingdom as the visible reign of the church. Many centuries later, they reassigned the kingdom to the invisible church of true believers. Some believed that the kingdom would come at the time of the Protestant Reformation. Others believed that the kingdom had begun, but that it was simply hard to see.

By the nineteenth century, however, Christians had embraced the idea that somehow God's people would bring about or build the kingdom through the good works they did on earth. Missionaries spread out across the globe with the words of the Lord's Prayer on their lips: "Thy kingdom come, thy will be done on earth as it is in heaven." They evangelized entire nations, built hospitals and schools, and sought to change economic and political structures grounded upon the principles of social justice. Probably no generation worked so hard or invested so much in order to make God's kingdom on earth than did those nineteenth-century believers. When World War I crushed their optimism, Christians retreated from the kingdom either by surrendering to failure or believing that their hope for a kingdom here on earth had been misplaced. Many abandoned a robust vision of the kingdom, trading it for theologies of escape and despair.

Rather than being a theology of retreat, spiritual practices actually pick up an ancient thread in our understanding of the reign of God. The dominant narrative of God's reign has been the one mentioned above: the first Christians believed that Jesus would restore the kingdom; medieval Christians believed that the church was the kingdom; Reformed Christians believed that true Christians embodied the kingdom in word and sacrament; and modern Christians believed that they could create the kingdom through their work. But there has also been another story about the reign of God—the notion that God's people anticipate and participate in the kingdom through spiritual practices.

Prayer, for example. Although a deeply personal practice, and in many ways the ultimate in "navel-gazing" spirituality, prayer connects an individual to God. Through it, we enter a conversation with God. But it also functions in a more universal and even eschatological way. To pray to God *anticipates* some future time when the supplicant will speak with God face-to-face. In God's kingdom, there will be no barrier of space or time between us and God's presence. Intimacy with God, as in the intimacy of prayer, will be the very nature of God's kingdom. In the here and now, prayer creates connection and relationship with God, even as it embodies the sure hope that God is our eternal friend.

All Christian practices work in this way. The practice of hospitality opens our hearts to those who are strangers; it anticipates that, in God's kingdom, there will one day be no strangers. The practice of forgiveness cleanses our souls from guilt and shame; it anticipates that, in God's kingdom, all will be forgiven. The practice of charity shares what we have with those who suffer want; it anticipates that, in God's kingdom, there will be no more hunger, pain, sorrow, or fear. The practice of stewardship creates a generous spirit; it anticipates that, in God's kingdom, money and possessions will cease to exist and that all is God's. Practices shape us to be better, wiser, more gracious people now, even as these very practices anticipate in our lives and communities the reality of God's kingdom that has entered into the world and will one day be experienced in its fullness.

Some may choose to participate in a certain spiritual practice because it is interesting, feels good, or gives their life new meaning, but every serious Christian practitioner soon discovers one of the deepest mysteries of these practices. Christian practices all contain within them the dimension of ethics—they all anticipate God's reign, in which the world will be made right according to God's love and justice. Practices are not merely spiritual activities we do to entertain ourselves. Practices enliven and awaken us to the work of God in the world. We anticipate each day, knowing that God is in the here and now, and anticipate, most assuredly, the human future in the Spirit's reign of peace. No matter which particular road we travel, if we practice our faith in imitation of Jesus, the outcome will be justice. Our actions witness to this hope. Practices are the connective tissue between what is, what can be, and what will be. Spiritual practices are living pictures of God's intentions for a world of love and justice.

## How *Revisited*

One warm summer day, I drove past a Lutheran church with a large banner in the front yard announcing a Vacation Bible School program. The colorful sign looked professional, with pirates promising an exciting search for biblical treasure. Funny thing, though. The sign was exactly like the one hanging at a Baptist church less than a mile away. The same program, just different dates and a different church name plastered on the mass-produced banner. Both congregations had purchased the same VBS program. In recent years, Christian publishing companies have developed VBS product lines bearing names like "The Plunge," "Holy Land Adventure," "Quest for Truth," and "Great Bible Reef." Prepackaged, these "complete Bible adventures" contain "everything you need" for a successful Bible school. One website boasts, "Just add kids"!

No doubt such programs entertain children and ease the creative burden of VBS teachers across the land. Buy Vacation Bible School, recruit teachers, unpack the can, and invite the children. Unlike my

childhood, when the women of the church and their children created Vacation Bible School with construction paper, oilcloth, magic
markers, yarn, buttons, and old socks, VBS has become a spiritual
commodity, a religious experience that can be purchased. Maybe
people have forgotten how to do a Vacation Bible School; maybe no
one ever taught them; maybe it is just too hard.

Sadly, much of contemporary church is the same. Successful
churches have also become products—bigger-is-better buildings
with slick programs that cater to an expanding religious market. Yet
spiritual commercialization creates a culture of sameness across the
country that subsumes local cultures in its wake, losing the quality
of neighborly faith. Want your church to grow? Attend the latest
pastors' conference offered by a celebrity minister. Offer an extensive array of programming. Put on a dazzling Christmas spectacular.
Buy Vacation Bible School in a can.

Not long thereafter, I was speaking at a conference about Christian practices.

"How do we pray?" asked one person. "Do you recommend a
program for learning prayer?"

"Practices aren't really programs," I replied. "You can't order a
practice online from Amazon." A few people laughed.

But the questioner persisted, "You mean I can't buy a program
like one of those Vacation Bible School kits? I've got to give my
church a program, so they know how to do it."

Whenever I say "practices are not programs," I see puzzled looks
on the faces of church folk. For many, faith means participating
in any number of church programs—from teaching Sunday school
from a purchased curriculum to mission trips organized by professional travel agents. There are children's programs, programs for
singles, for college students, for divorced people, for women, for
senior citizens. There are programs on how to pray, how to read
the Bible, how to evangelize, how to share your faith at work, how
to be a good Christian parent, how to survive grief, how to stop

drinking, or how to say no to sex. There are programs about renewing your faith, growing your church, and raising money for the next building campaign. Indeed, some congregations are actually clusters of programs—the programs entertain or inform, but the different subgroups in the church rarely relate to one another in a quest for spiritual maturity.

The ultimate model for programmatic church was Willow Creek Community Church, located north of Chicago. For three decades, the twenty-thousand-member congregation was structured around the idea that multiple programs would attract people to church and that frequent participation in church activities would "produce disciples of Christ."[11] However successful Willow Creek seemed to outsiders, church leaders sensed that something was amiss. They embarked on an intensive self-study to try to determine if attending church was making a difference in people's lives.

The study revealed that church programs had little to do with spiritual depth, maturity, or character. As one pastor commented, "Increasing levels of participation in these sets of activities does *not* predict whether someone's becoming more of a disciple of Christ. It does *not* predict whether they love God more or they love people more." Senior pastor Bill Hybels admitted, "We made a mistake" by being overly dependent on programs at the expense of "age-old spiritual practices of prayer, Bible reading, and relationships."[12] At Willow Creek, programs *about* Christianity had actually replaced *practicing* Christianity as a way of life. The result? A big building with lots of people, but little spiritual depth.

Programs are external to our lives, a kind of outsourced plan for transformation. They are action plans to gain a skill. Someone who lives far away and who does not know anything about you or your struggles creates a plan that promises to change your life—make you thin, help you find your true love, teach you to pray, or heal you. It might take a month, forty days, six weeks, or three months. How does this work? If you stick with the exact program, the results are guaranteed. And programs do work *if* you follow the steps; they work for a month or forty days or six weeks or three months. When the program ends, you will most likely go back to being exactly who you were before you started. You discover that you have not really changed at all. You are the same. And that struggle with the old sameness is especially disheartening for those seeking spiritual insight and change.

Spiritual practices are more like crafts than programs. They are activities you discern, choose, and learn, actions in which you develop skill and mastery to help you become a different sort of person and, as the Willow Creek pastor said, deepen your love of God and neighbor.

"Oh, I get it!" a church music director announced at a conference. "When I was little, my mother had a program for me: she wanted me to learn to play the piano. It was her idea. She took me to lessons and made me practice. I complained all the time." Sympathetic laughter filled the room. "But one day, I sat down at the piano without her telling me to do so. I liked it. I practiced on my own. Then I began to run home from school to practice piano. I began to improvise with the music, adding notes, changing keys, playing faster or slower, and writing my own tunes. My mother found me a more advanced teacher. I learned pieces by heart, and I learned to play them from my heart." She stopped for a second and then said with some deliberation, "Music started as my mother's program, but it became my passion. I went from being a person who knew how to play the piano to being a musician."

There are people in the world who teach and there are teachers; there are people who write and there are writers; there are people who swim and there are swimmers; those who paint and who are painters; those who love and those who are lovers. Spiritual practices are the bridge between doing something—such as engaging a hobby—and being someone shaped by mastery of an action. But how do you do it? What moves an activity, especially a spiritual one, from the realm of external plan to internal transformation? The two elements key to learning spiritual practices are *finding a teacher* and *time*.

Teachers can be found in all sorts of places. Some people bear the title "teacher" in schools, churches, colleges, and community centers as they share *how* with their pupils young and old. Religious communities are full of teachers. Not just the ordained clergy, but the wise elders who have spent a lifetime in prayer, the middle-aged deacons who have spent many hours visiting the sick, or choir members who have sung beautiful music since childhood.

Sometimes people complain to me that spirituality is "too individualistic, not focused on community." But if spirituality relates to practice, it is anything but individualistic. Indeed, all practice exists in a rhythm of relationships. For instance, if you want to learn yoga, how do you learn it? You might go and buy a yoga DVD and pop it in your DVD player. But it will not be easy. It is hard to watch the DVD and form your body in those poses at the same time. Some yoga poses are impossible to learn without an instructor. So you go find a yoga class. There, a teacher will show you. But she will not only show you. She will come up next to you, she will demonstrate it for you, and then she will shape your limbs into the correct position. You watch her. You watch your classmates. You will experience the position in your own body. You learn the spiritual practice in community. As you gain confidence, others will follow your example. You will be both student and teacher.

Parenting is another good example. Parents teach their children all sorts of practices; at the same time, the parents themselves are learning the practice of parenting. As they teach their children, the children grow, but they also question, challenge, and act in unexpected ways. The parents reach out and ask their own parents, friends, or trusted advisers. In turn, the wisdom they gain is brought back to their children through more mature guidance and insight. Children learn from parents; parents learn from children; children learn more from maturing parents. And so it goes in a process of reciprocal learning and teaching.

And learning takes time. In my seventh year as a college professor, I was sitting in my office reading when I realized that I was supposed to be in class in about thirty minutes. The schedule had slipped my mind. I thought it was Wednesday when it was actually Thursday. Panicked, I checked the syllabus for my Reformation History course. The announced topic for the day was John Calvin. My heart sank. My Calvin notes were at home. I raced across the campus, fretting about what to say. Should I cancel class? I walked into the lecture hall, looked at the students, and began talking. For more than an hour, without a single note in front of me, I held forth on Calvin and the Reformed tradition.

When it ended, I thought, "What just happened? I'm no expert on John Calvin! I don't even really like John Calvin."

What had happened was that I had put in seven years as a teacher, enough time to know my subject, to be confident in a classroom, and to deliver a lecture. Those who study human behavior, like Anders Ericsson and Michael Prietula, have discovered a tenthousand-hour rule of expertise. That is, if you devote ten thousand hours—approximately seven to ten years—to a craft, you will master that activity. Want to play violin at Carnegie Hall? Practice ten thousand hours. Join the ranks of professional tennis players? Practice ten thousand hours. Deliver a lecture without notes? Practice ten thousand hours.[13] Consistent, intentional practice actually can transform people's lives by moving them from being novices to mastery. As Ericsson and his team note:

> You need a particular kind of practice—*deliberate practice*—to develop expertise. When most people practice, they focus on the things they already know how to do. Deliberate practice is different. It entails considerable, specific, and sustained efforts to do something you *can't* do well—or even at all.[14]

Of course, Christian practice is a little different from learning to play golf or becoming a chess master. It is impossible to truly master the faith.

Yet the idea that practice takes time is an important insight for Christian spirituality. Those who embark on a spiritual path do not begin with confidence or deep knowledge or insight. Indeed, when initiates begin a practice, they generally do not do that thing very well. The Christian tradition speaks of progress in practice as maturity, what Paul referred to as the "meat" of the faith (1 Cor. 3:1–4). People who intentionally engage spiritual practices grow in their understanding and awareness of God, and they get better at prayer, forgiveness, discernment, hospitality, and stewardship. The path to Christian sainthood may not be as mystical as is often thought—it may be a matter of putting in the time to practice.

All of this makes me wonder if pews are misleading in churches. They trick people into thinking that Christians learn best by sitting quietly in rows, listening to lectures, and memorizing ideas about the faith. But churches should not be lecture halls. They should be more like a yoga class. Or, better still, like my dad's florist shop. A guild where a spiritual initiate becomes an apprentice, a novice, a journeyman or -woman, and finally a master. Unlike my family's florist shop, however, where the guild was ruled by assumption and inheritance, the contemporary guild of faith engages practices with intention, through imitation, and with a keen anticipation of a hope-filled future of peace and justice.

## Spiritual and Religious: Intentional Christian Practice

"Almost the end," I thought as I glanced up at the clock, looking forward to lunch at the conclusion of the workshop. "I'll take one more question," I said to the group.

A woman raised her hand. "Yes?" I said.

"Thank you so much for your book *Christianity for the Rest of Us.* We read it in church. We love the middle part of the book about the ten practices that make for a vital congregation." She stopped.

I smiled. "I'm glad you like it. I hope that it's helpful."

"Oh, it is," she said. "We learned that if we just do those ten things in your book, we'll fix our church. We've already started a ten-step program based on the practices!"

I sighed inwardly. Practices are not a checklist for church growth. They are not a fad or the latest gimmick for evangelism. Practices are not a technique or a Band-Aid for declining churches. Practices are fluid faith, a spiritual path, and a way of life. They are messy, inventive, and open-ended. They are not intended to be appealing (even if they often are); they are intended to be faithful. These are things that Jesus's followers do, regardless of their popularity or cultural relevance.

When religion—of the institutional and organized type—encounters spiritual practices, its first impulse is to transform them into a program that will attract more members to a church and increase the number of pledges. But, as Brian McLaren says, "The purpose of the ancient way and the ancient practices is not to make us more religious."[15] Nor are practices intended to stall decline in religious institutions. Practices are not instruments we use to accomplish our goals, like filling church pews or raising the money to fix the church's roof. Institutional religion may shelter spiritual practice, but as soon as institutional religion turns spiritual practices into programs, the life-giving energy of practice drains away. Religion and spiritual practice—in that order—are a combination that rarely sustains passion. With religion in the lead, practices always descend into a muddle of self-righteous dos and don'ts, often focused more on the actions of others than the state of our own hearts.

When the order is reversed, however, to spiritual practice and religion, then awakening becomes possible. When spiritual practices retain their commitment to intentionality, the wisdom of imitation, and a focus on God's reign, then they possess the ability to transform "religion" into *religio,* an experience of wonder, trust, and faith. Religious and spiritual? Not so much. But spiritual and religious? That is the path toward a new sort of Christianity. It is the way of awakening.

To be spiritual and religious when it comes to behavior means to be deliberate in choosing what we do, to do those things that imitate Jesus, and to act justly in the world. It is intentional Christian practice. We are to be learners on the way, then initiates, apprentices, skilled practitioners, and masters. Not just members of a church.

# CHAPTER SIX

# Belonging

AFTER MY MOTHER DIED, I became obsessed with family history. I spent days cruising the website ancestry.com looking for clues about the generations that went before. I traced one line back to the ancestor who came from Saxony to America—a Hermann Hochstadt, who arrived here in 1876 and settled in Philadelphia with his wife, Minna, and three young boys. In the 1880 census, he lists his profession as "florist." About five years later, he moved to Baltimore and started his own flower shop. However much I combed through online sources, I could not find the name of the ship that brought the family here or any trace of an immigration record. Even though I had the months and years of their births, searches of "Hochstadt" and "Saxony" turned up nothing in birth or christening records. I had no idea from what village or town the Hochstadts hailed. Then I remembered a snippet of conversation from my own childhood—my mother saying that the original Hochstadt (and eventually Hochstedt, replacing the *a* with an *e*) ancestor may have changed his name when he arrived in America and that no one in the family either remembered or would say what the family name had been.

The line was broken. Hermann and Minna's story was lost to me. What was their real name? Where did they come from? Why did they sail to America with such young children? I could not stop thinking about them, feeling historically dislocated as a terrible weight of sadness came over me. With the death of my own parents, I wanted to better understand myself by understanding where we had come from as a family. I wanted to know my name. I wanted to find my people. I needed to belong. But I had reached a dead end.

I shared my frustration about Hermann, along with my concern that I was spending too much time on Google looking for him, with a friend. She said, "Did you know it is quite a common thing to explore family history after parents die? Some people spend weeks going through old pictures, while others tear apart closets and attics looking for diaries and old letters."

I shook my head. No, I did not know.

She continued, "Grieving people try to connect, to remember who came before and what the past means for them as they go forward. It's about discovering who you are after loss. I guess that searching the Internet for family history is just a contemporary manifestation of the same. It is a very normal thing to do."

It is normal. Some people, however, view the search for identity as self-centered or indulgent. "Get over it and get on with life," they advise. But having a deep awareness of one's identity is one of the most important aspects of developing a lively spiritual life. As classical spiritual masters taught, knowing one's self is the beginning of understanding God, as we claim the deepest parts of our own beings and experience human soulfulness. The Roman Catholic mystic Teresa of Avila describes such self-knowledge in the first paragraph of her book *Interior Castle*:

> It is no small misfortune and disgrace that, through our own fault, we neither understand our nature nor our origin. Would it not be gross ignorance if when a man was questioned about his

name, or country, or parents, he could not answer? Stupid as this would be, it is unspeakably more foolish to care to learn nothing of our nature except that we possess bodies, and only to realize vaguely that we have souls, because people say so and it is a doctrine of faith. Rarely do we reflect upon what gifts our souls may possess, who dwells within them, or how extremely precious they are. Therefore we do little to preserve their beauty; all our care is concentrated on our bodies, which are but the coarse setting of the diamond, or the outer walls of the castle.

Or, as Jesus put it with such elegant simplicity, "Love God and love your neighbor as yourself." How can we love either God or neighbor if we know or love not ourselves?

## The Identity Gap

Belonging is an issue of identity. Searching out family roots, taking pride in one's nationality, joining a club or a church, participating in a movement or political party—all these things give people a sense of identity through belonging. I say: "I am a Hochstedt." "I have German roots." "I am an American." "I am an Episcopalian." "I am a Democrat." You will say it differently: Spanish or Indian family background; a Canadian or Australian or Bolivian or Mexican; a Baptist or Pentecostal or Catholic; Republican or Green. Yet we all mean the same thing in rehearsing the list. I am part of this family; I am related to these people; I throw my lot with this tribe. I both belong and I am. Belonging is intimately related to being. To belong is to be.

So what happens when old forms of belonging disappear? When the old labels no longer express who we are? When family ties are broken, when nationalities and ethnicities blur, and churches and denominations go into decline? People lose a sense of themselves—

that is what happens. Instead of being grounded, people feel unmoored. And with that comes grief, often unnamed, but still experienced in a myriad of ways.

In the United States, conventional Protestant, Roman Catholic, and Jewish identities are eroding. Protestants are taking on generic religious identities or leaving the faith entirely, Catholics are abandoning their churches, Jews struggle with intermarriage. Religious decline means countless numbers of people in the world today are suffering a sense of loss.

In 2007, I participated in a panel at the American Academy of Religion about the "emergent church," a discussion that became rather more heated than expected. Another panelist criticized mainline and traditional churches as moribund, lacking creativity, and resistant to change. Although I was certainly aware of the shortcomings of old churches, I did not agree with his characterization. Interrupting him, I said, "I've been in hundreds of mainline churches, and although they are not always open to change, that's not the primary feeling in the congregations. Their primary emotion is grief. They are grieving the fact that their churches are declining, that their children are going away, and that the traditions they love might disappear. They are in mourning." In short, they no longer know who they are or who their offspring might become.

If grieving individuals turn toward questions of identity, how much more is that true for groups of people feeling the weight of loss, of not belonging anywhere? If a community—a church, a town, an organization, a group of any sort—senses its end, the greater the need becomes to search out the family tree and to locate itself again in the larger story of continuity and change, to find where it belongs. Thus, at times of pitched cultural upheaval, a typical spiritual response includes heightened anxiety about identity—about who we are and the direction of our lives. Eventually, when something new comes into being, this anxiety will ebb. But, in the meanwhile, we are faced with a question that keeps many up at night: Who am I?

## The Religious Question: Who Am I?

Questions of belonging and identity have not always been as pointed as they are today. In medieval Europe, for example, there had developed a relatively stable sense of identity—you were who you were by accepting your place in a great chain of being, God's ordering of the universe from pope and king down through the ranks, and obeying those God had placed in authority over you. You belonged to God's order of things. Identity was fixed, divinely assigned, and communal. Questions of individual self-knowledge—as we know them today—probably did not exist for vast numbers of people. It is hard to imagine a medieval person even asking, "Who am I?" The answer would have been self-evident.

In the late Middle Ages, however, this began to change. Economic changes undermined the idea that God assigned people to a particular station as a new middle class experienced social mobility. A series of crises in the Catholic Church made many question the religious authorities they once believed spoke directly for God. Rising literacy enabled new readers to be more reflective, to consider words and ideas for themselves. A rediscovery of ancient knowledge of science, literature, and texts opened a new world of meanings with which people could interpret themselves and their surroundings. The old ways of understanding were passing, and as they died, they brought to the fore new questions of the self. "Who am I?"

In this context, Teresa of Avila wrote of searching out the interior life as a pathway to God. Her Protestant competitor, theologian John Calvin, made the same point: "Without knowledge of self, there is no knowledge of God. Our wisdom, insofar as it ought to be deemed true and solid wisdom, consists almost entirely of two parts: the knowledge of God and of ourselves. But as these are connected by many ties, it is not easy to determine which of the two precedes and gives birth to the other."[1] Although Teresa and John Calvin would come to exactly opposite conclusions about the self— Teresa concluded that the self was basically good and Calvin that it was basically bad—they nevertheless shared in the same quest for identity. Each asked, "Who am I?" To answer the question and find one's self was a way toward understanding God.

The modern thinkers who followed Teresa and Calvin offered many possibilities for understanding selfhood, the most influential of whom was the French philosopher René Descartes (1596–1650). Descartes's world was broadened by studies of mathematics and philosophy and aided by travel, all of which combined to undermine any sort of traditional religious certainty. He became consumed with doubt. For Descartes, nothing was self-evident. He felt the weight of the questions of his day—including a fundamental skepticism about human existence. With church authority rejected, religious division roiling Europe, evolving technologies changing daily life, and dizzying new sciences and humanities changing the nature of European society, Descartes struggled to find meaning and purpose. How do we know anything? How do we even know that we exist? His answer: "I think, therefore I am." Thinking— rationality—proved existence. Even doubting that one exists proves the case that one is. In a real way, Descartes built on the foundation laid by Teresa of Avila and John Calvin that the self is the starting place for spiritual understanding. He just particularized the "self" to the mind.

Over the last five centuries, philosophers and theologians either agreed with Descartes or argued with him. They developed answers to the question "Who am I?" by modifying Descartes's insight or rejecting it. An entire branch of philosophy called ontology, the study of being or existence, deepened to come to terms with the modern questions of self. And although some ancient philosophers asked questions of being, the search for understanding the self took on new urgency in Western Christianity around the time of Descartes. The word "ontology" itself did not even appear in European languages until 1606. Thus, the question "Who am I?" entered the forefront of Western consciousness and has remained with us since.

SPIRITUAL QUESTION 1:

## *Where Am I?*

When a college philosophy professor first introduced my class to the question "Who am I?" I thought he was less than completely sane.

"I'm Diana, of course," I thought. "Who needs to ask such a question?"

He continued, "How do you know that you exist?" Then, posing a question later artfully explored by the movie *The Matrix,* he said, "How do you know this isn't a dream? Or that you are living only in someone else's dream? What is real?"

Most people do not arrive at questions of identity through philosophy class, and if they do, their initial reaction might be like mine. Selfhood is self-evident. "Am" is a form of the verb "to be." Saying "I am" means my self comes from being. When I stopped to consider my professor's question, however, I realized that my selfhood might not be so evident. After all, who was I, really? What composed my being?

For generations, that question (if anyone had cared to ask it) had been answered in the same way by members of my family. We were the Hochstedts, a German family of florists who immigrated to Baltimore, who passed down a business, some real estate, a name, and traditions of hard work and hierarchy. To say "I am Diana" meant a host of things when I was a child. It meant that I was a girl (who would, of course, never inherit the family business and therefore did not need to attend college) and my father's daughter (which would entail marrying someone else's son). I was someone who was named not for an ancestor, a German hero (my great-grandfather was named Charles Magnus for the emperor Charlemagne—a case of bourgeois overreach or an ancestral line?), or a biblical character, but, in my parents' act of youthful rebellion, after a rock 'n' roll song. I had been a baby whose name, despite its pagan-sounding origins, was inscribed in a baptismal record of a Methodist church that her ancestors helped found. "Diana" located me in my family past, my parents' story, and what they supposed the future would be.

As it happened, we moved. We left Baltimore in 1972 and, except on rare occasion, I hardly saw my grandparents or cousins again; we purposefully disconnected from the family, leaving behind inherited understandings of identity and self and undoing the anticipated future. Years later, I asked my mother, who was no hippie radical, why we moved to Arizona. She replied simply, "Your father needed to discover who he was separate from his father. We needed to find ourselves." Although people talked about "finding themselves" in the 1970s—it came to be a cultural mantra that fashionable critics derided as narcissism—when my mother shared this, it sounded fresh, authentic, and natural. By moving to Arizona, we found new landscapes in which to locate ourselves—geographical ones to be sure, but communal, emotional, physical, intellectual, and spiritual ones too. From lived experience, and not the philosophy classroom, I learned that "Diana" was not a fixed or inherited self; instead, "Diana" could be discovered—and discovered again—in new and ever shifting geographies.

This experience was not unique to my family. In the 1960s and 1970s, scores of people moved in similar ways. Historians refer to this period of massive cultural migration, this intellectual and social relocation, by a number of names—they refer to it as "post-traditional," "postmodern," "emerging," or "late modern" society. Whatever its name, Western societies changed so profoundly that the links between past and present strained or broke, and older orders of family, work, religion, and politics gave way to new patterns of life. Like other times of change, this social shake-up was marked by the search for self.

Descartes's rational self—along with all its philosophical progeny—no longer seemed sufficient, as people grew increasingly skeptical with the limits of human reason and increasingly aware of the biological and chemical connections of body and mind. Both the end of the old world and the challenge of the new one opened up the need to explore and understand the territory of our selves. It is not narcissistic to ask "Who am I?" Rather, it appears to be popular common sense, as regular people—like my parents—responded to the spirit of the age and tried to choose what kind of life they would embrace. A few decades ago, people had to physically move to escape the old, to run away to find change or new possibilities; but, with ever increasing speed, change comes to us, no matter if we have lived in the same small town for the whole of our lives and still visit grandparents on Sunday. In this context of mobility, philosophers and theologians say that the most logical understanding of the self is that of a seeker, searcher, nomad, traveler, pilgrim, or tourist—identities of discovery and fluidity. Who am I? has become the question *Where* am I? I know that I am because *that* is where I was, *this* is where I am, and I *am going* somewhere else.

The impact of mobility on identity is profound, as it affects almost every aspect of our lives from where to live and shop, to whom we love and marry, to the churches and schools we attend. As journalist Bill Bishop argues, we live in a culture of the "big sort," where people move to sort themselves into affinity groups that provide comfort, meaning, and identity in an otherwise confusing and divided world.[2] But mobile identity can result in negative things such as hyperindividualism and isolation (the Unabomber) or the opposite in identity politics (cases of religious or political extremism). Many critics point out the unfortunate tendency of well-off Western people to shop for their identities by purchasing goods, products, and experiences to provide new avenues for self-discovery.

Problems and protests aside, however, the question "Who am I?" and its emerging answer, "I am my journey," appear to be new contours shaping our sense of selfhood. In the twenty-first century, it may be better to ask "Where am I?" as a path toward understanding who I am.

Going on a journey to find spiritual meaning is nothing new. The Hebrew and Christian scriptures are rife with such stories. Abram and Sarai leave their native land to follow an unnamed God. As they wander through the desert, they encounter God in surprising ways. They discover God's promises, God's faithfulness, God's quirky sense of humor, and God's power. In the process, God gives them new names—Abraham and Sarah—a new family and a new land. They roam from one life-giving place to another, sometimes trusting God, sometimes not. But in the process they find themselves. And they find God. Who are Abraham and Sarah? The first nomads of faith.

When I was a girl in church, we did not pay much attention to Abraham and Sarah's pilgrimage or their changing sense of identity. Instead, my childhood pastors emphasized Abraham's belief in and obedience to God. How hard it must have been for Abraham to leave home! He left everything to follow God! Look at his trust in God—he was willing to kill his own son because God commanded it! Abraham and Sarah were not consumed by spiritual wanderlust; they were steadfast (well, more or less) believers whom God tested and who, eventually, did as God commanded. When they learned to obey, God rewarded them by making them the parents of a great nation. Nice interpretation for training well-behaved Christian children or loyal church members, but not so good for restless spiritual seekers.

Movement energizes most biblical tales. Adam and Eve are forced from the Garden. Noah and his family embark on a nautical adventure. Hagar departs for the wilderness with her rejected son. Lot flees Sodom. Moses floats down the Nile, flees Egypt, and returns. The Hebrews escape Pharaoh to wander the desert for forty years. And Joshua sneaks into Israel, where he claims and fights for God's promised land. But that does not end the wanderings. The poets and prophets and historians tell continued tales of going and coming, of exile and return—like the story of Ruth, the young widow who leaves her own people to find a new identity in a new land and, in the process, becomes the great-grandmother of King David. The Hebrew scriptures are not—as many a pastor preached in my childhood—a story of Israel's failure to trust God and God's punishments for that failure. Instead, the Hebrew Bible is a sort of family spiritual pilgrimage memoir, a record of a communal journey to and from God and back again that reveals ever increasing faithfulness, deepening awareness of what it means to be a Jew, and a widening understanding of God and God's love and justice.

The Christian scriptures reveal the same passion for moving around. Indeed, Jesus is born on a road trip, and shortly thereafter his parents take their newborn to Egypt. In all the Gospels, it is rather hard to keep track of Jesus as he and his followers move from town to town, travel to Jerusalem, and retreat to the desert. Jesus himself goes away with some frequency to pray and encounter God afresh. And the entire Passion narrative is a story of movement—Jesus comes into Jerusalem, retreats to a garden, is arrested and taken to various officials, only to walk the Way of the Cross and be executed at Calvary. Even then, Jesus does not rest. He is taken to a tomb outside the city where, three days later, nobody can find his body. The women say he has risen from the dead and, to prove the point, he pops in and out of places for a time—including one memorable appearance on the road to Emmaus, where two of his followers find a new sense of themselves and Jesus through sharing a meal. Jesus does not stop moving even after he has died! He ascends to God in heaven saying that he will return.

As in the Hebrew Bible, the Christian story is also one of spiritual journey. The Holy Spirit descends on the new church. The apostles go out to spread Jesus's story. Paul is struck by spiritual insight on the road to Damascus, retreats to the desert for three years, and finally travels the known world teaching and preaching. The young churches of Paul's letters show a propensity to wander away from Jesus's teachings, and the apostle devotes himself to showing them the true way in Christ. Indeed, the first name for Christianity was "the Way"; and the book of Revelation shows the spiritual movements between heaven and earth, angels and demons, God and the devil, and the whole of human history culminates with a vision of the river of God's love flooding this world and the next.

In the midst of all this movement, the flow of history, the spiritual journeys retold in the pages of these holy books, there is one grounding point: God. And who is God? "I AM" (Exod. 3:14). All the wanderings to find our self, "Who am I?," lead to the One who is named "I AM." In the pages of ancient texts, journey, God, and selfhood are interwoven. God's being and human beings are intimately related.

SPIRITUAL QUESTION 2:

## Whose Am I?

In 1960, theologian Valerie Saiving wrote "The Human Situation: A Feminine View," proposing that traditional Christianity had misunderstood the doctrine of sin. Much of Western Christian teaching defined sin as pride, the human hubris of setting ourselves up as God, and a disease of disordered loves whereby human beings glorify themselves: "Man knows that he is merely part of the whole, but he tries to convince himself and others that he is the whole. . . . Sin is the unjustified concern of the self for its own power and prestige."[3] Saiving insisted that this may be how men experience sin, but it did not reflect women's perspectives on sin, which are "better suggested by such items as triviality, distractibility, and diffuseness; lack of an organizing center or focus; dependence on others for one's self-definition; tolerance at the expense of standards of excellence . . . in short, underdevelopment or negation of the Self."[4]

Saiving wrote in the earliest days of second-wave feminism some fifty years ago, so on the face of it much of the argument now seems dated. Who wishes to see sin as "male" or "female"? Yet with the experience of the last five decades, we can gain new insights through her observations. As Western society has been overtaken by faceless consumerism and seemingly uncontrolled technologies, do men still feel like gods? I doubt it.

Instead, in the last fifty years, most Europeans and North Americans—male, female, gay, straight, transgender, black, white, brown—have most likely succumbed to the sins of "triviality, distractibility, and diffuseness," having lost any real sense of self in a world of broken memories, entertaining technologies, and frenzied materialism. Indeed, philosophers and popular observers alike have noted that many people are now reconstructing their sense of self through nostalgia or consumerism. Saiving's description of female sinfulness has come to represent much of the human condition. Thus, "Who am I?" may well be the driving theological question of the day and the starting point for reflection on spirituality—that lived experience of God longed for by so many people in the once Christian West.

If sin was once seen as a twisted, self-centered quest to become God, then salvation was deliverance from the self in order to become other-centered. If the self is a problem, then the church's job was to help people diminish the self and make room for God. Thus, salvation was freedom from our selves, our humanity, and our ambitions.

The church taught that anything self-driven was evil and shaped communal prayer, ritual, worship, and penance around stamping out humanness and striving instead for divine ideals of goodness. In the West, Catholics and Protestants took different routes to the same end—Catholics emphasized confession, penance, and sacraments as the way out of the human dilemma; Protestants (depending on the sort of Protestant) emphasized right belief, reordered hearts, and moral action as the paths away from sin. Fundamentally, however, the outcome of salvation was the same: pushing back, replacing, or burying our human nature in favor of submitting to a transcendent—and often distant—God.

This, I suspect, is the root of many people's anxiety about church—that religion is the purveyor of a sort of salvation that does not address their lived struggles. So those who once "believed" in this sort of salvation migrate away from church, seeking instead something they call spirituality.

Pride and hubris do not particularly seem to be humanity's problem at the moment—they began to erode when the first atomic bomb fell on Hiroshima. In the last seven decades, a certain lostness has fallen over the human race, as if we are all stuck on an unnamed island in a place we do not know, not entirely sure how we arrived, where random, unexpected, unpredictable, and uncontrollable events happen to us for reasons we do not understand. In a very real way, we have come to the end of pride, living as we are in a posthubris world, and asking ourselves: Who are we in this story? How can we be saved from these dilemmas? Maybe we cannot get off the island, but perhaps, just perhaps, we might come to know ourselves—and God and our neighbors—more graciously and heroically while here.

Salvation is not being saved from ourselves, escaping some dreadful fate of judgment, damnation, and hellfire at the hands of a wrathful God; rather, it is being saved to ourselves, finding what was lost and the joy of discovery in the hands of a loving Creator.

Although the word "salvation" has come to mean "eternal life" in most religious circles, it is helpful to return to the word's Latin root *salvus,* meaning "whole," "sound," "healed," "safe," "well," or "unharmed," as a way to understand the spirituality of salvation.[5] Salvation and spirituality and self are related—spirituality connects us to the whole, allows us a glimpse into our place within God and God's world, giving a new sense of health and well-being in our situations and identities. The idea of salvation need not be rejected; rather, it needs to be brought back to a truer rendering of its root meaning. We need to come to an authentic sense of personhood, stitching together what was unraveled into a new whole. From a biblical perspective, that involves connecting to human well-being by asking "Who am I?" in relation to "I AM." And that might be our salvation.

A few years ago, I was leading a clergy event, and the topic was congregational identity. I made the case that churches with a clear sense of who they were and what they were called to do were more vibrant than those with a muddled identity. Toward the end of the talk, I stated: "Churches need to ask the question 'Who are we in God?' in order to move ahead."

During the question-and-answer, one minister stood up. "I've been a pastor for twenty years and know my church very well. We've been through many discernment processes to figure out who we are," he related. "I can tell you how many members we have, what their annual income is, their educational level, how they vote, what our neighborhood is like. But, in all the surveys we've taken and all the consultants we've hired, no one ever asked us who we are *in God*. They only helped us find out things *about* our church—who we are. I've never considered who we are *in* God. The preposition makes a difference."

When Descartes asked "Who am I?" and proposed "I think, therefore I am," most Europeans were Christians and assumed God existed. Even though things were changing in the 1600s, God was still in the background of every question and speculation. No one needed to add "in God" to deliberations of selfhood. God just was there, an unspoken part of both the question and the answer.

Over the next several generations, however, God slipped farther and farther into the background.[6] Most people did not take God out of the question, but the question moved away from God and more toward human experience. Eventually, as this shift occurred, it increasingly emerged as a human question, a question about "me" distant or disconnected from God, asked with little or no reference to a transcendent Being. As we moved through time, the once assumed phrase "in God" was forgotten. And we answered the question "Who am I?" in solely ethical, biological, psychological, social, and material ways with diminished capacity for the mystery and wonder of personhood.

Historians and sociologists call this process the "disenchanted" world. There is not anything qualitatively wrong with living in a disenchanted world. Indeed, most of us would rather live in a society where we can explain and treat cancer as a disease and not a spiritual punishment inflicted by demons. And it is a good thing that airplanes fly by laws of physics instead of the faithful prayer of pilots. But the search for self does not quite fit in the same category as curing cancer or flying airplanes. Despite everything suggested and discovered by research and social scientists in the last two centuries, we know we are more than our thoughts, actions, genes, demographics, or economic value. The quest to understand the self has brought many of us to an unsettled place, recognizing the contributions of nature and nurture to who we are, but feeling, oddly enough, as if we lost something along the way.[7]

Without intentionally adding the prepositional phrase "in God," we might forget that spiritual journeys are entwined with the Great I AM. "In" orients selfhood in a larger relationship; we are still ourselves, but we are not isolated individuals. We exist "in" something. In order to understand ourselves spiritually, we need to reinsert the

prepositions. Prepositions link words; they connect objects in a relationship, thus locating the subject in time and space. In the spiritual
life, they act as markers for reflection and discernment.

"Who am I in God?" This is one of the classical questions of
Christian spirituality, one rooted in the person of Jesus, the Gospels,
and the experience of early Christian community. In the Gospel of
Mark (the earliest of the four New Testament Gospels), Jesus asks
his followers, "Who do people say that I am?" and then quickly
shifts the question to "Who do you say that I am?" Peter answers,
"You are the anointed one," meaning the "Messiah" or "Christ"
(8:27–29). In a very real sense, however, that answer is as clear as
mud. Throughout the book, the disciples struggle to understand
what it means for Jesus to be God's "anointed one," a situation complicated by the fact that Jesus does not want them to tell anyone.

Although the question of Jesus's identity is one of the most
pointed themes in the Gospel of Mark, all four Gospels wrestle with
the same issue. As he traveled through Palestine, Jesus encountered
many people who wanted to know, "Who are you?" But the question is more than information or curiosity about Jesus. Instead, as
people in the Gospels meet Jesus, they gain new insights on themselves. The question "Who do you say that I am?" plunges Jesus's
friends into the corresponding self-query, "And who am I?"

Christians are used to reading the Gospels as focusing on Jesus,
mostly because our parents and churches have taught us that the purpose of those four books is to tell us who Jesus is, so that we might
believe in him. This Christ-centered focus is not necessarily wrong,
but it does limit our imaginations if we only understand the Gospels
as theological puzzles for which we only have to skip to the end to
find the correct answers. If we shift the focus, the stories open up in
new directions—what if the most important question is not Jesus's
identity per se? What if the most important question is the identity
of the other people in the story? How do Jesus's friends and acquain-
tances change or gain new insights when they find themselves *in* Je-

sus's company? Who are the disciples, the followers, the crowds, the nameless peasants, the children, the sick, the oppressed, the angry, and the anxious when they discover they are *in* God? For those who encounter Jesus, the Gospels are less like puzzles to be solved and more like good mysteries in which, through the process of intuition and discovery, we peel back layers of falsehood, dark motives, and hidden character to reveal the truth that has been there all the time.

Scholars and preachers often point to the fact that each of the four Gospels is very different from the others and that Jesus is depicted in profoundly different—and sometimes contradictory—ways in those accounts. As a result, skeptics, doubters, and scoffers dismiss the Gospels as inconsistent or untrustworthy. Indeed, the seemingly historical "facts" of the Gospels are a jumbled mess and almost impossible to harmonize into a single, coherent, chronological account. However, if you take Jesus's question "Who am I?" and read the Gospels through the theme of understanding identity, the four stories (and those in noncanonical writings like the *Book of Thomas the Contender,* where Jesus says, "For whoever has not known himself knows nothing, but he who has known himself has already understood the depth of all things"[8]) come into focus in a much more cohesive way. The Gospels are the "good news" that when we strive to answer Jesus's question "Who do you say that I am?," we plunge into the mysteries of ourselves, peeling away layers of self-delusion, deception, and deceit, to the unfathomable knowledge of who we really are when God is right there with us.

In John 4, Jesus meets a woman at a well. The conversation quickly turns to the question of Jesus's identity when she asks, "How is it that you, a Jew, ask of drink of me, a woman of Samaria?" (4:9). Jesus speaks of water, wells, and worship, and then springs it on her that he is the Messiah. How does the woman respond? She drops her water jar, runs back to town, and tells everyone, "Come and see a man who told me everything I have ever done!" (4:29). In this story, questions of Jesus's identity and her identity thread together in mutual revelation. Knowing who Jesus is leads her to know who she is—and, instead of feeling shame about her mistakes, she feels new freedom to tell her story. And so it goes throughout the Gospels. Almost everyone leaves Jesus's company saying: "He made me whole!" "I have been healed!" "I'm not a prostitute, a sinner, an outcast, or a leper. I now know who I really am!" "I may be a Samaritan, but I can still know God." "I am loved!" "I am accepted as I am!" Being "in" Jesus, in his presence or in conversation with him, pushes the other person beyond social roles and masks to deeper awareness of "Who am I?" transforming the question from an external one to a relational one that might be better rendered "Whose am I?"

Thus, the biblical query "Who am I in God?" is a starting point of Christian spirituality. Why do Christians pray? Christians do not pray to have wishes granted; rather, Christians pray to find themselves *in* God and that they might be more aware of their motives and actions. Why do Christians worship? Christians do not worship to be entertained; rather, Christians listen to sermons, sing, and partake of bread and wine in community to be *in* Jesus's presence and come to know themselves better. Why do Christians serve others? Christians do not act charitably to earn heavenly credit; rather, Christians find Jesus *in* their neighbors and such proximity enables greater insight to live fully in the world. Christians practice seeking Jesus *in* their lives because when they find themselves *in* God, pretense slips away to reveal the truest dimensions of selfhood and gives individuals the power to act in transforming ways.

Christian spirituality is comfortable with the preposition "in," which locates us in time and space near God or the person of Jesus. Christians are far less at ease, however, when the subject and object of the preposition are switched and a new question emerges: "Who is God in me?" For those who wish to retain a clear distinction between the mundane and the divine, this risky reversal smacks of pantheism, the idea that God is everything and everything is God.

In many ways, "Who am I in God?" is an analytical question, based in curiosity and the quest to know. Who is Jesus? Who am I related to God? What do I know of myself and of God? But the question "Who is God in me?" is the mystic's question, a spiritual query that is fearsome to utter. One might ask "Is God?" or "Who is God?" with some degree of confidence. But "Who is God in me?" Is that where God dwells? Asking the question in reverse is like Moses asking to see God's face, to behold God in person, and believe that God is in his own person. This inquiry moves us to holy ground.

Although Christians sometimes shy away from this question, it is found in the Gospels as well. In the Gospel of John, Philip asks Jesus, "Lord, show us the Father, and we will be satisfied." Jesus replies, "Have I been with you all this time, Philip, and you still do not know me? Whoever has seen me has seen the Father. How can you say, 'Show us the Father'?" (14:8–9). Despite the rebuke, Jesus continues:

> Do you not believe that I am in the Father and the Father is in me? The words that I say to you I do not speak on my own; but the Father who dwells in me does his works. Believe me that I am in the Father and the Father is in me; but if you do not, then believe me because of the works themselves. (14:10–11)

Although it is not in the story, Philip appears to have protested, "But you are going away? How will we see God then?" Jesus responds by saying that God is not only in him, but dwells in all who will follow him: "Very truly, I tell you, the one who believes in me will also do the works that I do and, in fact, will do greater works than these, because I am going to the Father" (14:12).

According to Jesus himself, he is not the only one in whom others see God. The apostle Paul follows Jesus in this emphasis on revealing God by urging the believers at Corinth: "Glorify God in your body" (1 Cor. 6:20). Sadly, too many Christians have read

Paul's letter to the Corinthians in a highly legalistic way and extrapolated from it a sort of religious list of dos and don'ts ("I don't drink, smoke, dance, or chew, and I don't go with guys who do"). But Paul's deeper meanings to his friends are found when one keeps the spiritual question "Who is God in me?" in mind. After writing of Jesus's resurrection, Paul states, "The body is meant . . . for the Lord, and the Lord for the body" (6:13).

In ancient times, the temple was not simply a building one went into to worship God; no, it was believed that the temple was the actual location of God, where one went to see God. When Paul reminds his friends at Corinth that they are temples of God (1 Cor. 6:19), he is not saying, "Repair your building, and you will be a pleasant place for God to visit." Rather, he is insisting, "You are sacred space; you are where the Divine One dwells. Others see God in you! Be aware that you are holy geography." Paul wants the Corinthians to hold the vision that God is in them at the forefront of their lives. Echoing Jesus's words to Philip, he is saying that if they act as Jesus, others will (not might) see God in them. Indeed, Paul's exhortation ends (several pages later) with a single, breathtaking statement: "Be imitators of me, as I am of Christ" (11:1).

In spiritual terms, "imitation" is not playacting, a false persona, mimicking, or a counterfeit. Rather, it is more like an imprint, an exact representation, or an image of God. Jesus and Paul both reminded their followers of the *imago dei,* that human beings are created in the image of God. Finding one's self in God is also to find God in one's self. Although Christian spirituality has often better understood the first half of the equation, the second half is the powerful—and even radical—substratum of experiential faith. The early Christian theologian Irenaeus affirmed Jesus's and Paul's teaching on this when he wrote, "The glory of God is the human person fully alive."

Through the monastic tradition, the writings of medieval mystics, and the Quakers and early evangelicals up to contemporary writers like Dorothy Day, Martin Luther King, and Oscar Romero, who saw God in the poor, the most vibrant practitioners of Christian spirituality have known that human beings are the face, hands, and feet of God in the world. Or, as Irenaeus would summarize, "God became man, so man could become like God."[9] From ancient martyrs who reenacted Jesus's death in gory arenas of violent sacrifice to a quiet monk named Brother Lawrence, who found God in the washing up of his pots and pans, to C. S. Lewis, who ruminated on the "weight of glory" that each of us carries in our physical bodies, to the urban gospel insights of Mary Mary's hip-hop "God in Me," a biblical spiritual identity is shaped from the clay of God within. God is not only "in" the Body of Christ, that is, the church, but God is in each and every human being ever born. That image is intrinsic to our identity. We belong to God, because God is in each and every one of us.

## Spiritual Insight: From Proposition to Preposition

Descartes argued that the self was a proposition: "I think, therefore I am." But Christian spirituality insists that the self is a preposition. We find and know ourselves in relation to our location on a journey and through the relationships that form the web of our lives.

Of course, "in" is not the only English preposition. As a locating word, it is certainly one of the most common and an appropriate starting point for spiritual reflection. A journey to understand one's self, however, needs a richer travel vocabulary. "Who am I *through* God?" is another question to consider. The apostle Paul writes, "I can do all things through him who strengthens me" (Phil. 4:13), and says that God is moving through the Philippians, enabling them "to will and to work for his good pleasure" (2:13). "Through" opens a new door to understand who we are. We are not only in God, but we exist *through* God—rather like the difference between standing in a doorway and walking through one. As a movement preposition, "through" reminds us that we are not static. Through God new possibilities open for growth as we move beyond our perceived limitations to new strengths, insights, and compassion. And the reverse question is equally helpful: "Who is God *through* me?" What does God actually look like to others when I enact God's love and justice in the world? What vision of God is moving through me? Christian spirituality of the self enjoins that God is not only located *in* us, but that God acts, speaks, heals, loves, touches, and celebrates *through* us.

The idea of journeying to find a deeper sense of identity is not new to Christian spirituality. In addition to biblical travelers who left everything behind to become nomads in and through God, the ancient Celts actually structured their understanding of Christianity around the practice of sacred journey. "God counseled Abraham," wrote St. Columba (ca. 521–97), "to leave his own country and go on pilgrimage to the land which God has shown him. . . . Now the good counsel which God enjoined here on the father of all the faithful is incumbent on all the faithful; that is to leave their country and their land . . . and go in perfect pilgrimage in imitation of him."[10] In order to share their stories of the journey, Celtic poets created a spiritual vocabulary of prepositions that invited all to reflect on God and the self. No poem expresses this impulse better than the eighth-century hymn *St. Patrick's Breastplate*:

> *Christ with me, Christ before me, Christ*
> *    behind me,*
> *Christ in me, Christ beneath me, Christ*
> *    above me,*
> *Christ on my right, Christ on my left,*
> *Christ when I lie down, Christ when I*
> *    sit down, Christ when I arise,*
> *Christ in the heart of every man who*
> *    thinks of me,*

*Christ in the mouth of everyone who*
*speaks of me,*
*Christ in every eye that sees me,*
*Christ in every ear that hears me.*

Who am I in God? With God? Before God? Behind God? Beside God? Who is God in me? With me? Before me? Behind me? Beside me? The holy texts present stories, poems, and songs that speak to all of these sacred locations. The contemporary mystery writer Nevada Barr makes the case: "It was a number of years of crashing and burning before I made the discovery that I was not God. Finally, I realized that though I was not God, I was *of* God."[11] Prepositions invite us to consider identity by exploring how we move, to whom we are related, and where we are located. Knowing one's self is not like finding a lost object that, once recovered, is protected that it might never be misplaced again. Rather, finding one's self on a journey, to quote J. R. R. Tolkien, is "there and back again." Back there once again. And again.

Many people today shy away from saying "I am a Presbyterian," and instead say "I am going to a Presbyterian church." I used to think that this was a sad commentary on theological ignorance, an inability to commit, or perpetual church shopping. Now, however, I rather like the switch in vocabulary. For such people, the Presbyterian Church is no longer a static or inherited identity; rather it is a locating device. Saying "I am going to . . ." indicates a sense of where one is heading and with whom one is moving. Church is no longer membership in an institution, but a journey toward the possibility of a relationship with people, a community, a tradition, a sacred space, and, of course, God. With complete and certain assurance, I confess that I no longer hold propositional truths about Christianity; rather, I experience prepositional truths of being found *in* God *through* Christ *with* others *toward* the kingdom.

The spiritual life is composed of verbs, orienting words, and movement prepositions. As Thomas Tweed, a professor at the University of North Carolina, notes in his book theorizing on the nature of religion: "Religions are active verbs linked with unsubstantial nouns by bridging prepositions: *from, with, in, between, through,* and, most important, *across.* Religions designate where we are *from,* identify whom we are *with,* and how we move *across.*"[12] Tweed also claims that religion is best defined as "an itinerary" in three senses: "a proposal for a journey, a representation of a journey, and the journey itself."[13] The pilgrimage to the self, and ultimately to God, is a spiritual itinerary.

## Spiritual and Religious: The Relational Self

"When I think of spirituality, I think of individualism," stated a Lutheran pastor. "Spirituality is all about 'me,' but religion is communal. It is about 'us.'"

I stopped for a moment. I had heard this comment many times during the months that I used the word-association exercise in church groups. On this day, however, I did not let it pass.

"I'm not sure about that," I replied. "How many times have you been at a church board meeting where someone comes in angry and threatens, 'If you don't do it my way, I'll take my pledge and leave the church.'"

People laughed uncomfortably, heads nodding.

"That's about as individualistic as you can get," I insisted. "Just putting a bunch of people together in a church building doesn't make them a community. Community is about relationships and making connections. That's spiritual work. And it may or may not happen in a church."

The sad fact is that many churches are not very good at being communities. They answer the *where* question by saying, "At First and Main." They answer the *who* question by putting up a sign that reads, "St. Peter's Episcopal Church." Some churches think this is an adequate explanation of identity, when millions report that they are searching for vibrant spiritual community. Almost three-quarters of young adult church members report that they long for community, while half of young adults outside of religious denominations say that they long for community. Indeed, Google "longing for community," and you will get more than 10 million hits.

In the 1930s, anthropologists, psychologists, and philosophers began to speculate that Descartes's formulation was a dead end for understanding the self. Indeed, social psychologist George Herbert Mead proposed that "the individual experiences himself as such, not directly, but only indirectly, from the particular standpoints of other individual members of the same social group."[14] By relating to others, human beings construct themselves. "The self is not something that exists first and then enters into relationship with others," he wrote, "but it is, so to speak, an eddy in the social current."[15] We are selves-in-process, formed and reformed as we relate to the communities we inhabit. We are, as two contemporary psychologists suggest, "entangled" selves, as "the self and personality are shaped largely by experiences with significant others."[16] Indeed, a better rendering of Descartes might be "I am because we are" or "I am only as we are connected."

Relational selfhood moves toward the territory of the mystical, the spiritual, and the theological. Indeed, the idea of relational selfhood is at the center of the African theology of Ubuntu. Ubuntu is a way of knowing the self and knowing God. The key concept in Ubuntu says, "I am because of who we all are." I am a person because you are a person. Archbishop Desmond Tutu explains:

> One of the sayings in our country is Ubuntu—the essence of being human. Ubuntu speaks particularly about the fact that you can't exist as a human being in isolation. It speaks about our interconnectedness. You can't be human all by yourself, and when you

have this quality—Ubuntu—you are known for your generosity.
We think of ourselves far too frequently as just individuals, separated from one another, whereas you are connected and what you
do affects the whole world. When you do well, it spreads out; it
is for the whole of humanity.[17]

Accordingly, our very existence is relational. We are *in, through,
with, next to,* and *with* one another.

For Christians, spiritual community, a living, renewed church,
begins with being *in* Christ, the first and primary relationship of
a vibrant faith life. The church is, therefore, not an institution, an
organization, or a building, but a community of relationships where
people's selves are *with* God and *with* one another, bound by love.
As theologian Emil Brunner wrote in 1939, "Man cannot be man
'by himself'; he can only be man in community. For love can only
operate in community, and only in this operation of love is man
human. . . . Only if he is loving can he be truly human."[18]

The church, therefore, is not only a community, but it is also
"communion," a "set of relationships making up a mode of being."[19]
In our world, these relationships extend beyond other human beings
and God. We are not only related to other people, but we are in
community with all of creation, with the animals who share life
on the planet as well as forests, rivers, oceans, the earth itself. Thus,
the self is discovered *in* Christ, *with* others, *through* the nature, *on*
the river of change. Everything is connected. A spiritual awakening
entails experiencing the full range of prepositional relationships in
which we live and move and discover our being.

In the territory of relational selfhood, the longing for spirituality, that is, "experience," and the role of religion, that is, the need
for the "communal," meet. The spiritual search for God and the
self wends its way toward others and the world, for without others
it is impossible to find God or know who we are. We must belong
in order to be and become. Religious institutions, even seemingly

ossified ones, hold the theological promise of being a community—mostly in their prayers, liturgy, the Lord's Supper, and songs. Yet belonging must be more than membership, a pledge card, the obligation to serve on a board, or occasional attendance at a religious service. This sort of belonging insists that the community must be a dynamic, ongoing love, a passionate romance between the divine and the mundane that seduces us into an intimate relationship with God, our neighbors, and our own deepest self.

## Moving Toward Where and Whose

My ancestors Hermann and Minna haunt me. I think of how they lived in a place called Saxony, a kingdom that existed for many centuries, and how, in 1870, it ceased to be, replaced by a new nation called Germany. Six years later, they left. Their homeland, and along with it their identities, had vanished beneath them, and they crossed the sea to find themselves in a new place. No wonder they took a new name. Whatever their original family name, they became "Hochstedt" in America, adopting a new identity in the new geography. They created a new web of relationships in which they became different people; and, I hope, they redeemed what had been broken or lost in the Old World by coming to the New. They certainly made a new future for all who would follow them. Changing *where* they were created new understandings of *whose* they were. Immigration is a spiritual journey as well as a geographical one.

Four generations and a century later, my parents did something similar. Their comfortable world of mid-century Baltimore had vanished and was replaced by a different sort of city, one more diverse, inclusive, and global. It was hard for them to understand. So they left. They escaped, really. Instead of embarking on a ship across the sea, they bought a 1972 Ford station wagon—yellow with wooden side panels—and journeyed upon a still new interstate highway system to a faraway desert called Arizona. They did not change their names, but they might have. In the move, they became different people from the ones they would have been, had they stayed home, and their family and future became different as well. In the desert, they discovered themselves in a different sort of community, with different people, different religions, different practices, and different languages. They found themselves in a new location, *in, with, among,* and *through* things and people they once would never have imagined. They fell in love with the mountains and desert and vast blue skies. They found a new place of belonging, new communities of faith. And there, they found themselves and God.

In his prison cell in 1944, Dietrich Bonhoeffer began a pilgrimage he never wished to take. He had been jailed by the Nazis, torn from family and friends and all he loved. An exile, really. And there, in a *where* so different from all he had ever known, he found that he had not really known himself:

> *Who am I? They often tell me*
> *I stepped from my cell's confinement*
> *Calmly, cheerfully, firmly,*
> *Like a squire from his country-house.*
> *Who am I? . . .*
> *Am I then really all that which other men tell of?*
> *Or am I only what I myself know of*
> *    myself? . . .*
> *Who am I? This or the other? . . .*
> *Whoever I am, Thou knowest, O God, I am*
> *    thine!*[20]

If we think of belonging only as membership in a club, organization, or church, we miss the point. Belonging is the risk to move beyond the world we know, to venture out on pilgrimage, to accept exile. And it is the risk of being with companions on that journey, God, a spouse, friends, children, mentors, teachers, people who came from the same place we did, people who came from entirely different places, saints and sinners of all sorts, those known to us and those unknown, our secret longings, questions, and fears. Whose am I? O God, I am thine!

# CHAPTER SEVEN

# The Great Reversal

I N 2009, A FRIEND sent me an e-mail with a YouTube link. "You've got to watch this one!" he wrote. "It made me see that there is hope."

I clicked the link. Up popped a clip. It looked neither promising nor professional. The words "Lost Generation"[1] appeared against a dark background, and the film scrolled down through the lines of this poem as they were being read by a young woman:

> I am part of a lost generation
> and I refuse to believe
> I can change the world
> I realize this may be a shock but
> "Happiness comes from within"
> is a lie, and
> "Money will make me happy"
> So in 30 years I will tell my children
> They are not the most important thing in my
>    life.
> My employer will know that

> *I have my priorities straight because*
> *work*
> *is more important than*
> *family*
> *I tell you this*
> *Once upon a time*
> *Families stayed together*
> *but this will not be true in my era.*
> *this is a quick fix society*
> *Experts tell me*
> *30 years from now I will be celebrating the 10th*
> *    anniversary of my divorce.*
> *I do not concede that*
> *I will live in the country of my own making.*
> *In the future*
> *Environmental destruction will be the norm.*
> *No longer can it be said that*
> *My peers and I care about this earth.*
> *It will be evident that*
> *My generation is apathetic and lethargic.*
> *It is foolish to presume that*
> *There is hope.*

"Hope?" I thought. "This is just depressing." Then the woman read a final sentence:

> *And all of this will come true unless we choose to*
> *    reverse it.*

Then she began reading the lines of the poem backward, as the film scrolled up instead of down. "There is hope," the young woman said. "It is foolish to presume that my generation is apathetic and lethargic. It will be evident that my peers and I care about this earth. . . ." She read the lines from the last to first, ending with "I can change the world, and I refuse to believe that I am part of a lost generation." Yes, my friend was right: hope.

Sometimes all you need to do is run the script backward.

## The Great Reversal

For the last few centuries, Western Christianity ordered faith in a particular way. Catholics and Protestants taught that belief came first, behavior came next, and finally belonging resulted, depending on how you answered the first two questions. Churches turned this pattern into rituals of catechism, character formation, and Confirmation. At birth, Christian children were either baptized or dedicated, with sponsors and parents answering belief questions on their behalf, promising to teach them the faith. As children grew, Sunday schools and catechism classes taught Christian doctrine and the Bible, ensuring that each generation knew the intellectual content of the tradition. Eventually, children moved from Sunday school classrooms to "big church," where they participated in grown-up church practices and learned how to pray, worship, sing, give alms, and act kindly. When a Christian child reached an age of intellectual and moral accountability—somewhere between seven and fifteen—the church would offer a rite of full membership in the form of Communion, Confirmation, or (in the case of Baptists) adult-believers baptism. Believe, behave, belong. It is almost second nature for Western people to read the religious script this way.

It was not always that way. About five hundred years ago, Western Christianity divided from a single church into five different major church families: Roman Catholicism, Lutheranism, Reformed Christianity, Anglicanism, and Anabaptist faith. Each group felt the need to defend itself against all the others, making clear its interpretation of the Bible and theology. Although religious diversity is common enough today, even the limited pluralism of the six-teenth century caused intense religious turmoil—including outright warfare. Competing religious claims turned into competing claims for political and economic power. Each religious group embarked on a process of ordering and systematizing its view of the faith. New theologies shifted away from emphasizing Christian practice toward articulating Christian teachings, as everyone attempted to prove that their group's interpretation was true or most biblical. Religion moved increasingly in the direction of defending philosophical truth claims. Wilfred Cantwell Smith notes that Christianity became intellectualized and impersonalized, as "decade after decade the notion was driven home that a religion is something that one believes or does not believe, something whose propositions are true or not true." He further states, "A legacy of it is the tendency still today to ask, in explanation of 'the religion' of a people, What do they believe?—as though this were a basic, even *the* basic, question."[2]

Thus, for several centuries, Western people have generally assumed that religious commitment begins when one assents to a body of organized doctrines. This holds true if you are considering changing churches or are having a faith crisis. If you are no longer comfortable being a Catholic, you look about to find a church that teaches divorce is acceptable. If you no longer want to be a fundamentalist, you find a church that teaches that the Bible is not literally true. You find out what a group teaches, and you wrestle with its ideas. Joining depends on whether or not you agree with its creed or statement of faith or doctrine. If you find its ideas about God sensible or truthful, then you reshape your life accordingly by learning new prayers, serving the poor, giving up smoking or drinking, and trying to be a better person. Finally, you become a member and join the church.

There is, however, something odd about this pattern. Other than joining a political party, it is hard to think of any other sort of community that people join by agreeing to a set of principles.

Imagine joining a knitting group. Does anyone go to a knitting group and ask if the knitters believe in knitting or what they hold to be true about knitting? Do people ask for a knitting doctrinal statement? Indeed, if you start knitting by reading a book about knitting or a history of knitting or a theory of knitting, you will very likely never knit.

If you want to knit, you find someone who knits to teach you. Go to the local yarn shop and find out when there is a knitting class. Sit in a circle where others will talk to you, show you how to hold the needles, guide your hands, and share their patterns with you. The first step in becoming a knitter is forming a relationship with knitters. The next step is to learn by doing and practice. After you knit for a while, after you have made scarves and hats and mittens, then you start forming ideas about knitting. You might come to think that the experience of knitting makes you a better person, more spiritual, or able to concentrate, gives you a sense of service to others, allows you to demonstrate love and care. You think about what you are doing, how you might do it better. You develop your own way of knitting, your own theory of the craft. You might invent a dazzling new pattern, a new way to make a stitch; you might write a knitting book or become a knitting teacher. In knitting, the process is exactly the reverse of that in church: belonging to a knitting group leads to behaving as a knitter, which leads to believing things about knitting.

Relationships lead to craft, which leads to experiential belief. That is the path to becoming and being someone different. The path of transformation.

It is also the path found in the New Testament; the Way of Jesus that leads to God. Long ago, before the last half millennium, Christians understood that faith was a matter of community first, practices second, and belief as a result of the first two. Our immediate ancestors reversed the order. Now, it is up to us to restore the original order.

In the last three chapters, I have argued that the response to contemporary spiritual longing can be discerned in tweaking the traditional religious questions. A larger task, however, is required: we must turn around the order in which the questions are asked. Instead of believing, behaving, and belonging, we need to reverse the order to belonging, behaving, and believing. And therein lies the difference between religion-as-institution and *religio* as a spiritually vital faith.

STEP 1:

## *Belonging*

Jesus did not begin with questions of belief. Instead, Jesus's public ministry started when he formed a community:

> As Jesus passed along the Sea of Galilee, he saw Simon and his brother Andrew casting a net into the sea—for they were fishermen. And Jesus said to them, "Follow me and I will make you fish for people." And immediately they left their nets and followed him. As he went a little farther, he saw James son of Zebedee and his brother John, who were in their boat mending the nets. Immediately he called them; and they left their father Zebedee in the boat with the hired men, and followed him. (Mark 1:16–20)

Over the centuries, theologians have argued that the Christian church began with Peter's confession to Jesus: "You are the Messiah" (Matt. 16:16). After Peter says that Jesus is the long-awaited redeemer, Jesus calls Peter "the rock" and says that upon this "rock" he will build his church. In a very real way, however, the church began long before that confession. It began when Jesus called out, "Follow me," and his friends and neighbors left their old lives and started a new community. A dozen men and a band of women joined Jesus and one another in a journey of faith and sharing and compassion. Christianity did not begin with a confession. It began with an invitation into friendship, into creating a new community, into forming relationships based on love and service.

What prompts any of us to drop what we are doing and heed the call into friendship and community? Curiosity? Fascination? C. S. Lewis once said, "Friendship is born at that moment when one person says to another, 'What! You too? I thought I was the only one.'" Belonging to a community starts with a flash of recognition, an intuition of connection: "I can't believe that I have found you! This is where my home has always been." We make friends, join a group, or enter into a romance because it is this person or these people who make our hearts lighter, bring joy and comfort, and make the world more interesting and bearable. Although once upon a time, people may have joined a church to make a business reputation or look respectable, it is hard to imagine either of those being a good enough reason for belonging to a faith community these days. People no longer join; instead, they join in. And when we join in, our heart leads the way.

Jesus began with the inner life, the heart. Indeed, when he said, "You will know the truth, and the truth will make you free," he was not speaking of a philosophical idea or a set of doctrines. The truth was that the disposition of the heart was the ground of truth. Spiritual freedom results from a rightly directed heart, the self as it moves away from fear, hatred, isolation, and greed toward love. And, as Jesus also said, love is shaped through a relationship with God and neighbor, steeped in self-love and self-awareness. Faith, truth, freedom—all of it—is relational, not speculative.

Early Christian writers knew this to be the case—even the most intellectual sorts, like the apostle Paul, who writes that even if we know everything, "but do not have love," we are nothing (1 Cor. 13:2). Indeed, both Jesus and Paul said that love was the *greatest* and *first* of all virtues, the womb of the good life. Right passion, the disposition of the soul, how we relate to God and neighbor is the starting place. The most ancient prayers of Christian faith have nothing to do with getting ideas about God right. Instead, they are prayers that reorder the heart, directing it anew. Ancient Christian prayers both recognize the disordered soul (sin) and point the soul toward mercy and restored relationships. "Forgive us our trespasses as we forgive those who trespass against us," or "Lord Jesus Christ, Son of God, have mercy on me, a sinner." Or, as desert monk Abba Pambo said, "If you have a heart, you can be saved." Vital faith begins with desire and disposition, not a doctrine test.

Spiritual awakenings always start within. From Augustine's aching longing, "Our hearts are restless until they rest in thee," to Mother Teresa's contemporary insight, "There is a terrible hunger for love. We all experience that in our lives—the pain, the loneliness. We must have the courage to recognize it." Those to whom the risen Jesus first appeared testified, "Were not our hearts burning within us?" (Luke 24:32). The scriptures are full of broken hearts, willing hearts, listening hearts, overflowing hearts, hardened hearts, and longing hearts. And, as Western religion increasingly became a matter of doctrine, spiritual movements emphasizing the heart tried to correct the course.

Love may start deep within, but it does not stay there. When asked what the greatest of all commandments was, Jesus replied it was to "love God" and "love your neighbor as yourself" (Matt. 22:37–39). Love is the connective tissue of relationship, the internal disposition that reaches up toward God and out toward others. It is impossible for love to exist in isolation. Love needs expression in relationships and communities. To love, one must risk belonging.

STEP 2:

## Behaving

The early community that followed Jesus was a community of practice. Jesus's followers did not sit around a fire and listen to lectures on Christian theology. They listened to stories that taught them how to act toward one another, what to do in the world. They healed people, offered hospitality, prayed together, challenged traditional practices and rituals, ministered to the sick, comforted the grieving, fasted, and forgave. These actions induced wonder, gave them courage, empowered hope, and opened up a new vision of God. By doing things together, they began to see differently.

It is profoundly important to grasp this. Jesus and his followers were poor; the vast majority of them were politically and religiously oppressed. There was little reason for them to hope for a better world, that the Romans would just let them be, or that the next ruler would change things. They were victims of one of history's most vicious empires; they lived in utterly hopeless circumstances. For someone to come along and say "Have faith; your lot will improve" would be a bit like someone spitting upon victims. Have faith? In what? Some long-promised messiah who seemed to be very late in arriving?

Jesus did not walk by the Sea of Galilee and shout to fishermen, "Have faith!" Instead, he asked them to do something: "Follow me." When they followed, he gave them more things to do. At first, he demonstrated what he wanted them to do. Then he did it with them. Finally, he sent them out to do it themselves, telling them to proclaim God's reign and cure the sick. When they returned from this first mission, they could not believe what had happened. They discovered that proclaiming the kingdom was not a matter of teaching doctrine; rather, the kingdom was a matter of imitating Jesus's actions. Jesus did not tell them to have faith. He pushed them into the world to practice faith. The disciples did not hope the world would change. They changed it. And, in doing so, they themselves changed.

Later in the New Testament book of James, the writer says, "Faith without works is dead" (2:17, 26). This verse has caused much consternation in Christian history. Does that mean we work our way to heaven? That good works save us?

It is a mistake to think that this verse is about some future salvation—about whether or not a person will go to heaven. The context is not eternal life; rather, the context is this life. When placed in the here and now, and in the context of following a spiritual path, the meaning is crystal clear: actions shape faith. Spiritual practices engender hope. Behavior opens the door for believing. Doing what once seemed difficult or impossible empowers courage to envision a different world and believe we can make a difference. Without practices, faith is but an empty promise.

## Step 3:
### Believing

Peter's confession of faith grew out of his friendship with Jesus and the things that they had done together—praying, eating, preaching, healing, giving, and feeding. In the Gospel of Matthew, before Peter's confession of Jesus as the Messiah (16:13–20), Jesus and his disciples had fed the great crowd that had been following their band (15:32–39). Together, they had practiced hospitality. Before he asks, "Who do you say that I am?" Jesus reminds them of this act of miraculous hospitality, saying that the action pointed to greater spiritual realities of God's power and presence in the world (16:8–10). In response to what he has experienced, Peter blurts out, "You are the Messiah, the Son of the living God." This is not an analytical or philosophical statement, not a hypothesis provable through the scientific method. Jesus says that Peter's insight comes from God's spirit, not any "flesh and blood" knowledge. Peter's participation in community and their shared practice set the stage for Peter's statement of faith. The confession is not an intellectually considered utterance of theological speculation. Rather, it is what the Bible refers to as "wisdom from above," the sort of knowing that comes from engagement with God, others, and the world. It is *credo,* "You are the One whom I trust for healing and love!" or "You are the One for whom my heart has waited!"

In the biblical pattern of faith, believing comes last. Indeed, this pattern repeats in both the Hebrew Bible and the Christian New Testament. From the calling of Abraham and Sarah through the great prophets and heroes of Israel to Jesus and the early church, those who walked with faith started by following, by becoming part of God's community, by enacting the practices of God's way, and finally by recognizing and proclaiming the glory of God.

## Christianity, Amish and African Style

When I was a little girl growing up in Baltimore, my family would often take a Sunday drive to the Amish country in Pennsylvania. The horses and buggies driven by the Amish fascinated me, as did their simple clothes, their houses not tethered to electric lines, their old-fashioned plows visible in the fields. We stopped at shops and markets to buy handcrafted goods, Pennsylvania Dutch relishes and pies and fresh farm produce. No church buildings rose from the rural landscape, only farmhouses, barns, shops, and schoolhouses. My mother explained that the Amish worshipped at home. And I was astonished. I had never heard of Christians without buildings or seminary-trained clergy. "Their faith," she said, "is the way they live."

The Amish descended from the Anabaptists, one of the Christian groups to emerge in the great reforms of the sixteenth century. All of the spiritual renewal movements in those days were concerned with the practical concerns of Christian living: salvation, sacraments, singing, reading the Bible, and shaping the faith community. The Reformation centered on the experience of encountering God. But, within a generation, Lutherans, Calvinists, and Anglicans as well as Roman Catholics moved away from experiential faith toward more defensive philosophical postures to explain their faiths, writing systematic theologies and compendiums of dogma. The long process of moving faith from the heart and hands to the head had begun.

That was not the case for the Anabaptists. Unlike other spiritual communities of the sixteenth century, they never embraced the new rage for systematizing faith. They wrote a few confessions, and their theologians tried their hand at writing. To be honest, the Anabaptists did not have the luxury of theological speculation and doctrinal debate. Persecuted by every other Christian group, they were too busy escaping one country for another, dodging authorities, praying for their friends in prison, and looking for a place to practice their faith in relative peace and freedom.

Many of the other Reformers had university educations and had been clergy or philosophers. Not so for most of the Anabaptists, who tended to come from the middle and lower classes. As a result, when they learned to read, they read the Bible unencumbered by ancient languages or Renaissance rhetorical theories. Instead, they read the Bible experientially. Early Anabaptists placed themselves in the Bible, imagining themselves as Jesus's disciples, and interpreted scripture in its most immediate ways. To the Anabaptists, when Jesus said, "Blessed are the peacemakers," that was exactly what Jesus meant. His followers must make peace and not participate in violence or war. When Jesus said, "Sell all that you have and give the money to the poor," the Anabaptists did it and established communal purses to serve the needs of the whole community.

Lutherans, Calvinists, and Anglicans did not agree with such simple, straightforward Bible reading. They argued that the Bible needed to be interpreted with the aid of tradition or a learned clergyman, a guide to temper the excesses of experiential faith. Indeed, Lutherans, Calvinists, and Anglicans loved the Bible and urged its wide reading, but they also found it potentially misleading and dangerous—not to mention politically inconvenient. Thus, for everyone but the Anabaptists, what began as a spiritual movement of encountering Christ the Word in the Word quickly became a matter of creeds and confessions and complex theological speculation.

The Anabaptists stayed the course, however. Next to the Bible, their most important theological book was not a theological tome at all. It was a book of testimonies called *The Bloody Theater, or Martyrs Mirror,* a collection of letters from prison and personal faith stories of early Anabaptist martyrs. It is a long book. A contemporary edition runs over a thousand pages and weighs a whopping five pounds. Despite its length, the stories in the *Martyrs Mirror* follow a similar narrative arc: a person encounters Jesus, joins with an Anabaptist community, embraces a life-changing set of practices, and experiences God in a personal, empowering way that involves understanding faith from the heart. The early Anabaptists testified to a way of life that made a radical difference in the world. This was a path of practical mysticism, of experiential Christianity, of the spirit-infused community.

Although it now seems more quaint than radical, the insight that Christianity is a way of life in community based on practices is still on display in Amish country. Through the mirror of contemporary Amish communities, it is easy to see that experiential faith can become as stilted as dogma. Human beings have a tendency to freeze practices around particular cultural expressions, as the Amish have around an early nineteenth-century way of life. Indeed, with the horses and buggies, prohibitions on buttons, and restrictions on dating and marriage, the whole business appears less an encounter with Jesus than a hyperconservative and closed tradition, one with as many downsides as other narrow religions.

That is, of course, until a gunman walks into an Amish one-room schoolhouse and shoots ten girls—and the community forgives him, attends his funeral, comforts his wife, and sets up a charitable fund for the family of the man who murdered their children. If they had been "conservative," in the political sense that most people understand, they would have demanded justice, marking the murderer's family as outcasts, or at the very least held a long and extended grudge against him and his relatives. The Amish experience of Jesus demanded otherwise, however. They were called to forgive, in an immediate and powerful way, as Jesus would have forgiven. No questions asked.

This is not to say that we should all become Amish. Nor is it to say that the Anabaptists were the only experiential Christian movement in history, or that they have always gotten it right. They were not, and they have not. They are only a familiar, close-at-hand example, nearer to our own time than the earliest Christian communities so similarly formed. The Anabaptists bear the memory that—even when aspects of their practice have become inflexible—Christianity is an experience of imitating Jesus. They represent a third path in Christian history other than ecclesial authority or salvation by doctrine alone, that of experiential faith: belonging, behaving, and believing. Being a people, practicing faith, and professing a story of God.

"Isn't it true that Western Christianity is dying?" a reporter asked me. "And that the conservative Christianity of Africa and Latin America is now the dominant form of Christian religion?"

It is one of those questions for which a reporter already has an answer in mind.

"Not really," I replied. "Christianity from those parts of the world is coming to dominate. But African and Latin American Christianity is more experiential and immediate than it is conservative in the sense that most of us understand the word."

Certainly, many Christians in Africa and Latin America have a difficult time with women ministers or accepting gay and lesbian persons in church, but that does not necessarily translate to "conservative." In the past decade, much of the global tension in Western Christian churches has revolved around these two issues. But Christians in Africa and Latin America are also deeply concerned with issues of oppression, economic exploitation, AIDS, global warming and climate change, pollution, the reduction in fish yields, corporate and consumerist colonialism, education, government reform and regulation, and universal health care. So, although they appear conservative from the angle of issues related to gender and sexuality (although ask some African church leaders what they think of plural marriage—you will not get a "conservative" answer), from the angle of economic development and environmentalism many Christians in the Global South seem rather liberal.[3]

What appears as an inconsistency, however, is better understood through the lens of experiential faith. Encountering the Bible at face value, as did the early Anabaptists, leads many Christians in the Global South to conclude that women should never teach *and* one should never own private property or that it is "unnatural" to love a person of the same sex *and* that Christians always must be pacifists. An experiential reading of Holy Writ does not easily conform to contemporary categories of liberal and conservative. It is something else altogether—an attempt to find oneself in the biblical story, to follow Jesus as his first followers did, to practice faith empowered by the Spirit, to change the world. Experiential faith does not always get this exactly right, as it can tend toward unhelpful literalism and misunderstand the context of ancient texts and practices, but experiential Christianity gets one thing very right: faith is not an intellectual exercise; it is a spiritual path.

## Experiential Christianity: The New Vision

Experiential Christianity is what Harvey Cox explains as the "Age of the Spirit," when "faith as a way of life or a guiding compass has once again begun."[4] The wind is blowing in Africa and Latin America and Asia, but in North America and Europe and Australia too. In the Global South, they struggle to keep up with the Spirit; in the West, we struggle to embrace it. The Age of the Spirit, this new-old experiential faith, is everywhere. In places where Christianity is very new and very old, where churches are being built and churches are being closed, "the experience *of* the divine is displacing theories *about* it."[5]

Relational community, intentional practice, and experiential belief are forming a new vision for what it means to be Christian in the twenty-first century, a pattern of spiritual awakening that is growing around the world. We belong to God and to one another, connected to all in a web of relationships, and there we find our truest selves. We behave in imitation of Jesus, practicing our faith with deliberation as we anticipate God's reign of justice and love. We believe with our entire being, trusting, beloving, and devoted to the God whom we have encountered through one another and in the world. We are; we act; we know. Belonging, behaving, and believing—shifted back to their proper and ancient order. This is the shape of awakened Christianity, a faith that is a deeply spiritual religion. No longer merely religion, but *religio*. The Great Reversal is the Great Returning of Christianity back toward what Jesus preached: a beloved and beloving community, a way of life practiced in the world, a profound trust in God that eagerly anticipates God's reign of mercy and justice.

# PART III

# *Awakening*

Jesus does not call men to a new religion, but to life.

DIETRICH BONHOEFFER
*Letters and Papers from Prison*

# CHAPTER EIGHT

# *Great Awakening*

**Santa Barbara, California**
**1979**

E VERY TUESDAY NIGHT, WE met in a college dorm room. We
called it Bible study, but it was really a church. My friends and
I, students at a small evangelical Christian college, had grown weary
of the praise choruses and narrow theology offered by most Santa
Barbara churches. College chapel was interesting when it challenged
us to think about controversial issues of the day, but not the rest of
the time. Most of us had read a book entitled *Call to Commitment,*
an account about a different sort of congregation in Washington,
D.C.[1] There, committed members participated in both small groups
that explored the inner life and justice groups that went out into the
world and worked for change. We wanted to be like that. And we
wanted to combine our newly discovered understanding of ancient
Christian theology, practice, and liturgy with our new passions for
global community, the environment, and gender equality. We felt
like the early church, as if we had each heard Jesus's call, "Follow

me," individually. It was all so immediate, so spiritually vibrant. We were the disciples, a first-century gathering all over again. We were the church of Armington Hall.

Such experiments popped up all over campus. There was an Evangelicals for Social Action group and an "alternative" dorm, where residents followed a rule of life akin to the monastic ones, ate vegetarian, and studied liberation theology. Another group dedicated itself to urban mission and spent weekend evenings ministering to the homeless. A small band of young men covenanted for a year to explore what Jesus meant when he called his followers to "die to self." Some women daringly began an evangelical feminist drop-in center on campus, replete with bean-bag chairs, a bookcase of feminist literature, and consciousness-raising prayer meetings. A few students began building an orphanage in Ensenada, Mexico. Arguments broke out in the dining commons about just-war theory and pacifism, about nuclear power and nuclear weapons.

Nobody told us to do these things. We just did them. It was all very spontaneous, all over campus at the same time. At its height, the Armington Hall church gathered nearly forty people in worship and prayer. We served each other Communion, shared in preaching the sermon, taught one another scripture, sang songs and hymns, and offered prayers for all who gathered and for the world. We held one another accountable throughout the week, encouraging each other to follow Jesus deliberately. We visited prisoners in the local jail, worked with prostitutes and drug addicts, and ministered to those with physical limitations. We tried to live simply. We read about the saints, studied classics of Christian spirituality, wrestled with theologians like Barth, Bultmann, and Tillich, and cried when Archbishop Oscar Romero was murdered. We experienced Jesus as our friend and daringly prayed to the God who was our Mother. We opposed the reinstated draft and worried about the new Moral Majority. In 1980, nearly every person in the church embarked on a summer mission project that we mutually supported in prayer and finances. We knew that we belonged to God and each other, we practiced our faith with deliberate passion, and we came to be-lieve—to trust—God in ways that we never expected.

We knew that we were part of the next Great Awakening, a revival of Christianity that would change the world.

## The Fourth Great Awakening

Looking back, it is tempting to think of this experience as typical college idealism, a "coming of age" story of young adults finding their way in the world. Although that was certainly part of it, the little Armington Hall church was more than a post-1960s hang-over; it was a microcosm of much larger trends in North America and around the world. Throughout the 1960s and 1970s, people experimented with new religious practices, founded new religious communities, and embraced new theologies. From the Jesus People and the charismatic movement to Christian feminism, to liturgical renewal, to interracial religious communes, to liberation theology, older forms of Christian thought and organization were questioned and challenged from within the ranks of church and from without.

The 1970s awakening, of which the Armington Hall commu-nity was but a tiny part, comprised vast movements of religious transformation, a massive break with the structures of conventional Christian practice, as people embraced more democratic, open, in-clusive, and experiential forms of faith. It took many forms, was present in evangelical churches, mainline ones, and Roman Cath-olic ones, in North America and around the world. And it went beyond the boundaries of Christian faith as well—indeed, some of the most dramatic spiritual changes occurred as religious traditions, once isolated, entered into sustained conversation with each other, and as Western and Eastern religions encountered one another and incorporated each other's practices into their respective faiths.

We were part of the next Great Awakening, yes. But it was far more sweeping, diverse, and wide-ranging than we could have ever imagined at our small Christian college in the late 1970s. William McLoughlin described its contours in *Revivals, Awakenings, and Reform* as an awakening grounded in a new understanding of justice, connection, pluralism, and inclusive democracy, summed up in a vision of what he referred to as a "Romantic" spirit of experiential, quest-oriented, self-aware religion. Since then, as pointed out in these pages, historians, journalists, and critics have named it everything from the "Next Christendom" to the "Great Emergence," claiming that the last forty years mark the most significant change in the Christian faith since the Protestant Reformation.

These global analyses are, no doubt, important. But there is a problem with them. They are so sweeping in scope that, if you happen to be a person of faith, it is hard to know what to do with them. Most of these books argue for such vast religious transformation that they leave people in the pews and pulpits with little to do other than watch the unfolding drama of a global paradigm shift. The tidal wave of history is simply overtaking us all.

It may seem as if religion is on a trajectory of unstoppable change, but genuine spiritual change does not result from historical determinism. Spiritual awakening is not ultimately the work of invisible cultural forces. Instead, it is the work of learning to see differently, of prayer, and of conversion. It is something people do. Awakening is the result of what New Testament writers referred to as *metanoia,* a change of perspective and outlook that moves human beings beyond chaos toward a new harmony with God and divine things. In some Christian circles, *metanoia* has been equated with a particular sort of revivalism wherein one recites a sinner's prayer and accepts Jesus in one's heart. But *metanoia* is a much richer concept. Ancient Christians, such as the writer of the influential second-century text *The Shepherd of Hermas,* defined *metanoia* as "the great understanding," or the practice of discernment through which human beings move from darkness toward the light. *Metanoia* necessarily implies human agency, and early Christian thinkers almost universally agreed that *metanoia* involved recognizing our estrangement from God and neighbor and a turning of the heart and mind toward love. Returning to a phrase used in an earlier chapter, *metanoia* is a "Great Turning" or a "Great (Re)Turning" toward the divine intention of harmony, unity, peace, dignity, and joy for all creation.

Having the grand perspective is necessary for *metanoia* to take place, but it is equally important to have a more discrete view as well. To explore the terrain of religious change from the angle of awakenings makes the landscape more navigable. Instead of being overwhelmed by the prospects of impersonal change, considering this awakening in the context of other awakenings reminds us that spiritual transformation is not simply the result of anonymous forces. Awakenings are also the hard work of people who have undergone *metanoia* and who seek to change their lives, communities, and the world around them in accordance with a renewed experience of God's love and justice. Awakening is a deeply personal realization. Everyone can experience the power of turning toward God's love—not as the threat of hell, but as the promise of paradise. The new spiritual awakening rehearses paradise, the awareness of love's liberating and healing power. God is with us in this world. Awakening is, of course, something transcendent. But awakening is also something that individuals can choose to participate in, can ask others to join in, can ignore, can reject, or can stop. When enough people experience *metanoia,* our sense of whose we are, what we are to do, and how we understand God changes.

As outlined previously, there have been three periods of intense religious revitalization, called "awakenings," in American history.[2] The first (ca. 1730–60) occurred in the years right before the American Revolution; the second (ca. 1800–1830), in the early decades of the America republic; and the third (ca. 1890–1920), as the United States became an industrial world power. During each one of these periods, religious, political, social, and cultural mores and institutions underwent profound change, as people searched for deeper understandings of selfhood, meaning, and purpose in the world. Awakenings are not unique to the United States; indeed, most cultures undergo similar processes when challenged with new ideas and technologies. "They are essentially folk movements," states William McLoughlin, "the means by which a people or a nation reshapes its identity, transforms its patterns of thought and action, and sustains a healthy relationship with environmental and social change."[3]

In the last fifty years, North America and Europe have experienced rapid social change. We have come a long way from the old industrial urban culture toward what Nobel Prize–winning economist Robert William Fogel calls the "technophysio evolution," in which technology and biology weave together in reshaping human life, the environment, and world economy. Our lives have changed to an astonishing degree when compared to human existence even a generation ago. "The incredible rate at which the economy and society are changing causes people to lose their bearings," states Fogel. "They fear not only for their safety but also for their livelihoods," leaving us in a culture marked by "the persistence of gloom." Not to mention malaise, failure, and foreboding as old patterns of faith, family, and work collapse.[4]

Very few people in the late 1970s would have been able to articulate—much less understand—a "technophysio evolution." There are many ways in which, before our daily lives were transformed by the digital technologies and global networks we now take for granted, we lived in an ignorant yet energetic bliss of an age coming to an end. But even without laptops, smart phones, or the Internet, many people in the 1960s and 1970s were developing a new worldview, one that can be understood as a romantic spirit; it included global conscience, environmental sensitivity, a passion for radical equality, an understanding of connection and community, an emphasis on beauty, art, music, and poetry, and an ethic of self-realization.[5]

Those who reached early adulthood in the 1960s and 1970s, born after the atomic bomb, were the children of cultural change, the first generation to come of age as "postmodern" (another word no one knew). Nothing was as it was; nothing was as it would be. Religion was not lagging behind the change. In many ways, people engaging new forms of faith drove much of the transformation. The 1960s and 1970s were a spiritual hothouse, a veritable garden of awakening, as people planted seeds of new forms of Christian belief and practice. Indeed, before Apple, Microsoft, Google, Facebook, or Twitter, there were small groups of committed people wrestling with ancient texts and traditions and trying to form community and meaning in a rapidly changing world. The spiritual revolution, with its emphasis on connection, egalitarianism, and human rights, could be credited with opening the path of acceptance of much techno-logical and social change.

"Since 1960, Americans have been in the midst of their Fourth Great Awakening," wrote William McLoughlin in 1978, likening our time to earlier times of challenge and change. "Once again we are in a difficult period of reorientation, seeking an understanding of who we are, how we relate to the rest of the universe, and what the meaning is of the manifold crises that threaten our sense of order at home and our commitments as a world power abroad." Yet these times have been particularly difficult: "We have been in the process of what may well be the most traumatic and drastic transformation of our ideology that has yet occurred."[6]

If the Fourth Great Awakening followed a pattern similar to earlier awakenings, McLoughlin speculated that 1978 was about the halfway point in the process of revitalization. He opined that in the early 1990s, "a consensus would emerge" that would result in "fun-damental restructuring" in American life and institutions. In "spiri-tual speak," enough people would have converted to restructure institutions and politics on a vast scale. McLoughlin explained it in terms reminiscent of *metanoia:*

Such a reorientation will most likely include a new sense of the mystical unity of all mankind and of the vital power of harmony between man and nature. The godhead will be defined in less dualistic terms, and its power will be understood less in terms of an absolutist, sin-hating, death-dealing "Almighty Father in Heaven" and more in terms of a life-supporting, nurturing, empathetic, easygoing parental (Motherly as well as Fatherly) image. The nourishing spirit of mother earth, not the wrath of an angry father above, will dominate religious thought. . . . Sacrifice of self will replace self-aggrandizement as the definition of virtue; helping others will replace competitiveness as a value; institutions will be organized for the fulfillment of individual needs by means of cooperative communal efforts rather than through the isolated nuclear family.[7]

This optimistic passage did, indeed, predict many of the developments in religion, theology, and church life over the next two decades, aspects of contemporary faith that existed only in incipient form in the 1970s. The Fourth Great Awakening would result in a more experiential, pluralistic, holistic, environmentally focused, and communal sort of American religion and politics. In 1978, William McLoughlin confidently asserted, we were almost there.

## The Mysterious Case of the Missing Awakening

When we graduated from college in 1981, the little church in Armington Hall disbanded. We went our separate ways, off to seminary and graduate school and marriage and children, off to work in the world. Ten years later, I returned to that same campus as a professor, and I searched for signs of what had happened a decade before. There was no vegetarian dorm, no students practicing the *Rule of St. Benedict,* no talk of global climate change, no peace fellowship, no Evangelicals for Social Action. The Women's Center was gone, replaced by a room full of video games. I found the evangelical feminist books integrated into the general library collection. The last time even one of them had been checked out was 1983. No talk of social justice and liberation theology. Students regularly gathered to listen to the campus-wide radio broadcast of one of their fellows who fancied himself an evangelical Rush Limbaugh. Little American flags decorated flower arrangements in the dining hall that celebrated a speech by the local candidate supported by the religious Right. Instead of professors pushing their conservative students toward more liberal readings of the Bible, conservative students led inquisitions against professors whom they deemed unorthodox.

In late 1991, over lunch in Chicago, my graduate adviser, a well-known historian of American evangelicalism, asked how the new job was going. I told him everything had changed from my years as a student. "What happened?" I asked forlornly. "What happened to the community I experienced as a student?"

He answered with two words: "Ronald Reagan."

I cast a puzzled glance. "What do you mean, 'Ronald Reagan'?"

He replied that Reagan represented a rejection of all the experiments of the 1960s and 1970s. Reagan re-created a mythic American past, giving people a sense of security when things changed too quickly or when people feared the results of change. That might have worked for a few years, my graduate professor suggested, but not long. He speculated, "You cannot move forward with nostalgia."

His remarks made me understand how much some people fear change and flee to leaders who promise to restore the glory of the past when the future is uncertain. Although it is actually impossible to do, people will often try to go back to what was in times of loss and uncertainty. There is no smooth path toward awakening; change is a journey of hard work.

As he spoke, I also remembered how angry people were with

President Carter. Not strong enough or not optimistic enough. Looking back, however, I understood that Carter anticipated many things that would matter greatly in the years to come—justice and equality; human rights; the impact of poverty on women and children; the need for a global worldview; the imperative to care for the earth and live simply; the limits of power in favor of reconciliation and peacemaking; the wisdom of Christian faith in conversation with other faiths.

In 1980, the choice between Ronald Reagan and Jimmy Carter was stark—not like some elections in which candidates are separated only by shades of gray. One offered to restore the faith of our fathers; the other offered the hard work of a future only dimly perceived. In 1980, in a close election, we opted to go back, in our imaginations at least, to an earlier time. Maybe we were tired. Maybe we did not completely understand at the time. Many certainly wanted to reject the changes of the 1960s and 1970s. A friend of mine refers to it as "1960s posttraumatic stress disorder."

As a result, the 1980s proved critical in the history of the contemporary spiritual awakening. Only two years before, McLoughlin rather confidently predicted that the Fourth Great Awakening was pushing toward the conclusion of its spiritual process, and that consensus and institutional change were just around the next American corner. Although he cited Jimmy Carter as a leader who, in many ways, embodied the spirit of the awakening, he also doubted that Carter's presidency would bring about the sustained institutional renewal needed for the future. McLoughlin wondered if there was enough grassroots consensus around concerns for justice, global community, multifaith religious understanding, and environmentalism. Not enough people had converted to the new vision. He opined that Jimmy Carter had been elected to tinker with the system, not transform it. "At some point in the future," he speculated, "early in the 1990s at best," Americans would elect a political leader with a mandate to embody the passions of the Fourth Great Awakening in policies and through our political institutions.[8]

What he never imagined, however, was that in two short years Americans would elect Ronald Reagan. He never imagined Jerry Falwell and Pat Robertson, or the Moral Majority or Christian Coalition for that matter. Or, eventually, Rush Limbaugh or Newt Gingrich or Glenn Beck or the Tea Party.

Perhaps, however, he should have. As he himself noted, "There almost always arises a nativist or traditionalist movement within the culture that is an attempt by those with rigid personalities or with much at stake in the older order" to organize a backlash to "return to the 'old-time religion,' 'the ways of our fathers,' and 'respect for the flag.'" Such movements scapegoat others (most particularly immigrants and outsiders), and they work to maintain high levels of fear among their adherents, since they feed off of "chronic stress."[9] If the defenders of the old system elevate anxiety to a fever pitch, they can actually block the growth of consensus and prevent necessary change from occurring. McLoughlin identified only the "nativists" he knew—those political and religious leaders from the 1960s, like William F. Buckley, Barry Goldwater, and a younger, more politicized Billy Graham, who worked to stop cultural change and who embodied a mythic past more than an innovative and inclusive future.

Jerry Falwell, Pat Robertson, Jim Bakker, and the host of other conservative evangelical leaders that Americans came to know in the 1980s and 1990s were *not* leading an awakening. Yes, the media reported the evangelical story as an awakening. Indeed, at the time, the media knew little or nothing of religion. Yet without much understanding of religious history they identified "revival" and "awakening" with this resurgent conservatism, not really understanding the difference between revivals of faith and spiritual movements of revitalization. Falwell, Robertson, and company claimed it was awakening, that God was calling America away from the hedonism, paganism, feminism, and theological impurity of the 1960s and 1970s in order to restore the nation's previous glory and re-create the Christian America of the past. The religious movement they led certainly resembled an awakening: conservative churches were growing; the old mainline and liberal churches were dying; the religious Right possessed the power to elect a president. American flags waving, hands upraised in ecstatic prayer, and eyes closed, people sang "Shine, Jesus, Shine" and fainted at altars as they experienced God's healing power. At one revival in 1995, I stood next to a man who started barking in the spirit, just as was reported during the camp meetings of the Second Great Awakening. It sure looked like a revival, an awakening—the flames of Pentecost were sweeping over the world.

A revival of conservative politics, yes. But not *the* awakening, the transformative spiritual revitalization needed to address the real challenges and struggles of the emerging world. Some of it might have been genuine awakening for individuals, of course, the broken-hearted and lost finding themselves in God, experiencing the power of faith afresh. The Falwell-Robertson revival was the backlash, however, a counterreformation of nativism against the emerging awakening of the 1970s. Much of the religious Right of those days was powered by shrewd manipulators who were using the emotions of the fearful to forward their own agendas and turn the course of history back toward their "absolutist, sin-hating, death-dealing" God. They certainly deluded many into thinking that theirs was the real awakening, not what had happened in the experiential, romantic movements William McLoughlin depicted.

During the First Great Awakening, pro- and anti-awakening parties became known as "New Lights" and "Old Lights." New Lights embraced the spiritual awakening of the eighteenth century, urging others toward an experience of God, personal transformation, and a more democratic church and society. Old Lights resisted this message, insisting that adherence to European creeds, ordered worship, and ministerial authority would reform society. Ever since, historians have referred to pro- and anti-awakening parties as New and Old Light. The distinction can be helpful now, if the terms are defined with contemporary realities in mind. In the twenty-first century, both pro- and anti-awakening proponents extol experiential faith, the need for personal spiritual renewal, and greater democracy. Their preachers sounding the need for spiritual and national transformation can often sound much the same.

However, the difference is threefold: the starting place of experiential faith, the end toward which it is directed, and the agency by which it is achieved. Today's New Light awakening starts with a vision of humanity created in the divine image and moves toward the hope of universal connection and wholeness through God's spirit. New Light spirituality emphasizes creation, restoration, and *shalom* (universal well-being and peace). For New Lights, the primary agency of experiential faith is the individual-in-community, following a freely chosen spiritual path, based on principles of empathy and compassion, and judged by internal authenticity. Today's Old Lights start with a vision of fallen humankind and push forward toward a world where ordered politics and an authoritative church shelter the sinful until their future reward of salvation in heaven. Old Lights emphasize the fall, rescue, and salvation. For them, the primary agency of faith is the mediating institutions of government, markets, and church. So, while Old Lights may claim to be "born again," speak in tongues, and honor spiritual mystics like Mother Teresa, all religious experiences need to be adjudicated and affirmed by external authorities. This is a very old argument. And, in a very real way, Americans have replayed New Light–Old Light arguments in every successive spiritual awakening since the eighteenth century.[10]

You can actually see patterns of this New Light–Old Light tension in sociological surveys. In their recent book *American Grace,* Robert Putnam and David Campbell trace patterns of social change in the United States in recent decades. Like McLoughlin, they also argue that, beginning in 1960, the United States entered a period of intensive social reorientation, something that can be shown by data in indices of cultural change. On page after page, in chart after chart, they demonstrate how America increasingly became a more "New Light" society, more open and inclusive, with greater flexibility in gender roles, a quest for liberation and social equality, a marked liberalism in attitudes regarding sexuality, increased religious diversity, commitment to a wide range of spiritual practices, and acceptance of difference. Using charts and graphs, Putnam and Campbell illustrate what William McLoughlin described in 1978 as the contours of the Fourth Great Awakening. Putnam and Campbell, however, do not call it an awakening or New Light. They simply call it "The Shock," a statistic picture of dramatic change.

Around the time I entered college in 1977, an "aftershock" was beginning to develop following the earlier change, a period of retrenchment that some people referred to as "a return to the fifties."[11] It could also be understood as an "Old Light" reaction. Through the late 1970s and early 1980s, Putnam and Campbell's indices of social change slow, level, and then drop as attitudes on significant issues move back toward pre-1960s levels. Indeed, they argue that the turn and the rise of conservative religion are roughly coterminous and that conservative religion was a major factor shaping the first cultural aftershock following the 1960s.

The case being made, the next conclusion is logical. Conservative religion, especially conservative evangelicalism, is *not* the awakening described by William McLoughlin, even if some aspects of it resemble characteristics of a typical awakening. Put simply, revivalist evangelicalism, the New Light faith of the First and Second Great Awakenings, has become the Old Light retrenchment of the contemporary spiritual movement. It resembles experiential faith mostly due to historical factors and inheritance, matters of theology and politics that have become ritualized but possess little genu-

ine power to engage the surrounding culture in deeply meaningful ways. But in the twenty-first century, New Light is passing by
the groups that once bore that name; the life-giving energy of the
spirit has moved on. Thus, conservative evangelical groups want to
claim that they are the awakening (mostly because of their heritage
they find it difficult to see things differently) while they embody so
little of the new awakening's vision of spiritual, social, and political
change.[12] Thus, the New Lights of the old awakenings have become
the Old Lights of the new one.

And perhaps even worse than simply being "Old Lights" (those
who ignore or resist change), some conservative evangelicals have
become an active *nativist* reaction against the new awakening. Using
McLoughlin's analysis, it becomes apparent that, over the course of
the last half century, they worked to reverse cultural change and
keep the forces of genuine social transformation at bay, as they played
to people's anxieties and, in many cases, actually worked to increase
fear of women, Islam, pluralism, environmentalism, and homosexuality through preaching, theology, and church discipline.[13] Putnam
and Campbell claim that many Americans found the new ideas
"deeply repugnant to their fundamental moral and religious views."
Thus, religious reactions to emerging social and cultural change
set in across faith communities, as significant groups of evangelicals, traditionalist Protestants, Roman Catholics, and Jews argued
for order and authority.[14] Few groups, however, were as vocal and
public as evangelicals in protesting the changes. The 1960s, Putnam
and Campbell state, formed a particular threat to their values, and
"heightened the appeal of conservative evangelicalism" for those
feeling adrift in the new world.[15]

Thirty years before Putnam and Campbell's analysis, McLoughlin worried about the potential of conservative evangelical religion—
even before it was called the "religious Right"—to derail a genuine
spiritual awakening, saying, "Too much narrow-minded authori-
tarianism and obscurantism is heard from its leading church spokes-

men to enable it in its current formulations to offer 'new light' for the future. . . . [It] is a divisive, not unifying force in a pluralistic world."[16] Yet McLoughlin also speculated that even "within" the backlash of the larger evangelical movement there "may well lie the seeds of this awakening's new light."[17]

He was right, as there existed many such communities of experiential and experimental evangelical religion like Church of the Saviour, Sojourners community, Evangelicals for Social Action, or the small church at Armington Hall. Unnoticed and unknown by most of the outside world, two sorts of evangelical religion emerged in the 1970s and 1980s. One type was that of Jerry Falwell and the other moral crusaders; the other type was that of evangelical liberation theologians and other innovators. I call these forms *dogmatic evangelicalism* and *romantic evangelicalism*. The first type is of an Old Light sort: those who want to shore up boundaries, reinforce creeds, and ensure group identity through theological purity and strict behavior. The second type, a New Light form of faith, is led by those who wish to connect with people and ideas that are different, to explore the meaning of story and history, and to include as many as possible in God's embrace. *Dogmatic evangelicalism* is the Old Light of belief-centered, externally bounded religion, a realm of authority and stability; *romantic evangelicalism* is the New Light of experiential, internally driven faith, the arena of adventure and spiritual fluidity.

*Dogmatic* and *romantic* forms of faith are not the exclusive purview of evangelicalism. Indeed, there are dogmatic Roman Catholics and Eastern Orthodox, dogmatic Jews and Anglican and mainline Protestants; I suppose that dogmatic Buddhists and Hindus exist as well. These are people who think that the Old Light is the best guide, who resist the new spiritual revolution. *Romantic* forms of religion contributed to the spiritual transformation of the world since the 1960s; *dogmatic* forms gained the upper hand in the reversals of that transformation from the late 1970s to the mid-1990s.

Clarifying the difference between Old Light dogmatics and New

Light romantics goes a long way to understanding contemporary faith—and religious decline and the growth of spirituality—in recent decades. For example, the Southern Baptist Convention (SBC) roiled with conflict in the 1980s. Commentators and combatants pitched the story as a fight between fundamentalists and liberals in the SBC, like the fundamentalist-modernist controversy of the 1920s. This time, however, the fundamentalists won instead of the liberals, who were chased out of their denomination with their theological tails between their legs. But that analysis does not really fit. If you know any Southern Baptists, you know that you would be hard-pressed to find many—even today—who could rightly be considered "liberal."

The Southern Baptists did not split over doctrine. They split between those who feared social change and wanted to reverse it and those who thought that much of America's recent social change was good and wanted to be Christians within the new context. They split between authoritarian creed-oriented Baptists and those who wished to recapture the original, and often radical, spiritual impulses of Baptist faith. The Southern Baptists split between dogmatics and romantics, not between conservatives and liberals. It was a split between serious, faithful, biblically minded Christians over varying dispositions—nativism or romanticism—toward the cultural awakening that began in the 1960s.

What is interesting, however, is that dogmatics are not necessarily politically or morally conservative. Dogmatics are the guardians of the old order; they want to return to the "faith of the fathers" in order to set things aright. In Roman Catholic circles, the dogmatics attempt to turn back the theological and liturgical innovations of Vatican II. In mainline churches, institutions that are generally theologically liberal, dogmatics regularly reject innovations in worship, church architecture, ordination, ministry, seminary education, hymnody, and polity. Many church leaders insist that the old ways were the best ways—and the best way to guarantee the future was to maintain and repristinate the past.

Nativist movements among dogmatic evangelicals, mainline Protestants, Roman Catholics, Orthodox, Jews, Buddhists, and Muslims are trying to put God back on His Throne, send Darwin, Einstein, and Stephen Hawking packing, quell the murmurings from the discontented rabble in the pews, elect godly men to be in charge, outlaw birth control and family planning, put women back in the kitchen, and shore up the bulwark of American exceptionalism. After the 1960s and 1970s, the turn toward nativism in the 1980s seemed like a sea change. As the old orthodoxies got born again, it appeared that enormous numbers of Americans opted for Old Light, wanting the security of their ancestors rather than to embark on an uncertain spiritual journey to the future.

Dogmatic religions make noise and grab headlines—and work hard to purify their ranks. Through the 1980s and 1990s, a crusading mentality set in, resulting in an exodus from evangelical churches and many Roman Catholic ones of some of the most innovative and insightful leaders of that generation. Many, many people got hurt.

With the spiritual carnage and the dogmatics' grab for power, increasing numbers of Americans came to equate the nativist faith with Christianity, indeed, practically with religion as a whole. By 2010, the polling data reflect that to be "religious" means that you reject a transcendent and open faith, are afraid to ask questions about the Bible, Jesus, or the creeds, turn your back on the planet, oppose women's rights, and dislike gays and lesbians, the poor, and immigrants. The experientialists, the romantics, the innovators—Christianity's creative class—suddenly were called "spiritual." In popular terms, "religion" stopped the real awakening, but the impulse remained, mostly around movements and practices that became increasingly shy of "religiosity" and that favored a self-understanding of being "spiritual."

Putnam and Campbell point out that the number of evangelicals was never as great as portrayed in the press. "The rise was real and statistically significant," they explain, "but it amounted to adding roughly one American in twenty to the ranks of evangelicals. Despite the mountains of books and newspaper articles about the rise of the evangelicals, in absolute terms the change was hardly massive."[18] There were many fewer nativists than most of us imagined. The trends revealed something even more surprising. The evangelical rise ended rather abruptly in the mid-1990s when "the number of evangelical adherents . . . actually slumped."[19] Thus, Putnam and Campbell make the startling claim: *The evangelical boom that began in the 1970s was over by the early 1990s, nearly two decades ago.*"[20]

In 1996, I covered the Republican National Convention for the *New York Times* regional newspaper syndicate. I followed Ralph Reed around the convention floor as he communicated with Christian Coalition delegates, trying to ask him about theology. I got close enough to Pat Robertson coming into the hall to shout a question, only to be pushed away by his legion of bodyguards. I attended an Operation Rescue rally of hundreds in a San Diego park, where the faithful proudly wore T-shirts boasting, "Intolerance Is a Beautiful Thing," while lifting high crosses, American flags, and photos of dead fetuses. I went to a luncheon where Phyllis Schlafly excoriated gay people and the audience applauded wildly. The members of the religious Right seemed invincible, with their high-tech devices and mobilization strategies, but something was amiss. They were too powerful, too political, too slick and prideful, and they had lost touch with the hearts and prayers of the good people who worshipped in small Baptist churches and at Pentecostal prayer meetings.

When I got home, a friend asked me how the convention had been.

"I think I witnessed the Gettysburg of the religious Right," I replied. "They can't go on as they are."

Indeed, sociologists and surveys would later prove this intuition right. Of course, they did not die then, but the tide was ready to turn. Despite some political victories, and even some rather considerable ones, their fortunes would ebb with the American public in the years to come.

In earlier awakenings, nativist movements started strong and threatened to derail the cultural change of the New Light. During all three previous awakenings, nativists took over political parties, elected candidates, started crusades, split churches, and thrust dangerous demagogues into the public theater. The dogmatics typically portrayed themselves as innovative purveyors of a true spiritual awakening, offering their followers the secret to a meaningful way of life. Eventually, however, nativist movements overreached, often breeding violence. Their insistence on the old ways seemed increasingly out of step with the daily lives of regular people, who begin to accept and adapt to economic, social, and technological change. As fear ebbs, and new forms of community, work, and family become more normal, nativist movements wither and retreat to the margins of society. Even those once comforted by dogmatic promises of authority and order begin to look for new forms of faith. Awakenings can be slowed by fear, but if enough people experience, understand, and practice a new way of the spirit, they cannot be stopped.

## Awakening and Romantic Religion: Self, Practices, and Community

A spiritual awakening is, of course, more than politics, warmed-over liberalism, or just the values of the counterculture. Awakenings typically embody the romantic elements of religion—adventure, quest, mysticism, intuition, wonder, experience, nature, unity, historical imagination, art, and music—as a protest against systematized orthodoxies and religious convention. During the First Great Awakening, heartfelt passion for Jesus displaced formalized covenants of faith and European liturgies. During the Second, individual heroism and attention to devotional practices replaced Calvinistic determinism and clerical authority. During the Third, a fascination with process, history, and archaeology led Christians to erect neo-Gothic cathedrals over sites once occupied by unadorned meetinghouses and opened the spiritual imagination to new understandings of soul in nature, poetry, and the past. The Reverend Henry Ward Beecher (1813–87), brother of Harriet Beecher Stowe and one of the greatest preachers of the day, fancied himself as "romantic evangelical" who, like many of his peers, found God in the unity of all things. The current awakening is marked by its insistence on connection, networks, relationship, imagination, and story instead of dualism, individualism, autonomy, techniques, and rules.

Some romantic movements of the past emphasized escape from the world in favor of utopian schemes. Indeed, the underside of the current spiritual awakening is the temptation toward "navel-gazing," isolated faith, sectarianism, and moral relativism. At its best, however, the contemporary awakening is a movement of *romantic realism*. The Fourth Great Awakening imbibes the romantic spirit, but it has been chastened by the overly optimistic movements that preceded it—like schemes to perfect human society through social engineering or Christian attempts to bring about the kingdom of God on earth. The new romanticists remember, however dimly, Reinhold Niebuhr's dictum: "Social justice cannot be resolved by moral and rational suasion alone. . . . Conflict is inevitable, and in this conflict, power must be challenged by power."[21] Thus, prayer must be twinned with a vigorous passion for doing good, and spirituality itself is increasingly defined as a life of contemplation and justice. Niebuhr's dark reminders of human sin and evil have proved increasingly truthful since 9/11, deepening the characteristics of pragmatism and realism that shape the new awakening.

The spirit of romantic realism is perhaps best developed by contemporary poets. In "The Vision," Wendell Berry captures the mood of romantic realism. Its words could be a hymn for this awakening:

*If we will have the wisdom to survive,*
*to stand like slow-growing trees*
*on a ruined place, renewing, enriching it,*
*if we will make our seasons welcome here,*
*asking not too much of earth or heaven,*
*then a long time after we are dead*
*the lives our lives prepare will live*
*here, their houses strongly placed*
*upon the valley sides, fields and gardens*
*rich in the windows. The river will run*
*clear, as we will never know it,*
*and over it, birdsong like a canopy.*
*On the levels of the hills will be*
*green meadows, stock bells in noon shade.*
*On the steeps where greed and ignorance cut*
      *down*
*the old forest, an old forest will stand,*
*its rich leaf-fall drifting on its roots.*
*The veins of forgotten springs will have opened.*
*Families will be singing in the fields.*
*In their voices they will hear a music*
*risen out of the ground. They will take*
*nothing from the ground they will not return,*
*whatever the grief at parting. Memory,*
*native to this valley, will spread over it*
*like a grove, and memory will grow*
*into legend, legend into song, song*
*into sacrament. The abundance of this place,*
*the songs of its people and its birds,*
*will be health and wisdom and indwelling*
*light. This is no paradisal dream.*
*Its hardship is its possibility.*[22]

The Fourth Great Awakening is not a quest to escape the world. Instead, it moves into the heart of the world, facing the challenges head-on to take what is old—failed institutions, scarred landscapes, wearied religions, a wounded planet—and make them workable and humane in the service of global community. No miracles here. God does not heal without human hands. The hard work is the possibility.

Romantic realism begins with the self-in-relationship, not the isolated hero, but the individual whose life is linked with other heroic lives in a quest for beauty and justice and love. Romantic realism is strengthened through spiritual practices that shape devotion, character, and ethics. These practices require attention, time, and teaching; they need to be formed and nurtured in a guildlike community of beginners, novices, craftspeople, masters, and innovators. Through the self, community, and practice, the awakened romantics experience God, discovering new possibilities of trust, devotion, and love directed toward their neighbors and dedicated to anticipating the future of God's peace, goodness, and justice at work in the world now. The goal is not to bring about a utopian kingdom; rather, the goal is to perform the reign of God in and for the life of the world.

## Awakening Now

As the end of Lent neared in 2011, I went to my local bank to deposit some checks. Three tellers were working that morning, all women. One woman wore a pale ivory *hijab* as a head covering; the second woman's forehead bore the dark red mark known as a *bindi;* the third woman had a small crucifix hanging around her neck.

I walked up and laughed. "You all look like the United Nations of banking!"

They exchanged glances and smiled.

"You are so right," said the Hindu woman. "You should meet our customers! But we cover a lot of languages between the three of us."

It was a quiet morning. They wanted to talk. I said something about being a vegetarian for Lent. The Hindu woman wanted to give me some family recipes; the Muslim woman wanted to know more about Christian fasting practices (the Catholic woman was, by now, on the phone in another office).

I shared how we had dedicated Lent that year to eating simply and exploring vegetarian foods from different parts of the world. "When we eat Indian food," I explained, "we try to talk about the church in India or pray for people in India. The same for African and Asian and Latin American countries."

"What a wonderful idea!" the Muslim woman said. "We need to love our traditions and be faithful to our God; but we teach the beauty and goodness of the other religions too."

Her Hindu colleague chimed in, "That is the only way to peace—to be ourselves and to create understanding between all people."

For the next few minutes, they shared how much they appreciated living in Virginia, where they had found religious freedom. "Here, it is like Thomas Jefferson promised," the Muslim woman said. "Very good. People here are very tolerant, curious about different religions. Much better than other places. Here there is real respect. I can be a good Muslim here."

I glanced at my watch. I needed to get to an appointment. I thanked them for their insights.

"I would wish you a Happy Easter," I said hoping they would hear the sincerity in my voice, "but, instead, I wish you both peace."

I started to walk away when the Muslim teller said to me, "Peace of Jesus the Prophet. And a very happy Easter to you."

And the Hindu woman called out, "Happy Easter!"

When I reached my car, I realized that I was crying. I had only rarely felt the power of the resurrected Jesus so completely in my soul.

Sometimes it is hard to see the awakening that is happening all around us, because this awakening is quite different from those in the past. Unlike the awakenings in American history books, this one was not concluded in thirty or forty years. No one spiritual renewal has reshaped us; there is no political consensus and no genuine institutional renewal. We have experienced almost two generations of religious conflict, most often with people in our own religious traditions. We still feel lost, we are divided, and our institutions are failing us. Things are different, especially those things of the spirit, but the road ahead is not clearly marked.

Part of this can be explained by the strange historical process of this particular awakening—in an age of swift change, this awakening is taking a very *l-o-n-g* time. Certainly unanticipated by William McLoughlin or anyone leading religious change in the last five decades, the Fourth Great Awakening has unfolded in two distinctive periods, with an interlude in between: the Fourth Great Awakening 1.0, from 1960 to 1980; a powerful nativist backlash from 1975 to 1995, which is most obviously embodied in the religious Right and which set up rival and contradictory versions of revival; and the Fourth Great Awakening 2.0, beginning around 1995 and continuing to today.

Although the first phase set a social and ideological vision of equality, care for the earth, and authenticity, two things have changed significantly since the earlier phase. Each of those two things contributed to muting the nativism of the 1980s, and each altered the course of the emerging spiritual awakening. First, technology has exponentially increased our ability to connect and communicate, to share information, and to be aware of events and concerns around the world. Indeed, technological advances have played a role in major American awakenings since the days when George Whitefield mounted his horse and rode from one colonial village to another, acting as a human networker and sharing the good news of revival. Technology was always a means of awakening, a form of communication that carried information *about* new possibilities and ideas.

In the eighteenth century, technology changed the way people did things, but there was not quite an immediate and intimate relationship between technology and personhood. Today, however, technology is shaping us; we are in the process of internalizing and integrating technology in ways that make us different than we were—even to the point of enhancing human wisdom, opening us all to new dimensions of spiritual experience. Technology is not only enabling an awakening; it is an important dimension of it. That shift was not possible in the 1960s and 1970s before microtechnologies, digital information, and the Internet.[23] Many twenty-first century technologies are, by definition, about connection and community, both of which are central to the nature of spirituality and to this awakening. Indeed, much of the promise of the Internet is profoundly spiritual.

Second, religious pluralism is much more widespread and deeply ingrained in American culture than it was in the 1960s and 1970s, during the first phase of the awakening. In the mid-1960s, the U.S. government lifted immigration quotas on Asian, African, and South American countries, allowing for people of non-Christian, non-Western faiths—as well as Christians from countries where Pentecostal forms of both Protestantism and Catholicism were pronounced—to move here more easily and become citizens. During the first stage of awakening, pilgrims had to go to Tibet, Japan, or India to learn to meditate or experience Buddhism or Hinduism. Only a small number of American communities of these religions existed, and practitioners of Eastern spiritualities were considered exotic.

Now, however, if one is curious about another religion, most of us can walk across the street and ask neighbors about their prayer practices. You can ask your aunt or your sister-in-law. Indeed, religious diversity is so strong in the United States that we have developed a practice of "bridging," whereby we befriend, marry, and work with people of a wide variety of faiths. This pragmatic diversity is actually changing the way most Americans view what it means to be "a good American," as individuals and religious groups creatively engage the tension between devotion and diversity.[24]

The Reverend Dr. James Forbes, the noted Protestant leader and former pastor of the venerable Riverside Church in New York City, believes we are in an awakening of spiritual renewal and social transformation that embodies a holistic understanding of self and God, is expressed through a life of "balance" and in community, and draws from all faiths, not just one. He claims:

> The great awakenings in American history were all Christian revitalization movements that brought personal piety and also brought transformation in the society. But the next great awakening will have to be an interfaith awakening.

Forbes continues, sounding remarkably like the tellers at my neighborhood bank:

> Will an interfaith Great Awakening look like a watered-down version of spiritual or religious life? Or does it look like challenging every religious tradition in this nation simply by the question, "What does your tradition have to say about how we achieve and maintain balance necessary for full human existence?" I want to ask my Christian church, don't water down your religion. Interfaith awakening will probably not be about comparative soteriology, doctrines about salvation. It will not be about what names we use. It will not probably be about our comparative eschatology, study of the end times. It has to be about what gives us balance. And I am convinced that just as it is in my body, also in the body politic. There is a gyroscopic mechanism that would

incline us to seek balance, and that is why it is likely that a great awakening is going to happen. In each of the great awakenings there has been a perceived sense of out of balance, out of kilter, insecurity, change beyond our capacity to cope. I think we are a prime suspect for a great awakening because we surely meet that requirement. Out of kilter, broken down, scared, not able to even believe that our ideals are feasible.[25]

An interfaith awakening does not mean that everyone will surrender their distinctiveness or that churches, mosques, temples, and synagogues will cease to exist. Nor does it mean that the world's people will suddenly convert to a single and imperialistic religion— whether that religion is Protestant fundamentalism, Roman Catholicism, Islam, or something else. We are slowly, painfully, and patiently learning what it means to live in particular faiths while honoring the wisdom of others in a mutual, spiritual quest toward "full human existence."

Because of religious mixing, the Fourth Great Awakening might better be understood as the Fourth Great Awakenings, plural. Throughout these pages, I have described a Christian awakening mostly of a Protestant sort. In the past, Great Awakenings have served to renew American Protestantism and revitalize a largely homogeneous culture. But this awakening is not only an evangelical Christian or even a larger Protestant Christian event. Catholics, Jews, Muslims, Hindus, and Buddhists have been undergoing similar revitalizations as they pay renewed attention to the spiritual dimensions of their traditions, emphasizing communal identity, faith practices, and experiential belief—often over against authoritarian leaders and inflexible religious structures. Belonging, behaving, and believing are undergoing profound transformations in every religious context. These multiple spiritual awakenings are parallel events across faith boundaries. Just now, people are realizing that there are walkers on another nearby path heading in the same direction. Not the same path, but a close enough path that travelers can make friends with others on a similar (but not identical) journey that will eventually bring new life, new hope, and new possibilities to the larger culture.

We live in a time of Christian spiritual awakening, of Jewish spiritual awakening, of Muslim spiritual awakening, of Hindu spiritual awakening, of Buddhist spiritual awakening, of spiritual awakening that bears no religious label, of spiritual awakening of the "nones." Harvey Cox describes this multireligious awakening as the Age of Spirit, an effusive, experiential, practice-centered impulse of faith sweeping across the globe. This is an age of great awakenings. With such spiritual scope, it may not be the "Fourth" of anything, for nothing quite like it has happened before in history.[26] This may be the Great Global Awakening, the first of its kind. The American or Canadian or English or Australian or West African or Korean or Latin American forms of this sort of spiritual revitalization are local expressions of vast, multinational religious shifts, in which each cultural family is exploring new connections between the divine story and their own story. What is happening in the United States is a spiritual node in a global network of faith. Indeed, Christianity is also a spiritual node in this network of awakening. In my country and in my faith tradition, we are merely a part of a much, much larger web of God's wondrous work.

## Nativism Now

All of this, however, poses risks. Awakenings can be slowed—or potentially stopped—if people fail to understand the times in which they live and respond with fear instead of hope. Awakenings are both the work of God, and they are hard work. Every spiritual awakening gives birth to counterawakenings, those nativist movements seeking to restore older forms of authority and power. In the 1980s, the fundamentalists slowed, and in some cases stopped, the momentum of the revival of my college days. In Pentecostal and charismatic churches across the United States, leaders who prayed in tongues to an awesome God morphed into political preachers instructing their folks in the evils of Democrats, feminism, homosexuality, environmentalism, and abortion. Conservative leaders used the revival to baptize a single political agenda to establish their vision of a godly society. What was once a liberating experience of God devolved into a checklist of political litmus tests. The leaders did not tolerate questions or deviation and used spiritual intimidation, threats of hell, and ecclesial authority to support their theocratic longings. They found a religious audience eager to launch a crusade against women's rights, separation of church and state, homosexuals, and environmentalism. "Return to a Christian America!" shouted the nativists, which they believed to be America of the 1950s or 1840s or 1770s. For the first time in the history of American awakenings, a rearguard movement nearly succeeded in hijacking spiritual revival in favor of narrowing human rights and making American religion less inclusive, rather than more so. And they did so by claiming that they alone constituted American faith and that those who opposed them were ungodly or demonic.

Between roughly 1980 and 1995, the counterawakening was powerful in American life, but it never entirely succeeded. American attitudes toward women, birth control and abortion, premarital sex and interreligious marriage, prayer and Bible reading in public schools, and acceptance of gays and lesbians never returned to 1950s levels. Although President Reagan took the solar panels off the White House that President Carter had installed, Americans have never managed to completely shake environmental awareness. Indeed, although measures of social change showed small reversals in some cases during the heyday of the religious Right, many Americans continued to embrace social values shaped in the 1960s. Although the religious Right grabbed headlines, a religious, cultural, and social substratum took shape, a spiritual impulse that started to emerge in the mid-1990s and began to exert grassroots pressure on the religious and political establishment, mostly by the means of local renewal, community organizing, the Internet, and social networking.

These movements burst into public consciousness with President Obama's election in 2008, much as the religious Right had with the election of Ronald Reagan in 1980. But unlike the old religious Right, this new movement has no name. The media sometimes, and rather unimaginatively, refer to it as the religious Left. "Spiritual progressives" may be closer to the mark, but that moniker does not fully capture its essence either. Whatever it may be called, it is the wind of the Fourth Great Awakening, version 2.0, the America part of the Great Global Awakening: a generative spirit, a creative and innovative openness, a sense of hope-filled realism, of pragmatic idealism, of an interconnectedness of all things, of urgency and wonder, and of experiencing the divine in the here and now.

Whatever it's called, it is powerful and real, it is changing the lives of countless millions, and it is the motivating source for change in North America, in Europe, and around the world. And it is, like the earlier phase of the awakening in the 1960s and 1970s, spawning powerful nativist movements that seek to turn back history as completely and definitively as they can by whatever means necessary.

In early autumn 2010, I was visiting my friends Lisa and David in Seattle. Lisa is a pastor, and David a university professor. The conversation quickly turned to the upcoming midterm elections, especially the strong backlash against President Obama. David, whose academic work covers rhetoric, religion, and politics, had spent the previous summer leading a research project studying the Tea Party.

"In 2008, I was excited as anyone for Barack Obama," he confessed. "Not only professionally, but personally. He created a brilliant narrative of what it meant to be American. Grounded in history, drawing off some of the deepest themes and spiritual longings of our nation. But it was open, inclusive, inviting, oriented toward the future, not the past. He articulated what millions hoped for, dreamed of—an American future for peace and the planet."

David sighed. "I went to those rallies. I thought, 'This is it. The new American story. We've moved ahead. Finally. There is no going back. The door to the future has opened.'"

He paused. "What I never imagined was that a counternarrative, a story as passionate, as deeply held, as full of meaning, as fraught with spiritual *and* American meaning, would come from another source. I was completely blindsided by the Tea Party."

I do not recall if he used the word "nativist" to describe the Tea Party. That was, however, what he clearly discovered in his research. A religious-political movement, like the one McLoughlin describes, of "reactionaries who look backward to a golden time, when the system worked; they insist that it will still work if only everyone will conform to the old standards."[27] Fear is a powerful motivator, and the good old days seem pretty good to those caught in a web of economic change, collapsing industries, and social insecurity. Many people in such movements sincerely love God, their families, and their country, longing for the best for their communities and the future. Reactionary religions often understand themselves to be truly compassionate faiths, offering clear paths of authority and order in days that seem unhinged. To them, complete conformity to a singular interpretation of the Bible or Constitution or both— whether freely embraced or legislated by those in power—is the only way to health, happiness, and salvation.

Yet coercion and fear are never compassionate. The only test of compassion is love-in-practice. In the Middle Ages, Christians claimed to be loving God and neighbor when they converted others at sword point or sent heretics to burn on stakes so that their souls would be purified. The priests and crusaders who inflicted such mayhem sincerely believed that these were loving acts, but common sense and human decency clearly say otherwise. These were the acts of a fear-filled people, anxious about early death, overwrought by economic change, the failure of the feudal system, the challenge of Islam, or the need to control women. Periods of intense social change and periods of intense religious encounters between different faiths often resulted in historical tragedies when fear-based religious groups gained political power. In such cases, we might empathize with their fear or desire order ourselves, but it is necessary to recognize that sincerity and claims to love do not count for much in the larger scheme of things. When nativism threatens, having compassion on the fearful is an important spiritual practice, but it always must be coupled with an ability to speak the truth in love. Fear-filled religions stand in sharp contrast to compassion-based spiritual awakenings. The distinction must be made clearly in pulpits and in public.

The Tea Party, the schismatic movements in mainline churches, evangelical leaders charging innovative young pastors with heresy, the Vatican investigating nuns and silencing theologians, the Taliban and their like closing girls' schools and blowing up Buddhas, Jews attacking Jews because of different views of Israel, violent jihadists terrorizing millions, religious dictators shutting down the Internet, West African fundamentalists killing gay people and torturing children as witches—contemporary history is full of fear-filled, backward-looking, violent believers. But these are not wars of religion versus religion, like Christianity versus Islam. Rather, a new inquisition has been unleashed, and some of the worst violence is directed within. The greatest pressure points in the religious world are between dogmatics and romantics, between Old Lights and New, between those who wish to shore up the old religions and those who embrace the new spiritual awakening.

The nativists have returned with fury. As David told me, "This is the worst version of religious and political hatred in American history for at least one hundred and fifty years." Harvey Cox calls it the fundamentalist rearguard action of those clinging to "belief-centered" faith, the fearful opposition to the Age of the Spirit. A death rattle? The last stand? The global spiritual awakenings of hope and possibility have created global nativist movements of fear and dread. We live in a time of dangerous religious warfare, but not of the expected sort of warfare between different religions, interreligious warfare; rather, we live in a dangerous time of intrareligious warfare, between those with differing versions of the same faith. Nativists of all sorts are doing their best to halt the spiritual awakening of romantic realism and undo the future it might create.

That is a lot of bad news, I know. We all feel the weight of it. Every day, newspapers and the Internet bring more stories of fear, failure, political crisis, and violence than they do of hopeful change and compassion.[28] The bad news, however, is an important current of the change that is happening in these times. Our society, sadly enough, is divided into Old Lights and New Lights—not necessarily cleanly or neatly or even self-consciously. The groupings may be messy, confusing, or surprising. But division is real and it is increasing, rather than lessening, cultural anger and fear. It is easy to call dogmatic or nativist opponents crazy or evil; it is far more difficult to discern that their reaction against spiritual and social change is part of the predictable pattern of awakening. Dismissing or ignoring these movements diminishes our ability to discern the signs of the times in which we live.

This is the good news: there would be no backlash if there were no spiritual awakening. Indeed, the presence of backlash movements actually indicates how widespread and compelling an awakening has become. Human beings rarely move toward the future without the fear of loss or the fear of risk, and the anxious deserve both compassion and pastoral care. Often, individuals who are most fearful are spiritually closest to real change. Anxiety is frequently the mark of personal transformation, for anxiety is a primary emotion when the heart feels disoriented and lost. Indeed, awakenings and the backlash they spawn may not happen with great regularity, but when they do happen to individuals and societies, great tension and division is a normal (if disconcerting) part of the process of spiritual and cultural revitalization.

In this situation, leaders and spiritual communities are not needed to comfort people feeling lost in times of change. Instead, spiritual leaders need to help transform these fears into urgency and courage. People cannot stay in a state of perpetual fear. To enable and empower people to move ahead calls for wisdom and love, two qualities we seldom speak of in political leadership. It also calls for patient insight twinned with the ability for prophetic proclamation of the new world. The genuinely good news is that the spiritual awakening itself offers ways beyond anxiety and division through meaningful practices that embody faith, hope, and action. Prayer, discernment, hospitality, service to others, forgiveness, testimony, conversation, and friendship—all function to create new connections between neighbors and revitalize public discourse. Renewed spiritual practice gives the anxious an ability to reach out to those who are different, to experience friendship and community, to reconcile, heal, and serve. In an awakening, we actually *wake up* and see ourselves, our neighbors, and our world from a different perspective. Awakening opens the imagination toward what might be, instead of only what was.

Most of all, awakening calls for a change of heart. "Repent (*metanoeite*)!" cried Jesus, "for the kingdom of heaven has come near!" (Matt. 4:17). Jesus invited those who dared to follow on an adventure, a life-giving spiritual work to craft "health and wisdom and indwelling light" in this world.

"What can we do? How can we change? How can this happen?" asked those who heard the invitation. Awakening is not a miracle we receive; it is actually something we can do.

## CHAPTER NINE

# Performing Awakening

Iᴎ 1734, ᴀ ʀᴇᴠɪᴠᴀʟ swept through the town of Northampton, Massachusetts. Three hundred people experienced a spiritual awakening and joined the local Congregational church, where Jonathan Edwards was the minister. As rumor of the revival spread, friends pressed Edwards to write an account of the event. Four years later, he published *A Faithful Narrative of the Surprising Work of God,* a book that recounted both the history of the town and spiritual histories of its inhabitants. Edwards, with keen psychological insight, identified four steps of spiritual awakening that had enlivened members of his flock: a general stirring toward moral living, an awareness of personal shortcomings and sins, an experience of "converting grace," and a palpable sense of joy from encountering the "new light" of God.

The book was an immediate bestseller, going through twenty printings in its first year. Clergy who wanted to imitate Edwards's spiritual success eagerly read *A Faithful Narrative.* Across England and throughout English colonies, religious leaders wanted to know how to stir slumbering churchgoers and inspire awakening. Would dramatic preaching awaken the church? Would instilling a sense of

fear rouse the sinful? How could preachers help others experience
the new light of God?

Edwards, a Calvinist who believed that God initiated all acts of
the soul, rejected the idea that people, pastors included, could do
much of anything to bring forth a revival. The "surprising work"
was, indeed, God's work. Edwards could discern only a pattern of
God's activity in the awakening and argued that his flock had merely
responded to God. According to Pastor Edwards, however, there
was one thing that people could do to prepare for spiritual awakening: pray. Prayer opened the heart to sense God and opened the
eyes to see God's activity. "The future advancement of the church,"
wrote Edwards, "would come to fruition as multitudes from different towns resolve to unite in extraordinary prayer."[1] That was all
the faithful could do. Pray.

During each spiritual awakening, people have asked the same
questions: What do we do to bring about renewal? How do we experience new light? Can we participate in God's work? As a result,
in each successive period of awakening, Christian folk—pastors and
lay leaders alike—wrote volumes on these concerns, all explaining
how to promote the spiritual work of revitalization.

Although there were often arguments about nurturing renewal between proponents of and participants in the awakenings,
a significant insight stands out in each. In the First Great Awakening, Edwards's Calvinist insistence that prayer alone could forward
God's work emerged as central to spreading the revival. Ministers
across the colonies and in England and Scotland formed "concerts
of prayer" that focused attention on God's power to renew weary
hearts.

During the Second Great Awakening, preaching was the primary practice to foster revival. Pastors and revivalists alike emphasized the power of the word, often full of emotions and vivid im-
agery, to propel lukewarm souls into a new experience of God's
passionate embrace. The results stunned ministers across the land,

as unnumbered masses flocked to camp meetings and tent revivals, where they sat, under the spell of the preached word, quaking anxiously on benches and surrendering their hearts to Jesus during newly introduced altar calls.

The Third Great Awakening was a complex affair, involving two spiritual impulses interwoven into a cloth of experiential faith. Among some, new Pentecostal gifts—speaking in tongues and miraculous healings—marked the trail toward awakening. In other communities, a new emphasis on human progress, accepting and adapting to the insights of science, history, psychology, sociology, theology, and biblical criticism formed a pathway toward spiritual enlightenment and the kingdom of God. Although often hostile to each other, as participants came from very different social worlds, Pentecostalism and progressivism nevertheless displaced conventional churchgoing and dazzled the Christian world with new visions of faith and faithfulness at the dawn of the twentieth century. The twin streams of awakening flowed through both church life and politics, remaking religious practices of prayer and worship toward justice and the common good for much of the last century.

Prayer, preaching, Pentecostal gifts, and progressive theology and politics—these were the pathways of past awakenings. What is the way today? How can people participate in the spiritual renewal that is reshaping the world now? What can we do about it?

## Acting Out

Every Memorial Day, thousands of motorcyclists descend on Washington, D.C, for an event called Rolling Thunder. One year, as my husband and I drove down a major suburban street, a rider came up in the lane next to us. Sitting on an impressive Harley-Davidson bike sporting a pair of America flags, he was wearing a black T-shirt, with many tattoos visible on his arms and neck. An attractive woman in shorts sat behind him, her arms encircling his waist in intimate fashion. The man was smoking a very large, very fat cigar. I glanced at my husband and laughed. "Well, that's one impressive display of testosterone, isn't it?"

The philosopher Charles Taylor argues that the contemporary quest for authenticity has given rise to a culture of "mutual display," through which "people grasp themselves and great numbers of others as existing and acting simultaneously." He explains the culture of display through the use of fashion:

> I wear my own kind of hat, but in doing so I am displaying my style to all of you, and in this I am responding to your self-display, even as you will respond to mine. The space of fashion is one in which we sustain a language together of signs and meanings, which is constantly changing, but which at any moment is the background needed to give our gestures the sense they have.

Taylor continues, "It matters to each of us as we act that the others are there as witnesses of what we are doing, and thus as co-determiners of the meaning of our action." The contemporary world, Taylor observes, is constructed of stages—that is, the public spaces—where strangers "rub shoulders" and form "the inescapable context of each other's lives." Such stages include neighborhood festivals, subways, stadiums, city streets, shopping malls, coffeehouses, parks, and the virtual geographies of television and the Internet—all are the public spaces where we perform our lives. "Here each individual or small group acts on its own," writes Taylor, "but aware that its display says something to the others, will be responded to by them, will help build a common mood or tone that will color everyone's actions." As a result, he suggests that authenticity and display are creating "a new way of being together in society," one that could promote a positive vision of both individual selfhood and communal benefit.[2]

Given this cultural setting, the Rolling Thunder motorist was both expressing his own understanding of personhood—bike, tattoos, girl, and cigar—and participating in a communal event—a rally intended to raise political awareness of prisoners of war and the needs of military veterans. His display served both purposes, self-expression and political action. In order to find our truest selves and to make meaningful social change, we act out on public stages (and there are fewer and fewer "private" spaces all the time) in full view of others, those who we hope will react to our performance and will respond in some mutually beneficial way.

The culture of display is a theater to enact spiritual longings, connection, and awe. Take, for example, flash mobs. At the beginning of the Christmas shopping rush in 2010, a Philadelphia opera company unexpectedly performed a portion of Handel's *Messiah* at a Macy's department store. Six hundred singers mingled anonymously in a crowd of shoppers. At a specified time, the singers began a rousing version of the "Hallelujah Chorus." With no clear division between performers and audience, regular shoppers joined the chorus, turning the department store into a massive stage of song and celebration. People were stunned, laughing, crying, raising hands in ecstasy, teaching their children the lyrics, or standing still reverently to listen.[3] What happened in that Macy's was a "random act of culture," but it was also a random performance of spirituality, an act of connection, memory, joy, and perhaps even conversion.

Performance has always been important to awakening. In the First Great Awakening, George Whitefield's preaching was the ultimate colonial theater. In the Second, the camp meetings were theaters of improvisation, where the converted acted out their encounters with the divine. In the Third, both Pentecostals and progressives displayed the public possibilities of racial integration, women's leadership, and caring for the poor and outcast in the theaters of pulpit and political gathering. American religious history is marked by theatricality, and religious leaders display the faith as much as teach it.

But a spirituality of display is in no way limited to American Christianity. Indeed, performance has a long Christian history beginning with Jesus's acts of healing and the staging of early Christian liturgies. It was made visible through icons and rehearsed in medieval mystery plays. Mystics acted out apostolic poverty and simplicity, and followers of Luther and Calvin protested against the established church. Every spiritual awakening to transform Christianity over the last two thousand years has been accompanied by radical, perspective-altering public performances by saints, theologians, preachers, and faithful folks enacting the life of God or teaching of Jesus in shared spaces to express their own spirituality, create a communal theater of faith, and invite others into a new way of life.

The difference between performance then and now is obvious: in earlier ages, there existed a more distinct boundary between public and private space, thus shielding some aspects of personhood from display.[4] As a result, past awakenings always involved public performance, but were not entirely fostered, composed, or constructed in and through display.[5] The new global Great Awakening is not contained by the stage of the local Congregational church, in small groups, at camp meetings or tents, or at Pentecostal tabernacles or progressive political meetings. This awakening is being performed in the networked world, where the border between sacred and secular has eroded and where the love of God and neighbor—and the new vision of belonging, behaving, and believing—is being staged far beyond conventional religious communities. Although churches seem the most natural space to perform spiritual awakening, the disconcerting reality is that many people in Western society see churches more as museums of religion than sacred stages that dramatize the movement of God's spirit.[6]

What do you do to participate in awakening? To rouse others? To move to spread the good news of a new spiritual awakening?

Perform faith. Display the kingdom in all that you do. Anticipate the reign of God in spiritual practices. Act up and act out for God's love.

## Prepare, Practice, Play, Participate

Performing faith involves four important actions: *prepare, practice, play,* and *participate.* Preparing by learning the story, rehearsing a new way of life, having fun, and joining with others are key to acting out spiritual awakening. These actions happen in the context of the great reversal as the new experiential community forms, acting out its spirituality in practice, and discovering new insights of loving and trusting God.

If you don't know what's going on, it is very difficult to take part. You must *prepare* by learning the overall religious story of our time. And that story is deceptively simple. Conventional religion is failing and a new form of faith, which some call "spirituality" and can also be called *religio,* is being born. This is a new spiritual awakening, in line with other American awakenings, part of a complex web of spiritual renewal throughout the world, which is in the process of reshaping most religions by emphasizing relationships, practices, and experience that connects people to a deeper awareness of self, to their neighbors in global community, and to God. There are powerful new forces of egalitarianism, communalism, environmentalism, economic life, and mutual responsibility being born from the emerging spirituality, opening the possibilities for new forms of compassion toward others and toward the planet. We are living at a time of great turning in which we have the opportunity for *metanoia,* to see differently and to create a global common good that reflects a divine dream of reconciliation, peace, dignity, and justice. Christians refer to this as the reign of God; other faiths refer to it by other names. Yet all seek to somehow enact the Golden Rule as the way of compassion to renew our communities and save us from despair, dehumanization, and destruction.

In order to embody the story and help others experience it, we need to *practice* our faith intentionally in ways that anticipate compassion and justice. When Jesus said, "Thy kingdom come, thy will be done on earth as it is in heaven," he was directing his followers to do something. God's reign does not fall from heaven to those who wait. The people of God must live the kingdom by purposefully *doing* actions that rehearse love, charity, kindness, goodness, mercy, peace, forgiveness, and justice. Thus, like actors preparing for a play, we have lines to memorize, movements to master, stage directions to follow, emotions and feelings to portray. At first, these things might seem unnatural, but as we practice, we begin to feel them, we become the characters we play, and, to borrow from Shakespeare, the play becomes the thing. All the world's a stage, the theater of God's divine drama. The more we rehearse, the better we become at our parts.

Performance involves the hard work of practice, but it also entails *play*. Sometimes movements of change bog down, because those involved become so serious about the work that they forget about the basic human need for fun, delight, and joy. Awakening cannot occur without laughter and lightness. Mirth is essential to vibrant spirituality. Making a difference in the world, worshipping God, embracing new friends, feasting together, celebrating small successes, doing meaningful work—these are all things that make people happy. Performance is not always drama; rather, play includes irony and improvisation, self-deprecation and satire. Indeed, performance is "entertainment" in its original sense, which meant "to hold together, stick together, or support." The purpose of entertainment was to create a community focused on the story at hand. Laughter enables people to move in concert toward difficult ends, and comedy is often as profound as the most compelling tragedy.

Finally, performance requires that we *participate*. In some circles, there exists a temptation to divide the performers from the audience; performers enact the play, while the audience watches and appreciates their work. Performers are professionals, and audiences are amateurs. But the dichotomy between actor and audience is a false one. Performers and viewers inform, inspire, and respond to one another. Ideally, there is no such thing as a passive audience. Instead, audiences conspire with actors to create unique performances. To perform awakening means we all must participate—sometimes as actors, sometimes as audience, as directors, writers, stagehands, set designers, ushers—rather like a community theater, all with interchangeable roles. Awakening is not professional performance, but it involves everyone acting his or her parts, as a shifting script demands.

As was the case with the motorcyclist at Rolling Thunder, performance is both individual and communal. We must each act our parts, but there must be corporate display as well. This may well be the role of church in the emerging awakening. At its best, church is holy performance. Churches cannot be clubs for the righteous, institutions that maintain religious conformity in the face of change, or businesses that manage orthodoxy and personal piety. Churches must be more like Rolling Thunder or holy flash mobs. They must grasp—in a profound and authentic way—that they are sacred communities of performance where the faithful learn the script of God's story, rehearse the reign of God, experience delight, surprise, and wonder, and participate fully in the play.

## What to Do?

In summer 2011, my family spent a week at Ring Lake Ranch, an ecumenical retreat center in the Wyoming wilderness. Situated in a valley of glacial lakes once used by Sheepeater Indians as a site for their sacred vision quests, Ring Lake Ranch exudes an unexpected power of spiritual awe. Guests stay in simple log cabins, scattered on the hillsides with views of mountains and water. The days of the week follow a simple pattern: a communal morning prayer, community meals, hikes, fishing, or horseback riding, and quiet time. Before dinner, someone shares a passion, hobby, or story with the group. And after dinner, a speaker explores topics in scripture, poetry, theology, nature, art, music, or spirituality.

There are few guidelines—things like put trash in the bear-safe containers, help with the dishes, and don't drink the lake water. The camp directors, Carl and Joyce, are not overly directive; they plan prayers, make announcements, and offer options for the day. Each person decides what, if any, activity to engage in. There are few clocks, limited wireless, and no cell service.

With so little planned activity—the only "program" being the evening lecture—I wondered if the whole business was a retreat for individualistic introverts. A funny thing happened, however. From this minimal structure, the forty strangers who gathered began to make a community as we discovered shared passions and connections between our lives. In less than a week, and without difficulty or planning, we performed the spiritual awakening. We learned a new script in the telling of personal stories, biblical stories, and stories about nature and the world; we engaged in spiritual practices of our own choosing (mine were daily morning prayer and hiking); we played (feasting and dancing); and together we made a microcosm of God's reign, an experience where the divine and mundane interwove, not only in the glories of nature, but in the human exchanges while walking, sitting on porches, and chatting over tables. Like the ancient Sheepeaters, who came to the valley thousands of years ago on their vision quests, we left having encountered the spirit, our eyes opened wide to different possibilities for our own lives and the world. We both experienced and created awakening.

There is no specific technique that can be employed, no set program to follow to start a great awakening. If you want it to happen, you just have to do it. You have to perform its wisdom, live into its hope, and "act as if" the awakening is fully realized. And you have to do it with others in actions of mutual creation.

That is, of course, the rub. In recent decades, the sorts of places where such communities can develop have declined—the locales where strangers meet and spontaneously begin to do the sacred work of listening, learning, laughing, and leading together. It can be hard to find strangers, or even friends, willing to do this kind of work. In the face of daunting problems and fear, many people have retreated from even the hope of real community into "self-contained private realm(s)" where "we can pursue our own happiness without regard for the needs of others."[7] Even many churches, sadly enough, are not really communities of belonging; they have, instead, created religious "private realms" where each member maintains personal theologies with little concern for the larger world. As a result of this cultural erosion, temporary and ad hoc communities like Ring Lake Ranch have gained in popularity across North America. Open monastic houses, denominational retreats, cathedral and urban church communities, and spiritual centers of all sorts attract throngs of people—not only those who want to escape from the noise of contemporary life, but also those who are seeking to find connection with others who are enacting awakening.

In his recent book, *Healing the Heart of Democracy,* Parker Palmer points out that intentional retreat is not the only option in finding places to experience and create life-giving community. Despite the overall erosion of community, there are still spaces where strangers gather and "act with dignity, independence, and vision."[8] Those settings include neighborhoods, community gardens, city streets, public transit, parks, cafés, and coffee shops; galleries, museums, and libraries; festivals, fairs, and farmer's markets; rallies and debates; public schools, congregations, and social networks.[9] Each of these locations offers the possibility of community and is potentially the sacred stage upon which awakening can be performed.

Performing, of course, entails doing something—not only waiting for a magical form of community or the kingdom to arrive. At a place like Ring Lake Ranch, performing awakening is amazing, where nature and eager participants willingly take part in sacred theater outside their normal structures. But in the real world? What to do there?

During spring 2010, I decided that I wanted to spend most of my family's food budget at the local farmers' market. After reading Michael Pollan's *Omnivore's Dilemma,* I wanted to do something to make the world different regarding food, sustainability, and the future. Every Tuesday morning, I went to the nearby market, buying from the same fifteen vendors. As the weeks progressed, I got to know the farmers—old-time Virginians working family farms, new immigrants from Mexico, well-off retirees growing organic crops or raising free-range animals. They told me about farming practices and managing land, about their hopes and fears for the future of American farms, sharing their passion for good food and the way of life it embodied. They taught me how to cook unfamiliar vegetables and how to grill buffalo. I picked up tips from the local gardening club, which maintained a booth at the market, talked with grassroots political activists, ran into local clergy—including a Methodist pastor who had just bought an SUV-full of apples for a congregation-wide pie contest—and chatted theology, and shadowed local celebrity chefs to see what produce they purchased. Regulars recognized me, asking whether the recipes had worked, if my family had enjoyed vacation, and how my book was going. Pretty soon, I realized that the farmers' market was more than a place to shop—it was a community, and a lively spiritual one at that. Every Tuesday morning, the people who gathered learned stories, shared practices, celebrated food, and created a microcosm of a different kind of world.

The Great Global Awakening is a matter of big questions—belonging, behaving, and believing—rightly reordered to enliven the heart and empower people to transform the world. But it is also a matter of four actions that we can take together in extraordinary places like Ring Lake Ranch and in ordinary ones like the local farmers' market. What to do now to nurture awakening?

First, prepare for awakening. Not by posting billboards announcing that the end is near or by frightening people with predictions of doom and gloom. Instead, prepare by reading and learning the holy texts of faith in new ways. Read a Bible, one written in contemporary style as if it were a novel—the Common English Bible or *The Message* are good versions for such reading. If you are a longtime churchgoer, try to read it as if you have never heard it before, looking for surprising bits that you have never noticed. Challenge yourself by listening to sermons from other traditions, read holy texts from other faiths, pick up books from controversial authors. Preparing to take part in a performance is not a matter of imitating other actors, but of delving into the material and discovering from within a fresh interpretation of ancient stories. But these stories cannot be read in isolation from the culture. Theologian Karl Barth once said that Christians should read the Bible along with the newspaper—a good suggestion still. Reading sacred stories and understanding the world in which we live are of a piece. When you read, always ask, "Where is God's spirit active here?"

Second, engage two new practices of faith. One should be an inner practice, such as prayer, yoga, or meditation, and the other, an outward practice, such as offering hospitality to the homeless or learning to be a storyteller. Join with a community of people who already engage the practice at a congregation, at a community center, or through a nonprofit group. Explore dimensions of the practice by going to a workshop, listening to a teacher, reading a book. Invite a friend or family member to join you. Take time with these things, and remember that you get better at doing things as you practice. Practices are not things you do when you are good at something; practice is what you do to become good at something.

Third, have fun. Play. Even in an age of anxiety and division, whatever their political opinions and religious views, Americans like two things: sports and eating. Games and feasting make the heart glad. Get out of the usual routine by cheering on a favorite team or gathering your neighbors for a softball game. Go out to a restaurant or hold an old-fashioned potluck at home. Coach in a children's league. Shoot some hoops at the local park. Volunteer at a community garden. Teach a friend how to make one of your family's favorite recipes. These are hard times, worrisome times, and serious times. Try to enjoy the life you have and play along the way.

Fourth, participate in making change. Show up for the awakening. It may seem self-evident, but every person has to make the choice to act. Spiritual transformation does not happen by watching a self-help guru on a DVD, studying about prayer, or listening to a great speech. No one can do it for us. Spiritual transformation happens only as we jump in and make a difference. Parker Palmer refers to this as the "Rosa Parks decision," named after the black woman who, in 1955, refused to give up her bus seat to a white man and, in doing so, helped forward the Civil Rights Movement. Palmer describes the "Rosa Parks decision" as "the moment a person acts on the decision to live an undivided life."[10] Experiential faith demands action. It is not enough to sit quietly in private and pray or meditate. Experiential faith happens in the world. Act out in public. It is risky, yes. But if you act in and with community, others take the risk with you. You are not alone.

## Great Awakening on Display

In May 2011, President Obama began a speech by telling a story about Miami Dade Community College, a school where immigrants from 181 different nations had earned degrees. "At the com-

mencement ceremony," he said, "181 flags—one for every nation
that was represented—were marched across the stage, and each one
was applauded by the graduates and the relatives of the graduates
with ties to those countries." He explained, "When the Haitian flag
went by, all the Haitian American kids shouted out; when the Guatemalan flag went by, all the kids of Guatemalan heritage shouted
out." So it went with 181 different nations, 181 different flags, and
181 different ethnic groups cheering their native places. "But then,"
the president continued:

> The last flag—the American flag—came into view and everyone
> in the room erupted in applause; everybody cheered. It was a re-
> minder of a simple idea as old as America itself: *E Pluribus Unum*.
> Out of many, one. We define ourselves as a nation of immigrants,
> a nation that welcomes those willing to embrace America's ideals
> and America's precepts. That's why millions of people, ancestors
> to most of us, braved hardship and great risk to come here so they
> could be free to work and worship and start a business and live
> their lives in peace and prosperity.[11]

This, President Obama concluded, was the American future: *out of
many, one.*

PEOPLE OFTEN ASK ME to describe this awakening. In response, I
tell stories, parables of spiritual renewal, of a world transformed by
God's love. I tell stories about surprising congregations and relate
conversations I have had on airplanes, at coffeehouses, and with
bank tellers. I share insights from my friends and family. I show
people polls, surveys, and trends. I preach from scripture. I read
poetry. I teach about the people of the past. I confess my own struggles and regrets. In these pages, I have described the end of an old
religious world, and invited you to see the contours of the new one

that is being born all around us. You may wish to mourn the loss of
what was, but there is no need to fear what will be, for the future is
here only in part, and there is much work to be done. We can make
a new way of faith.

I think the awakening might be a little like graduation at
Miami Dade Community College. In a very real way, we are all
religious immigrants now, faithful people who have—willingly or
unwillingly—left the old world for a new one, a place that exists
largely in the hopeful risk taking of those seeking a meaningful
way of life that offers peace and prosperity for all. This is especially
true when it comes to faith. The old religious world is failing, but
the Spirit is stirring anew. On the stage of awakening, I imagine
Christians carrying high the cross, all the different varieties with
their Bibles, prayer books, icons, and rosary beads; Jews holding the
Torah; Muslims bearing the Qur'an; Buddhists with their Dharma
wheel; Native peoples beating their drums; and so on, each group
cheering its own flag. But then, the reign of God shows itself, as
promised in these ancient words from the prophet Isaiah:

> In days to come
>     the mountain of the Lord's house
> shall be established as the highest of the mountains,
>     and shall be raised above the hills;
> all the nations shall stream to it.
> Many peoples shall come and say,
>     "Come, let us go up to the mountain of the Lord,
>     to the house of the God of Jacob;
> that he may teach us his ways
>     and that we may walk in his paths."
> For out of Zion shall go forth instruction,
>     and the word of the Lord from Jerusalem.
> He shall judge between the nations,
>     and shall arbitrate for many peoples;

> *they shall beat their swords into ploughshares,*
>      *and their spears into pruning hooks;*
> *nation shall not lift up sword against nation,*
>      *neither shall they learn war any more. (Isa. 2:2–4)*

And everyone applauds wildly. Everybody cheers. This is the new spiritual awakening. We proudly carry our own flag across the stage, and we shout for our team. But when the time comes, we will all be one in communion with God, in harmony with the cosmos, loving each other.

Of course, faithful people have been looking for the kingdom for many millennia and have been disappointed. Jesus said to look within. And he said that we should do it. Instead of waiting around, we can display awakening in our lives, churches, and communities. We cannot bring the kingdom with this awakening, nor can we make Isaiah's ancient promise come true. But we can embody some of its ideals and precepts more fully in this world. We can love God and neighbor better. Every spiritual awakening seeks to make visible, even if only in some incomplete way, God's dream for creation. And each has succeeded in some way in doing so, as awakenings have resulted in greater compassion and equality in history. Jonathan Edwards imagined each awakening as ripples in the pool of history; throw a pebble in the water and each successive wave moves farther and farther toward the shore. This awakening will not be the last in human history, but it is our awakening. It is up to us to move with the Spirit instead of against it, to participate in making our world more humane, just, and loving.

# ACKNOWLEDGMENTS

In the fall of 1980, I was a student at an evangelical Christian college and read a book entitled *Dynamics of Spiritual Life,* by Richard F. Lovelace, in a religious studies class. The book, praised by both evangelical and mainstream Protestants, proposed that the United States was in the midst of a new Great Awakening and wove together then-contemporary trends, history and theology, and biblical interpretation in a map of practical wisdom that could guide spiritual renewal. It was my introduction to the study of American revivals, religious history, and spiritual awakening—subjects I would continue to explore through seminary and graduate school. Although I could not know it at the time, the issues raised by the author and the then-young professor of the course, Curt Whiteman, regarding spirituality and social justice, personal faith and institutional vibrancy, and living tradition and transformative Christian practice, would frame the next three decades of my vocation, work, and passions. In a very real way, *Christianity After Religion* unfolds my views, academic and personal, of the dynamics of the current spiritual awakening, as these pages explore religious trends in sociology, history, and theology. It is also a map for spiritual renewal for Christians and faithful friends in other traditions. These pages are my long-considered answers to questions a book and a teacher raised during my senior year in college. Books, professors, and college classrooms shape lives, and I am profoundly grateful to both Richard Lovelace and Curtis Whiteman for helping to shape mine. I do not know if they will approve of the dynamics I see or the answers offered here or how my former mentors would grade this extended essay. I do suspect, however, both would award an A for effort.

Many of my friends and colleagues contributed to this project, some intentionally, others less purposely so through the grace of conversation. Special thanks go to Marcus and Marianne Borg, Anne Howard, Pat DeJong and Sam Keen, Michael and Frannie Kieschnick, Brian McLaren, Lisa and David Domke, Eric Elnes, David Felten, Jeff Procter-Murphy, Phyllis Tickle, Joe and Megan Stewart-Sicking, Alexander Shaia, Teresa Thompson Sherrill, Robert Jones, Carol Howard Merritt and Brian Merritt, Julie Ingersoll, Linnae Himsl Peterson, Peter and Kate Eaton, Tony Jones, Mary Ray, Angela Cannon, Adrian Pyle, Gretta Vosper, Philip Brenner, Reginald Bibby, members of the Episcopal House of Bishops, my legion of clergy friends, and my insightful and always rambunctious Facebook and blog communities. As always I am indebted to all those who have attended speeches, workshops, and retreats I have given, and those churches and groups who have invited me to share with them. Thank you for your provocative, thoughtful, and often emotional insights, stories, and questions, many of which I wrestle with in these pages. I greatly appreciate the support, creativity, and community of the SeaburyNext project, a seminary that has taken on the challenge of becoming a theological community for the twenty-first century, especially in its leadership of Robert Bottoms and Elizabeth Jameson, and through the generosity of Nicholas and Eleanor Chabraja. I appreciate being invited to dream with you about the future.

This is my third book with Roger Freet, editor at HarperOne. Writers love complaining about editors, but I will not join that chorus. Instead, I quote Theodore White: "There are two kinds of editors, those who correct your copy and those who say it's wonderful." White, evidently, did not know Roger, who is the sort of editor who says your copy is wonderful while he is correcting it, simultaneously encouraging and challenging his authors. Our collegial friendship is of an old-fashioned sort, one not found in many publishing houses these days, and has made this book much, much better than it otherwise would have been. Thanks to Roger, Christina Bailly, Suzanne Quist and the production team—especially copy editor Ann Moru—and the marketing and art department folks at HarperOne for all their good and hard work.

This work is dedicated to Marcus and Marianne Borg, and their wonderful dogs, Henry and Abbey. The book owes much to a long Sunday-afternoon conversation with Marianne, an Episcopal priest who sees with keen insight the spiritual dynamics of the world in which we live. She convinced me of the project's importance when I was rather depressed about the whole thing. Marcus and Marianne have been good friends to me and to my family, embodying the swift love and hasty kindness in the words of a prayer they often share.

For whatever conventional reason, the most important thanks come last. To Richard, Emma, Jonah, and our dog, Rowan, you are my most cherished community, those with whom I struggle to perform faith, and the ones who teach me to belove God. Thank you for making it possible for me to write, speak, and travel, sharing the good news of awakening with the world. And thank you for holding me accountable to practicing what I preach. When it comes to a journey of belonging, behaving, and believing, no companions could be more delightful, supportive, or honest than you.

*Diana Butler Bass*
*Alexandria, Virginia*

# NOTES

## Chapter 1: The End of the Beginning

1. Jon Meacham, "The End of Christian America," April 3, 2009, www.news week.com/2009/04/03/the-end-of-christian-america.html.

2. Meacham, "End of Christian America."

3. Meacham, "End of Christian America."

4. Mark Chaves, "The Decline of American Religion?" ARDA Guiding Paper Series (State College: Association of Religion Data Archives at The Pennsylvania State University, 2011), www.thearda.com/rrh/papers/guidingpapers .asp.

5. Harvey Cox, *The Future of Faith* (San Francisco: HarperOne, 2009); Phyllis Tickle, *The Great Emergence* (Grand Rapids, MI: Baker, 2008); Brian McLaren, *A New Kind of Christianity* (San Francisco: HarperOne, 2010).

6. Vida Scudder, *Socialism and Character* (Boston: Houghton Mifflin, 1912), p. 346.

7. Dietrich Bonhoeffer, *Letters and Papers from Prison* (London: Fontana Books, 1959), p. 91.

8. Anne Rice, *Called Out of Darkness* (New York: Knopf, 2008), p. 183.

9. Comments made on Diana Butler Bass, "Ex-Catholics and Ex-Evangelicals: Why Did You Leave?," Belief.net, posted August 16, 2010, blog.beliefnet.com/ christianityfortherestofus/2010/07/ex-catholic-ex-evangelical-why-did-you-leave.html.

10. Robert N. Bellah et al., *Habits of the Heart* (Berkeley: Univ. of California Press, 1985), p. 221.

11. Bellah et al., *Habits of the Heart,* p. 235.

12. Nancy Gibbs, "Looking Back to the Future," *Time,* December 6, 2010, p. 33.

13. Which, of course, are the same forces driving religious renewal, to be more fully explored in Chapter 8, "Great Awakening."

14. Michael Elliott, "Was It Really So Bad?" *Time,* December 6, 2010, p. 78.

15. William McLoughlin, *Revivals, Awakenings, and Reform* (Chicago: Univ. of Chicago Press, 1978), p. 2.

16. McLoughlin, *Revivals, Awakenings, and Reform,* p. 2.

17. Historians argue over the extent, nature, and duration of these "awakenings," some to the point of suggesting that "awakening" is a creation of theological fiction, a phantom of ministerial anxiety, the result of gender-constructed paradigms, or a neat arrangement of narrative convenience. Certainly, each of these interpretations has merit, as the conception of "awakening" has been occasionally overplayed in American religious history, often in support of a particular form of revivalist Protestantism. That said, I find myself in the school of historians who recognize that periods of significant change have occurred in the history of Christianity, changes that respond to, are shaped by, and help to reshape other cultural institutions and political movements. In the historical, anthropological, and ideological sense that William McLoughlin speaks of awakenings, I am most comfortable and am quite willing to leave both divine and more fully secular explanations of spiritual awakenings up to their respective adherents.

The North American movements had corresponding and counterpart movements of awakening in other Protestant countries and in various mission settings. These Protestant awakenings were often twinned with spiritual renewal in Catholic settings as well; the Catholic movements typically focused on new sorts of piety, deeper attachment to Mary and the saints, and the formation of new Catholic monastic or lay service communities.

18. McLoughlin, *Revivals, Awakenings, and Reform,* pp. 12ff.

## Chapter 2: Questioning the Old Gods

1. Greg Garrison, "Many Americans Don't Believe in Hell, but What About Pastors?" August 1, 2009, www.usatoday.com/news/religion/2009-08-01-hell-damnation_N.htm.

2. Will Herberg, *Protestant, Catholic, Jew: An Essay in Religious Sociology* (Garden City, NY: Doubleday, 1955), p. 72.

3. Herberg, *Protestant, Catholic, Jew,* p. 74.

4. American Religious Identification Survey (ARIS), 2008, www.american religionsurvey-aris.org/reports/ARIS_Report_2008.pdf.

5. Pew Forum, *U.S. Religious Landscape Survey,* June 2008, religions.pewforum .org/pdf/report2-religious-landscape-study-full.pdf, p. 26.

6. The number of people who respond that they are "none of the above" or unaffiliated has been growing steadily and shows no sign of reversal. In 2008, Pew reported 16.1 percent of Americans were unaffiliated and the General Social Survey found that number to be 17 percent. In 2011, Public Religion Research reported that number as 20 percent. See also, Dan Cox, Scott Clement, et al., "Non-believers, Seculars, the Unchurched and the

Unaffiliated," presented to American Association for Public Opinion Research, May 2009. www.publicreligionresearch.org/objects/uploads/fck/file/AAPOR%20Paper%Final.pdf.

7. A good section on this can be found in Robert D. Putnam and David E. Campbell, *American Grace* (New York: Simon & Schuster, 2010), pp. 16–18.

8. American Religious Identification Survey (ARIS), 2001, prog.trincoll.edu/ISSSC/DataArchive/index.asp.

9. Paul Froese and Christopher Bader, *America's Four Gods* (New York: Oxford Univ. Press, 2010).

10. Cathy Lynn Grossman, "View of God Can Predict Values, Politics," *USA Today,* September 11, 2006, www.usatoday.com/news/religion/2006-09-11-religion-survey_x.htm.

11. Pew Forum, *U.S. Religious Landscape Survey,* p. 3.

12. Pew Forum, *U.S. Religious Knowledge Survey,* 2010, pewforum.org/other-beliefs-and-practices/u-s-religious-knowledge-survey.aspx.

13. Barna Group, "New Research Explores How Different Generations View and Use the Bible," October 19, 2009, www.barna.org/barna-update/article/12-faithspirituality/317-new-research-explores-how-different-generations-view-and-use-the-bible.

14. A good example of this is John Micklethwait and Adrian Wooldridge, *God Is Back* (New York: Penguin, 2009).

15. Kirk Hadaway and P. L. Marler, "Did You Really Go to Church This Week? Behind the Poll Data," *Christian Century,* May 6, 1998, pp. 472–75; also on religion-online.org.

16. Philip S. Brenner, "Exceptional Behavior or Exceptional Identity? Overreporting of Church Attendance in the U.S.," *Public Opinion Quarterly* 75, no. 1 (spring 2011).

17. Putnam and Campbell, *American Grace,* p. 75; emphasis theirs.

18. Hadaway and Marler, "Did You Really Go to Church?"

19. Pew Forum, "Many Americans Mix Multiple Faiths," December 9, 2009, pewforum.org/Other-Beliefs-and-Practices/Many-Americans-Mix-Multiple-Faiths.aspx#1.

20. Gallup, "Americans' Church Attendance Inches Up in 2010," June 25, 2010; www.gallup.com/poll/141044/Americans-Church-Attendance-Inches-2010.aspx?version=print.

21. Putnam and Campbell, *American Grace,* p. 71.

22. James P. McCartin, *Prayers of the Faithful: The Shifting Spiritual Life of American Catholics* (Cambridge, MA: Harvard Univ. Press, 2010), p. 3.

23. Diana Butler Bass, *Christianity for the Rest of Us* (San Francisco: HarperOne, 2006).

24. Pew Forum, "Many Americans Mix Multiple Faiths," p. 8.

25. McCartin, *Prayers of the Faithful,* p. 4.

26. This section closely follows my own work in *A People's History of Christianity: The Other Side of the Story* (San Francisco: HarperOne, 2009), pp. 294–96.

27. Pew Forum, *U.S. Religious Landscape Survey*, p. 23.

28. Raimon Panikkar, from *The Intrareligious Dialogue* (New York: Paulist Press, 1978), see raimon-panikkar.org/english/biography-3.html.

29. Putnam and Campbell, *American Grace*, pp. 148–52.

30. "Revealing Statistics: America in *Decline:* The Present Costs of the War Against God," www.jesus-is-savior.com/Evils%20in%20America/statistics.htm.

31. McLoughlin, *Revivals, Awakenings, and Reform*, p. 12.

32. Robert Wright, *The Evolution of God* (New York: Little, Brown, 2009); Richard Dawkins, *The God Delusion* (Boston: Houghton Mifflin, 2006).

## Chapter 3: When Religion Fails

1. To be fair, Virginia Beach also has a lesser-known history as an alternate spiritual center, noted for the community that gathered there in the 1930s and 1940s around psychic Edgar Cayce.

2. The number of those who are "not religious and not spiritual," i.e., atheists and agnostics, is higher in Australia and Great Britain than in the United States and Canada. For an interesting summary of British attitudes toward religion, see www.bbc.co.uk/news/magazine–12507319. For Canadian attitudes, see Reginald Bibby, *Beyond the Gods and Back: Religion's Demise and Rise and Why It Matters* (Lethbridge, AB: Project Canada Books, 2011). For Australian attitudes, see the International Social Survey Program (2009), via Philips Hughes, Christian Research Association, Nunawading, Victoria; see also David Tracey, *The Spirituality Revolution: The Emergence of Contemporary Spirituality* (Melbourne: HarperCollins, 2003).

3. The World Values website contains a wealth of information on social values, attitudes, and ethics around the globe: www.worldvaluessurvey.org.

4. *Newsweek* Poll, "A Post-Christian Nation?" Princeton Survey Research Associates International, April 3, 2009, www.psrai.com/filesave/0904%20ftop%20w%20methodology.pdf.

5. Robert Fuller, *Spiritual but Not Religious: Understanding Unchurched America* (New York: Oxford, 2001), p. 6.

6. C. Sedikides and J. Gebauer, "Religiosity as Self-Enhancement, A Meta-Analysis of the Relation Between Socially Desirable Responding and Religiosity," *Personality and Social Psychology Review* 14, no. 1 (February 2010):17–36 (20); originally published online November 25, 2009.

7. This has been found to be the case in not only my impromptu group exercises, but also in social scientific studies. See, for example, Kenneth I. Pargament, "The Psychology of Religion *and* Spirituality? Yes and No,"

*International Journal for the Psychology of Religion* 9, no. 1 (1999): 3–16; Brian Zinnbauer, Kenneth Pargament, et al., "Religion and Spirituality: Unfuzzying the Fuzzy," *Journal for the Scientific Study of Religion* 36 (1997): 549–64; and Penny Long Marler and C. Kirk Hadaway, "Being Religious or Being Spiritual in America: A Zero-Sum Proposition?" *Journal for the Scientific Study of Religion* 41, no. 2 (2002): 289–300.

8. Pargament, "The Psychology of Religion *and* Spirituality?" p. 6.

9. Bob Smietana, "Southern Baptist Evangelism Plan Facing Setbacks," December 18, 2008, www.usatoday.com/news/religion/2008-12-18-southern-baptist_N.htm?csp=34; Martin Marty, "Decline in Conservative Churches," *Sightings,* December 14, 2009, divinity.uchicago.edu/martycenter/publications/sightings/archive_2009/1214.shtml; Christine Wicker, *The Fall of the Evangelical Nation* (San Francisco: HarperOne, 2008).

10. "Willow Creek Repents?" October 18, 2007, www.outofur.com/archives/2007/10/willow_creek_re.html.

11. Matt Branaugh, "Willow Creek's 'Huge Shift,'" May 15, 2008, www.christianitytoday.com/ct/2008/june/5.13.html.

12. Marler and Hadaway, "Being Religious or Being Spiritual in America," p. 298.

13. Dean Hoge and Jacqueline Wenger, *Pastors in Transition: Why Clergy Leave Local Church Ministry* (Grand Rapids, MI: Eerdmans, 2005), p. 29.

14. I borrow the term "participation crash" from Canadian sociologist of religion Reginald Bibby in *Beyond the Gods and Back.*

15. Jim Lobe, "Conservative Christians Biggest Backers of Iraq War," October 10, 2002, www.commondreams.org/headlines02/1010-02.htm.

16. Christopher Hitchens, *God Is Not Great* (New York: Hachette, 2007), p. 13.

17. Pew Forum, *U.S. Religious Landscape Survey,* June 2008, p. 7, religions.pewforum.org/pdf/report2-religious-landscape-study-full.pdf.

18. Gallup, Honesty/Ethics in Professions, November 19–21, 2010, www.gallup.com/poll/1654/honesty-ethics-professions.aspx.

19. Robert D. Putnam and David E. Campbell, *American Grace* (New York: Simon & Schuster, 2010), pp. 501–15.

20. Putnam and Campbell, *American Grace,* pp. 120–33 and 401–18.

21. See, for instance, David Gushee, who wonders if scandals in Baptist churches are only "shielded more deeply from view" than those in the Roman Catholic Church, in "The Churches and Sexual Abuse," *Associated Baptist Press,* March 29, 2010, www.abpnews.com/content/view/4997/9/.

22. Putnam and Campbell, *American Grace,* pp. 91–133.

23. David Kinnaman and Gabe Lyons, *unChristian: What a New Generation Really Thinks About Christianity . . . and Why It Matters* (Grand Rapids, MI: Baker, 2007), pp. 28ff. Although the survey information in *unChristian* is helpful, the interpretation in this book could be offensive to many Christians. Kin-

naman thinks the primary problem for churches is "image" and that a sort of theological public relations campaign would make things better. The data is interesting, but the analysis is very thin and biased in the direction of a conservative evangelical social agenda.

24. Mark Chaves, *American Religion: Contemporary Trends* (Princeton, NJ: Princeton Univ. Press, 2011), pp. 75–77. In the early 1970s, approximately 35 percent of Americans said they had a "great deal" of confidence in religious institutions; in the last forty years, the number shows overall decline, with an increase only in the decade from 1990 to 2000, and a brief, but slight rebound in 2004 and 2005 before declining again. Interestingly enough, even in the radical 1970s, Americans trusted religious organizations *more* than they trusted other sorts of conventional institutions—that is no longer the case. Americans rank religious institutions as poorly as they do other sorts of organizations. Religious leaders fare even worse than religious institutions.

25. Chaves, *American Religion,* p. 79.

26. This dynamic is very similar to that which occurred during the Great Depression. According to historian Robert T. Handy, "it was an already depressed Protestantism that was overtaken by the economic crisis." See his now-classic article, "The American Religious Depression, 1925–1935" in *Church History* 29 (March 1960), 3–16. For specific data on the recession and religion, see "Holy Toll: The Impact of the 2008 Recession on American Congregations," faithcommunitiestoday.org/holy-toll-2008-recession.

27. Putnam and Campbell, *American Grace,* pp. 167–69.

28. Adapted from a prayer by Robert Raines that first appeared in 1971 in *Wittenberg Door.* See video version at Living the Questions, www.youtube.com/user/livingthequestions#p/u/2/LgL4X1hNWPY.

29. Linda Killian, "Independent Voters Fed Up with Entire Political System," November 1, 2010, www.politicsdaily.com/2010/11/01/independent-swing-voters-fed-up-with-entire-political-system/.

30. Killian, "Independent Voters Fed Up." Killian is writing a book called *The Swing Vote: The Untapped Power of the Independents* (forthcoming).

31. Robert Wuthnow, *The Restructuring of American Religion* (Princeton, NJ: Princeton Univ. Press, 1988); Martin Marty's two-party paradigm in Martin Marty, *Righteous Empire: The Protestant Experience in America* (New York: Dial Press, 1970). This, however, is something that I have argued against in most of my books.

32. Dan Cox, Scott Clement, Gregory Smith, Allison Pond, and Nega Sahgal, "Non-believers, Seculars, the Un-churched and the Unaffiliated: Who Are the Non-religious Americans and How Do We Measure Them in Survey Research?," paper presented at a meeting of the American Association for Public Opinion Research, Hollywood, FL, May 14–17, 2009.

33. Kinnaman and Lyons, *unChristian,* pp. 28ff.

34. Indeed, it has. See, for example, Jeffrey B. Russell, *A History of Medieval Christianity: Prophecy and Order* (New York: Crowell, 1968).

35. Personal e-mail conversation, December 2010.

36. Marler and Hadaway, "Being Religious or Being Spiritual in America," p. 297.

37. Gallup, "Americans Remain Very Religious, but Not Necessarily in Conventional Ways," www.gallup.com/poll/3385/americans-remain-very-religious-necessarily-conventional-ways.aspx.

38. *Newsweek* Poll, Princeton Survey Research Associates, April 2009, www.psrai.com/filesave/0904%20ftop%20w%20methodology.pdf, p. 11.

39. Although no national data exist for this in Canada, a survey of Alberta indicates that 43 percent of the people in that province identify with "spiritual and religious"; see Bibby, *Beyond the Gods and Back,* pp. 124–25.

40. David Korten, *The Great Turning: From Empire to Earth Community* (Bloomfield, CT: Kumarian; San Francisco: Berrett-Koehler, 2006), p. 3.

41. Korten, *Great Turning,* p. 3.

42. Korten, *Great Turning,* p. 72.

43. R. F. Ingelhart et al., *Human Beliefs and Values* can be found online: books.google.com/books?hl=en&lr=&id=UVPMESnqY0AC&oi=fnd&pg=PR15&dq=world+values+survey+religion&ots=2LPlmPHN7T&sig=jWOGJNqPk7uEpRv0xIuDgGZF-iU#v=onepage&q=world%20values%20survey%20religion&f=false. See also the shorter report, www.worldvaluessurvey.org/wvs/articles/folder_published/article_base_110/files/WVSbrochure4.pdf; David Korten has a short discussion of the WVS in relation to the Great Turning in *Great Turning,* p. 80.

44. Hitchens, *God Is Not Great,* p. 12.

45. Wilfred Cantwell Smith, *The Meaning and End of Religion* (New York: Macmillan, 1962), p. 40.

46. Smith, *Meaning and End of Religion,* pp. 21–23.

47. Smith, *Meaning and End of Religion,* p. 191.

48. Smith, *Meaning and End of Religion,* p. 29.

## Chapter 4: Believing

1. Harvey Cox, *The Future of Faith: The Rise and Fall of Beliefs and the Coming Age of the Spirit* (San Francisco: HarperOne, 2009), pp. 5–6.

2. Cox, *Future of Faith,* pp. 213, 221.

3. Nathan Schneider, "Age of Spirit: An Interview with Harvey Cox," October 30, 2009, blogs.ssrc.org/tif/2009/10/30/age-of-spirit-an-interview-with-harvey-cox.

4. Cox, *Future of Faith,* p. 2.

5. Dwight Friesen, "Orthoparadoxy: Emerging Hope for Embracing Difference," in Doug Pagitt and Tony Jones, eds., *An Emergent Manifesto of Hope* (Grand Rapids, MI: Baker, 2007), p. 204.

6. This paragraph follows the argument laid out by Parker J. Palmer, *Healing the Heart of Democracy: The Courage to Create a Politics Worthy of the Human Spirit* (San Francisco: Jossey-Bass, 2011), pp. 119–50.

7. Wilfred Cantwell Smith, *Believing: An Historical Perspective* (Oxford: One World, 1998), p. 40. First published as *Belief and History* (Virginia: Univ. Press of Virginia, 1977). Marcus Borg has written about the shift of the language of belief. See his *The Heart of Christianity: Rediscovering a Life of Faith* (San Francisco: HarperOne, 2003), chapter 2, pp. 26–42; and *Speaking Christian,* chapter 10.

8. Smith, *Believing: An Historical Perspective,* p. 41.

9. Smith, *Believing: An Historical Perspective,* p. 44.

10. Smith, *Believing: An Historical Perspective,* p. 58.

11. Smith, *Believing: An Historical Perspective,* p. 65.

12. Smith, *Believing: An Historical Perspective,* p. v.

13. Smith, *Believing: An Historical Perspective,* p. 69.

14. Grant Wacker, *Heaven Below: Early Pentecostals and American Culture* (Cambridge, MA: Harvard Univ. Press, 2001).

15. Wacker, *Heaven Below,* p. 4.

16. Friedrich Schleiermacher, *Addresses on Religion* (1799), quoted in Kedourie, Elie, *Nationalism* (Praeger University Series, 1961), p. 26.

17. William James, *Varieties of Religious Experience* (London, New York, and Bombay: Longmans, Green, 1911), p. 31.

18. James, *Varieties of Religious Experience,* p. 515.

19. Leigh Schmidt, *Restless Souls: The Making of American Spirituality* (San Francisco: Harper San Francisco, 2005), pp. 170–71.

20. George Marsden, *Jonathan Edwards: A Life* (New Haven, CT: Yale Univ. Press, 2003), p. 285.

21. Marsden, *Jonathan Edwards,* p. 284.

22. Marsden, *Jonathan Edwards,* p. 288.

23. Marsden, *Jonathan Edwards,* p. 288.

24. Palmer, *Healing the Heart of Democracy,* p. 6.

25. Martin Buber, *I and Thou,* trans. R. G. Smith, 2nd ed. (London and New York: Continuum, 1958), pp. 88, 89.

## Chapter 5: Behaving

1. Richard Sennett, *The Craftsman* (New Haven: Yale Univ. Press, 2008), p. 51.

2. Charles Taylor, *Varieties of Religion Today* (Cambridge, MA: Harvard Univ. Press, 2002), pp. 63–107.

3. Brian McLaren, *Finding Our Way Again: The Return of the Ancient Practices* (Nashville: Thomas Nelson, 2008), p. 14.

4. Craig Dykstra and Dorothy Bass, "Times of Yearning, Practices of Faith," in Dorothy Bass, ed., *Practicing Our Faith,* 2d ed. (San Francisco: Jossey-Bass, 2010), p. 5.

5. Dykstra and Bass, "Times of Yearning, Practices of Faith," p. 4.

6. Another third attend only one religious community; and the remaining third do not attend any religious community at all; Pew Forum, "Many Americans Mix Multiple Faiths," December 9, 2009, pewforum.org/Other-Beliefs-and-Practices/Many-Americans-Mix-Multiple-Faiths.aspx#1.

7. In his book *Drive: The Surprising Truth About What Motivates Us* (New York: Riverhead, 2009), Daniel Pink explores how external forces do not prompt human beings to do their best work. Instead, three things—autonomy, mastery, and purpose—motivate people to use their imagination and creativity in "crafting" new ways of being themselves, working, and making a difference in the world. The thesis in *Drive* easily translates into the world of faith.

8. This point is nicely made in two Christian classics of the late Middle Ages, still popular today: Brother Lawrence's *Practicing the Presence of God* and Thomas à Kempis's *The Imitation of Christ.*

9. Taylor, *Varieties of Religion Today,* p. 94.

10. Although to be fair, I am pretty certain she said "kin-dom," a less hierarchical and sexist term for God's kingdom favored by many UCC pastors.

11. "Willow Creek Repents?" October 18, 2007, www.outofur.com/archives/2007/10/willow_creek_re.html.

12. "Willow Creek Repents?"

13. This idea has been popularized by Malcolm Gladwell in *Outliers: The Story of Success* (New York: Little, Brown, 2008) and is based on research by K. Anders Ericsson, Michael J. Prietula, and Edward Cokely, "The Making of an Expert," *Harvard Business Review,* June 7, 2007, www.coachingmanagement.nl/The%20Making%20of%20an%20Expert.pdf.

14. Ericsson, Prietula, and Cokely, "The Making of an Expert," p. 3.

15. McLaren, *Finding Our Way Again,* p. 182.

## Chapter 6: Belonging

1. John Calvin, *Institutes of the Christian Religion,* Book I, chapter 1, section 1, www.reformed.org/books/institutes/books/book1/book1ch01.html.

2. Bill Bishop, *The Big Sort: Why the Clustering of Like-Minded America Is Tearing Us Apart* (Boston: Mariner Books, Houghton Mifflin Harcourt, 2009).

3. Valerie Saiving, "The Human Situation: A Feminine View," in Carol P. Christ and Judith Plaskow, *Womanspirit Rising: A Feminist Reader in Religion* (San Francisco: Harper & Row, 1979), p. 26.

4. Saiving, "The Human Situation," p. 37.

5. Marcus Borg discusses the rich meanings of the word "salvation" in his book *Speaking Christian: Why Christian Words Have Lost Their Meaning and Power—And How They Can Be Restored* (San Francisco: HarperOne, 2011), chapter 3.

6. Charles Taylor, *A Secular Age* (Cambridge, MA: Harvard Univ. Press, 2007).

7. But not all of us—contemporary atheists are perfectly content accepting selfhood in material terms.

8. *The Book of Thomas the Contender,* translated by John D. Turner, www.gnosis .org/naghamm/bookt.html.

9. Quoted in Bass, *A People's History of Christianity,* pp. 36–40.

10. Quoted in Bass, *A People's History of Christianity,* p. 99.

11. Nevada Barr, *Seeking Enlightenment . . . Hat by Hat: A Skeptic's Path to Religion* (New York: Putnam, 2003).

12. Thomas A. Tweed, *Crossing and Dwelling: A Theory of Religion* (Cambridge, MA: Harvard Univ. Press, 2006), p. 79.

13. Tweed, *Crossing and Dwelling,* p. 164.

14. George Herbert Mead, *Mind, Self, and Society* (Chicago: Univ. of Chicago Press, 1934), p. 138; quoted in Stanley J. Grenz, *The Social God and the Relational Self* (Louisville, KY: Westminster John Knox, 2001), p. 307.

15. Mead, *Mind, Self, and Society,* p. 182; quoted in Grenz, *The Social God and the Relational Self,* p. 310.

16. Susan M. Anderson and Serena Chen, "The Relational Self: An Interpersonal Social-Cognitive Theory," *Psychological Review* 109, no. 4 (2002): 619–45.

17. Ubuntu Women Institute USA, "Ubuntu Women Institute USA (UWIU) with SSIWEL as Its First South Sudan Project," accessed May 2, 2011, www .ssiwel.org/?page_id=83.

18. Emil Brunner, *Man in Revolt* (New York: Scribner, 1939), p. 106; quoted in Grenz, *The Social God and the Relational Self,* p. 313.

19. John Zizioulas, "The Doctrine of God the Trinity Today: Suggestions for an Ecumenical Study," in *The Forgotten Trinity: The BBC Study Commission on Trinitarian Doctrine Today* (London: CTBI, 2011); quoted in Grenz, *The Social God and the Relational Self,* p. 334.

20. Dietrich Bonhoeffer, *Letters and Papers from Prison,* p. 173.

## Chapter 7: The Great Reversal

1. Jonathan Reed, "The Lost Generation," www.youtube.com/watch?v= 42E2fAWM6rA.

2. Wilfred Cantwell Smith, *The Meaning and End of Religion* (New York: Macmillan, 1962), pp. 39–40.

3. Harvey Cox makes the point that Global South Christianity is not as conservative or reactionary as many Western observers think; see *The Future of Faith* (San Francisco: HarperOne, 2009), pp. 199–211.

4. Cox, *Future of Faith*, p. 19.

5. Cox, *Future of Faith*, p. 20.

## Chapter 8: Great Awakening

1. Elizabeth O'Connor, *Call to Commitment: The Story of Church of the Saviour, Washington, D.C.* (New York: Harper & Row, 1963).

2. These roughly parallel other religious revitalization movements in Canada and parts of western Europe. See Mark Noll, *A History of Christianity in the United States and Canada* (Grand Rapids, MI: Eerdmans, 1992), and Richard Carwadine, *Transatlantic Revivalism: Popular Evangelicalism in Britain and America, 1790–1865* (London: Paternoster, 2007).

3. William McLoughlin, *Revivals, Awakenings, and Reform* (Chicago: Univ. of Chicago Press, 1978), p. 2.

4. Robert William Fogel, *The Fourth Great Awakening and the Future of Egalitarianism* (Chicago: Univ. of Chicago Press, 2000), pp. 74–83.

5. According to Fogel, the quest for "self-realization" is one of the most distinctly postmodern traits of the search for meaning in emerging technophysio culture. He defines "self-realization" as "the desire to find a deeper meaning in life than the endless accumulation of consumer durables and the pursuits of pleasure" (*Fourth Great Awakening*, p. 176).

6. McLoughlin, *Revivals, Awakenings, and Reform*, pp. 1–2, xv.

7. McLoughlin, *Revivals, Awakenings, and Reform*, pp. 214–15.

8. McLoughlin, *Revivals, Awakenings, and Reform*, pp. 212–14. One cannot read McLoughlin's section on presidential leadership without thinking of the election of 2008 and President Barack Obama.

9. McLoughlin, *Revivals, Awakenings, and Reform*, p. 14.

10. I am well aware that contemporary historians have ably demonstrated that during periods of intensive religious argument and awakening, many Americans were in the middle and did not choose sides between the extreme parties. That is certainly the case. But a large middle does not invalidate the fact that rival parties (and variations within the rival parties) contended—and are contending—over the spiritual and political future.

11. Robert Putnam and David E. Campbell, *American Grace* (New York: Simon & Schuster, 2010), p. 101.

12. The dynamic is remarkably similar to that of the Republican Party. In the nineteenth century, the Republican Party was the party of reform and racial inclusion, marked by an insistence on creativity and social justice. Slowly, however, the Republican Party became the establishment party of business

and social elites, abandoning its historical passion for the poor and marginalized in favor of defending the status quo. The Republican Party was once a "new light" political party, but it became an "old light" one—all the while still insisting that it is the "party of Lincoln." It may well be historically true that the Republican Party is that of President Lincoln, but this bears little relevance to bringing his spirit, insights, and commitments to bear on contemporary politics. Lincoln's mantle has become a ritualized identity rather than a living practice of engaging the world.

13. This is why "hell" is so important a theological category to conservative evangelicals—you need hell as a physical, literal place to reinforce fear and support the authority of preachers, theologians, and church leaders who claim to hold the keys of eternal salvation. Without hell, fear diminishes.

14. Ironically, they often argue for authority with an appeal to experience, thus proving the larger case for a spiritual shift toward experiential faith!

15. Putnam and Campbell, *American Grace,* pp. 113–14.

16. McLoughlin, *Revivals, Awakenings, and Reform,* p. 214.

17. McLoughlin, *Revivals, Awakenings, and Reform,* p. 214.

18. Putnam and Campbell, *American Grace,* pp. 104–5.

19. Putnam and Campbell, *American Grace,* p. 105.

20. Putnam and Campbell, *American Grace,* p. 105, italics in original.

21. Reinhold Niebuhr, *Moral Man and Immoral Society: A Study in Ethics and Politics* (Louisville, KY: Westminster John Knox, 1932, 2002), p. xxvii.

22. Wendell Berry, "The Vision," in *Clearing* (New York: Harcourt, 1977).

23. See, for example, Marc Prensky, "H. Sapiens Digital: From Digital Immigrants and Digital Natives to Digital Wisdom," www.wisdompage.com/Prensky01.html.

24. Putnam and Campbell, *American Grace,* pp. 516–50.

25. James Forbes, "The Next Great Awakening," *Tikkun,* September/October 2010, www.tikkun.org/article.php/sept2010forbes.

26. Although earlier awakenings have often been multireligious affairs, with similar spiritual impulses reshaping a variety of religious traditions at the same time. The best example might be the move toward a "religion of the heart" that transformed European Protestantism, Catholicism, and Judaism in the early to mid 1700s. In England and the United States, the Protestant form of that spiritual event became known as the First Great Awakening (or Evangelical Revival). The difference between then and now, however, is that *then* the multiple awakenings remained separate and distinct ecclesial events, with little communication and connection across religious boundaries. *Now,* such religious "silo-ing" is nearly impossible, given immigration, technology, and communication.

27. McLoughlin, *Revivals, Awakenings, and Reform,* p. 14.

28. For a sociological study of fear in America and the possibility of creativity in the face of fear, see Robert Wuthnow, *Be Very Afraid: The Cultural Response to Terror, Pandemics, Environmental Devastation, Nuclear Annihilation, and Other Threats* (New York: Oxford Univ. Press, 2010).

## Chapter 9: Performing Awakening

1. Edwards, *An Humble Attempt* (1747).
2. This section follows Charles Taylor, *Varieties of Religion Today* (Cambridge, MA: Harvard Univ. Press, 2002), pp. 84ff.
3. The video "The Opera Company of Philadelphia, 'Hallelujah!' Random Act of Culture," can be viewed on YouTube, www.youtube.com/watch?v=wp_RHnQ-jgU.
4. It can be well argued that public-private divide was a creation of Enlightenment culture and that the medieval world was much more like ours in the porous boundary between "private" and "public" space, especially as space related to sacred things. See my discussion of this in *A People's History of Christianity;* see also Elizabeth Drescher, "Medieval Multitasking: Did We Ever Focus?," *Religion Dispatches,* July 12, 2010, www.religiondispatches.org/archive/culture/2942/medieval_multitasking:_did_we_ever_focus/.
5. Although George Whitefield in the First Great Awakening might be the exception to this claim. See Harry S. Stout, *The Divine Dramatist* (Grand Rapids, MI: Eerdmans, 1991).
6. I write about some churches that are enacting the awakening through spiritual practices in *Christianity for the Rest of Us.*
7. Palmer, *Healing the Heart of Democracy,* p. 92.
8. From Sara Evans and Harry Boyte, *Free Spaces: The Sources of Democratic Change in America* (Chicago: Univ. of Chicago Press, 1992), p. 17, quoted in Palmer, *Healing the Heart of Democracy,* p. 97.
9. Palmer, *Healing the Heart of Democracy,* p. 97.
10. Palmer, *Healing the Heart of Democracy,* p. 185.
11. "President Obama on Fixing Our Broken Immigration System: 'E Pluribus Unum,'" May 10, 2011, www.whitehouse.gov/blog/2011/05/10/president-obama-fixing-our-broken-immigration-system-e-pluribus-unum.

# INDEX